BROTHERTON

**New Jersey's First and Only Indian Reservation and the
Communities of Shamong and Tabernacle That Followed**

GEORGE D. FLEMMING

Plexus Publishing, Inc.
Medford, New Jersey

First Printing, 2005
Copyright © 2005 George D. Flemming

Published by: Plexus Publishing, Inc.
143 Old Marlton Pike
Medford, NJ 08055

Publisher's Note: The author and publisher have taken care in preparation of this book but make no expressed or implied warranty of any kind and assume no responsibility for errors or omissions. No liability is assumed for incidental or consequential damages in connection with or arising out of the use of the information contained herein.

Library of Congress Cataloging-in-Publication Data

Flemming, George D., 1935–
  Brotherton: New Jersey's first and only Indian reservation and the townships of Shamong and Tabernacle that followed / Geroge D. Flemming
    p. cm.
  Includes bibliographical references and index.
    ISBN 0-937548-61-8 (hard) - ISBN 0-937548-57-X (soft)
  1. Indians of North America--New Jersey--Brotherton Indian Reservation--History. 2. Indians of North America--New Jersey--Brotherton Indian Reservation--Social life and customs. 3. Indians of North America--New Jersey--Shamong (Township)--History. 4. Indians of North America--New Jersey--Shamong (Township)--Social life and customs. 5. Brotherton Indian Reservation (N.J.--History. 6. Shamong (N.J. : Township)--History. I. Title.
  E78.N6F54 2005
    974.9'61—dc22

                                         2004028029

Printed and bound in the United States of America.

President and CEO: Thomas H. Hogan, Sr.
Editor-in-Chief and Publisher: John B. Bryans
Managing Editor: Amy M. Holmes
VP Graphics and Production: M. Heide Dengler
Book Designer: Kara Jalkowski
Cover Designer: Amanda Beland
Copy Editor: Dorothy Pike
Sales Manager: Pat Palatucci
Proofreader: Pat Hadley-Miller
Indexer: Sharon Hughes

TABLE OF CONTENTS

FOREWORD

Ed Rutsch, the archaeologist, once said, "We must be the new story-tellers." Ed was excavating an Indian site on the island of St. John in the U.S. Virgin Islands and had invited me down to help him. Ed then told the class a long story using the artifacts that had been excavated that day. He ended his story by cupping his hands to his lips and making the sound made by a helmet conch trumpet. If I close my eyes I can still hear that sound.

George Flemming is a storyteller. He has been telling the story of Brotherton for 50 years. Now it is in print. It is a small story that is part of a much larger picture. It begins in the distant past when New Jersey had a different name. It is a story of what happened to those people, and the people who came after them. In a juxtaposition of language, Brotherton is about the first group of people. Shamong is about those that replaced them.

Flemming's story is a journey through time, from the prehistoric to the recent past. The main story is set in the 18th century and evolves into a story of the 19th century. Parts have been constantly added to the story as new evidence has been found; parts have been deleted. Much of the myth has been separated from the prehistoric past. Much could still be added to the historic story.

Brotherton falls into that period of time when someone else spoke for the Indians: William Franklin, the governor, Charles Read, the Indian Commissioner, Rev. John Brainerd, the missionary. There were a few who spoke for themselves: Mahamickwon, Okokathseeme, and a few Indians with Anglecized names, such as Stephen Calvin, Bartholemew Calvin, and Moses Tatamy.

While the Brotherton section of the book is a narrative, the Shamong section is a series of short stories about organizations, work places, church-es, schools, taverns, mills, and factories. Flemming's journey is completed with essays about specific people, like Indian Ann, and the brothers James and William Still.

The Lenape, a first nation, became known as the Delawares. A remnant of the Delawares is placed on a reservation named Brotherton. A smaller group leaves 43 years later and walks to New York. There they live along the Chemung River with the Seneca Indians. Indian Ann's father, Elisha Ashatama, returns to Burlington County. Indian Ann is born circa 1805. Shamong Township is created in 1852. One hundred and fifty years later, a new regional high school is called Seneca.

By the edge of old Edgepillock
By the shining pure, clear waters
Stood the wigwam of the hunter.

Budd Wilson
Green Bank, New Jersey
July 4, 2004

INTRODUCTION

My initial interest in Shamong Township began in 1953 while doing research on the Brotherton Indian Reservation. In recalling my first visit to Indian Mills, I was immediately fascinated, and yet saddened at the thought, that nearly 200 years ago this land had been the last home of the native Indians of our state. Now only the quiet hamlet of Indian Mills surrounded by farmland and pine forest remained. Nothing was evident to even hint where one of the earliest Indian reservations in our country had been founded in 1758. There were no markers to tell of the noble humanitarian efforts that had taken place. Gone were the once thriving sawmill and gristmill that had provided sustenance to the natives. Gone, too, were the log mission church and dwelling place of the Reverend John Brainerd, who had preached to the Indian natives as well as to early white settlers. What remained appeared similar to most rural farm communities in central and southern New Jersey. Even the once thriving iron furnace community of Atsion was rapidly passing into oblivion.

Sensing the need for recognition of the reservation, I made a suggestion to the Archaeological Society of New Jersey (ASNJ), in 1957, to erect a suitable marker commemorating the 200th anniversary of the reservation founding. I was 22 at the time and had been a member of the ASNJ since 1954 and thus, I thought the chances of approval were slim. To my surprise and delight the suggestion was approved. I was asked to serve on the marker committee with such distinguished members as Dr. Charles Philhower, Dr. Henry Bisbee, Dr. Lewis Haggerty, and Dr. Dorothy Cross. We met at Indian Mills and sat in a circle on the front lawn of the Methodist Church. The marker was ultimately unveiled at impressive ceremonies that took place at the Indian Mills Methodist Church on October 26, 1958. The day may well be recalled by many of the older residents. It was damp and cold with rain threatening at any moment. New Jersey State Troopers were directing traffic at the normally quiet intersection near the church. More than 300 persons were in attendance, most noted of whom were the numerous descendants of Indian Ann Roberts, the last full-blooded Lenape to reside in this state. It was a glorious day for those who recognized the need to preserve the heritage of this forgotten chapter in the history of New Jersey.

Previous to and following the placement of the marker, I had been accumulating considerable material about the history of the area with the ultimate goal of writing a detailed account of the Brotherton Reservation, heretofore glossed over in local and state histories. During the formation of the Indian Mills Historical Society in 1973, it became quite evident to me that such an account should encompass and preserve not only the history of the reservation, but also the story from prehistoric times to the early colonization of Shamong Township and surrounding areas. Many modern writers had touched on these subjects, but the full story had yet to be told and some misinformation had been spread. We needed a book that could set the record straight.

Much original research for the book involved endless hours of reviewing original documents wherever possible. This encompassed numerous early property deeds, census records, mortgage records, wills, estate proceedings, early church and burial records, diaries, legislative proceedings, school records, and vital statistics. Examining these records made history come alive for me. It is my fervent wish that others will share this feeling when reading the book and experience this same journey back in time.

The reader should keep in mind that this book will focus on the area within the boundaries of the original Shamong Township as it was incorporated in 1852. This includes part of present day Tabernacle Township, which was formed in part from Shamong in 1901. Emphasis has been primarily placed on the time period preceding the year 1900, with the thought in mind that future historians will meet the challenge of continuing this history. The text is intended as a reference work and every effort has been taken to ensure its accuracy. The folk tales and legends of the pines are entertaining, but for the most part have been omitted. While folklore has a place in history, I decided not to include it.

No history is ever really complete, as new information is constantly being uncovered. This story is a beginning, and I trust only a beginning. Many problems and areas of concern still remain to be researched and recorded. The future appears promising in this regard, owing to the wealth of new material being made available through microfilming techniques, dedicated archivists, and the new breed of archaeologists.

This introduction passage would not be complete without extending my heartfelt thanks to all those who made the book possible. In particular I want to thank Mrs. Gail Currier, founder of the Indian Mills Historical Society. Her bright spirit, dedication, and love of history are a credit to the community. I also wish to thank the staffs of the Burlington County Library, Savitz Library of Rowan University, Burlington County Clerks and Surrogates Office, Burlington County Historical Society, Gloucester County Historical Society, Gloucester County Clerks and Surrogates Office, New Jersey State Library and Archives, and the Truncer Library at Batsto, New Jersey. I am grateful as well to the residents of Shamong Township and members of the Indian Mills Historical Society whose tireless efforts in gathering photos and sharing of personal knowledge of the area, helped make my dream a reality. Additional acknowledgments are made throughout the text for information supplied and photographic material obtained.

Last, but by no means least, a sincere thank you goes to my dear wife, Doris, for her patience, understanding, and willingness to listen to my end-less tales of what once was around every nook and cranny of South Jersey.

CHAPTER 1

The Dawn of Man

PALEO MAN

When did man, the hunter, first come upon the area we now call New Jersey? This has been a question of considerable debate in the scientific community. For many years it was thought man had only been here for some 4,000 or 5,000 years. This time estimate seemed to coincide with interpretations of biblical sources regarding the creation stories. As time went on, though, certain archaeological sites began producing finds that indicated a greater antiquity for man in the New World.

In 1932 archaeologists found a mammoth kill site near Clovis, New Mexico, dating back some 12,000 years. Also found were fluted projectile points that have since been termed Clovis points. Naturally there were skeptics of these early dates, but as time went on there appeared little doubt that man had indeed entered the New World approximately 12,000 years ago, having migrated from Siberia into Alaska over a land bridge called Beringia. This land bridge was caused by the presence of massive glaciers that lowered the level of the Bering Sea. The land bridge created a corridor some 1,000 miles wide. In Pleistocene times mammals consisting of woolly mammoths, mastodon, musk oxen, caribou, elk-moose, and others had been native to the Americas for thousands of years. Ancient man, the hunter, in his quest for the meat of these large mammals, migrated across this land bridge. The glaciers covered most of Canada and the Arctic; however, an ice-free corridor eventually opened up between Alaska and the northern United States, permitting man to proceed south throughout the continent, all the way down to the southernmost tip of South America.

Hunting bands of 25 to 50 people continued to escalate through the Americas in many waves of migration. Numerous sites of these early hunters

Clovis type projectile points used by early man, the hunter, 10,000 to 12,000 years B.P. (before the present). (Photo by the author.)

emerged all over the Americas, with Carbon 14 tests indicating an age in the 10,000- to 12,000-year-old range. The Clovis type projectile point became the hallmark indicator of the time period known as the Paleo Indian Period.

Dr. Herbert C. Kraft of Seton Hall University documented the first habitation site of this period found in New Jersey in 1970. It became known as the Plenge Site and was located near the town of Washington along the Musconectong River in Warren County. It yielded the entire tool assemblage of Paleo Man. No Carbon 14 dating tests were possible here, as these were not excavated finds, but rather surface finds due to the site being under active farm cultivation. In recent years Paleo habitation sites have been discovered on the Inner and Outer Coastal Plain of New Jersey, yielding the debitage of fluted Clovis type points, scrapers, and knives of obvious antiquity. Isolated finds of Clovis type points have also occurred throughout the state including the Pine Barrens.

In respect to New Jersey, the southernmost point of the Wisconsin glaciation was near Belvidere. This is known as the terminal moraine. As a result of so much of the land being locked up in ice, the coastline of New Jersey was then 90 miles east of its present location. For many years, scallop fishermen and dredging activities have recovered hundreds of fossilized bones of Pleistocene mammals. Archaeologists have recently identified an Early Man site known as the Corcione Site off the coast of Sandy Hook, which produced stone tools and flakes clearly indicating the presence of Early Man. The finds are still being evaluated and mark only the beginning of what may provide lasting proof of man's emergence in New Jersey at a very early date, possibly preceding the settling of Clovis people here.

PRE-CLOVIS / PRE-PALEO INDIAN

In 1974 radio carbon dates of 13,000 to 16,000 years ago were found at a site since known as the Meadowcroft Rock Shelter. This lies south of Pittsburgh, Pennsylvania, and was thoroughly excavated by Dr. James Adovasio, a prominent and well-respected archaeologist. His dating results were obtained from a charcoal hearth at a very low depth of the rock shelter.

Vertabrae of the Pleistocene Musk-Ox Symbos and fragment of a Mastodon tooth. Both were dredged up by scallop fishermen off the coast of Tuckahoe, NJ. (Photo by the author.)

Since then, other dates have been obtained as far back as 19,000 B.P. (before the present), associated with stone tools and projectile points pre-dating the Clovis type point. This site has attained worldwide notoriety as one of the oldest known Early Man sites in North America.

More recently, a mastodon kill site near Saltville, Virginia, yielded dates of 14,000 B.P. A site at Cactus Hill, Virginia, along the Nottoway River has provided dates of 15,000 B.P. Numerous other sites have been found in the Northeast and Middle Atlantic States that predate the Clovis sites, and with entirely different unfluted projectile points. In New Jersey there have been hundreds of mammoth and mastodon remains found, but to date none can be reported as a kill site. There seems little doubt, though, that man did hunt these large mammals as a food source. It may be only a question of time before this is proven. It will also come to be shown that man emerged in New Jersey long before the arrival of the Clovis People.

New theories on man's earlier arrival abound. Ample evidence has been produced to indicate that, in addition to arriving in the New World by the land bridge, man may have proceeded south from Siberia down the Pacific Coast. Another theory postulates the arrival of Early Man from Southwestern Europe. A particular culture known as the Solutrean disappeared from Europe some 19,000 years ago. There are many similarities in the tools they made and the tools found in the Eastern United States.

Other scientific disciplines support a Pre-Clovis theory. Theodore Shurr of Emory University, a geneticist, found that Early Man must have entered the Americas at least 30,000 years ago. He and others have been studying genetic markers and DNA to determine how Native Americans and natives of Siberia are related.

A prominent linguist, Johanna Nichols of the University of Berkley, has studied more than 140 language families of Native Americans. She has determined it would take at least 30,000 years or possibly 40,000 years to generate as many languages as exist among the Indian populations of the Americas today. These two scientific disciplines lend considerable credence to the premise of ancient man populating the Americas prior to the Clovis people of 12,000 to 13,000 years ago. It seems increasingly clear that the long-accepted land migration of these people from Siberia will no longer survive.

The archaeology of the New World is in an exciting time in prehistory, especially in New Jersey. New finds are being made constantly along with the advanced technology of locating and identifying the sites of ancient man. The time is fast approaching when there will be startling discoveries made in the coastal waters of New Jersey, where the mammoth and mastodon kill sites associated with the tools and weapons of ancient man will be found.

THE ARCHAIC PERIOD

After the Paleo Period came the Archaic, which traditionally began about 10,000 years ago and lasted until about 3,000 years ago. It is difficult to set exact dates because there were many situations occurring that caused regional overlapping of time periods. As the glaciers began to melt some 10,000 years ago, the melt waters slowly inundated the Continental Shelf. Possible Paleo and Pre-Paleo sites are now under water off the coast of New Jersey. The Clovis style projectile point ceased to exist or was greatly diminished, and was replaced with shorter unfluted points. Theories abound on the reasons for this change. As the glaciers melted, the large mammals may have retreated to the north, with the Clovis people following them as well. The climate was rapidly changing, becoming warmer, and as the glaciers disappeared altogether, the climate became much as it is today. The large mammals either became extinct from excessive hunting or moved northward into oblivion.

The Archaic people seemed to have favored smaller projectile points. Some say this was because the game being hunted had decreased in size. The Late Pleistocene mammals were gone, leaving behind many of the animals we see today. In New Jersey there were still herds of elk, smaller bison, bear, the ever-present deer, and most of the smaller mammals that still survive. People continued to be hunters and food gatherers, remaining as they had for many thousands of years. The open grasslands and subarctic terrain gave way to expansive stands of spruce, pine, and oak forests.

A curious land phenomenon was also present as a reminder of the influence made by the extensive glacial activity. Known as periglacial features, they represent variously sized round or oval depressions in the terrain,

Bifurcate-based projectile points from early Archaic Period, 6,000 to 8,000 years B.P. Some may also have been used as hafted knives.
(Photo by the author.)

sometimes as large as several acres. In Paleo times, these depressions were bogs or freshwater ponds. Such depressions are, for the most part, now devoid of water except during heavier periods of rain, when they still contain water for days and sometimes weeks. Around the rims of these depressions Early Man frequently made campsites. Invariably the stone tools, weapons, and traces of fire-cracked stones from campfires can be found from Paleo-Indian times through the Archaic Period. These periglacial features are seen throughout the Inner and Outer Coastal Plains of southern New Jersey, including the Pine Barrens. Many an unsuspecting farmer has had his tractor imbedded in these depressions, and they are now usually avoided.

The Archaic people dominated the area we now call New Jersey. The population of Early Man increased substantially, although the people still remained essentially nomadic and ventured far and wide in quest of game. Sites of Early Man are evident on the sandy knolls of streams throughout the state. It has often been said that the banks of the Rancocas Creek in Burlington County and its tributaries seem to be one continuous band of occupation by prehistoric man.

*Full-grooved axes. These were hafted onto wooden handles and utilized as
woodworking tools as well as weapons during the Archaic Period. (Photo by the author.)*

*Three-quarter grooved axes from the late
Archaic Period, 1,000 to 4,000 years B.P. (Photo by the author.)*

The area we now know as the Pine Barrens was once thought to be a place of foreboding, a strange and uninhabited land where even Early Man seldom ventured, except to hunt game. This premise has been proven quite wrong. Habitation sites in the Pine Barrens and environs were rarely discovered because farming was not prevalent there. The soil was lacking in sufficient nutrients to produce most truck crops, hence Early Man sites were not readily found in plowed fields, as they were elsewhere. Today most of the Pine Barrens lie within a national reserve and is protected from development. Since this protection occurred, numerous archaeological studies have been done that identified thousands of sites from the Paleo-Indian Period 12,000 years ago until Late Woodland times in the 1700s. Mankind had indeed occupied the Pine Barrens, much of which still remains today in a wilderness state. The Pine Barrens remain a veritable treasure from an archaeologist's standpoint and will hopefully provide the answers to many questions, if intensive archaeological work is ever undertaken.

Various styles of weaponry and tools characterized the Archaic people. It is apparent that waves of migrating peoples from varied and sundry places entered New Jersey, stayed for possibly decades or substantially longer, and then moved on. Their stone tool sources and the variety of projectile point styles seem to indicate this. There are certain areas of central and southern New Jersey that had an influx of a band of hunters that stayed for hundreds of years and then either moved on or assimilated with others already here. This circumstance was known as the Koens-Crispin Complex, which was initially identified in 1915. Workmen were digging marl on the Crispin Farm along Ark Road in Medford, when they discovered crescent-shaped stones and large aboriginal projectile points. The University of Pennsylvania Museum was hastily summoned. Shortly thereafter, excavations were begun under the direction of E. W. Hawkes and Ralph Linton.

A portion of a village site was excavated on the joint properties of Petrus Koens and George Crispin, which yielded a complex of caches containing bannerstones, large argillite blades, and animal bones. The fine workmanship of the bannerstones and the fact that the caches were placed in definite rows around a central fire pit led the excavators to conclude that the complex had some ceremonial significance.

*Koens-Crispin projectile points and variants,
circa 4,000 years B.P. (Photo by the author.)*

In 1915 scientific methods of excavation and evaluation were in their infancy. Financing of archaeological projects was meager and sadly remains so even to this day. As a result, only the central portion of this large aboriginal village was investigated and all digging ceased. Today this site remains in a wooded area; however, custom-built homes now occupy this 4,000-year-old native village.

It was not until the years of the Great Depression, in the 1930s, that further archaeological work was done. In order to create work for the unskilled and unemployed, the Federal Government formed the Works Progress Administration. New Jersey began its state project under this program by creating the Indian Site Survey. The New Jersey State Museum and the Archeological Society of New Jersey were their sponsors.

In November 1937 it was decided to continue excavation of the Koens-Crispin site. Test trenches were dug throughout the area. They determined the village site extended some 2,000 feet along a branch of Mason's Creek, a tributary of the South Branch of Rancocas Creek. In the more productive areas, these test trenches were expanded into full excavations. The work continued, weather permitting, for one year. An area of 29,295 square feet was excavated, producing six pits, 41 caches, 2,605 stone artifacts, and 437 potsherds. The work was considerably hampered by the fact that the most productive trenches were located in a heavily wooded area, which meant chopping through roots of trees and dense undergrowth. The author has excavated under similar conditions and can well appreciate the difficulties encountered.

Specific artifacts recovered at the Koens-Crispin site made it unique. Quantities of large broad-bladed bifaces or projectile points, exquisite bannerstones, and numerous flat slabs of sandstone with circular grooves, called shaft-smoothers, were found.

In 1938 the artifact known as a bannerstone was considered by scientists to be problematic, and its exact use was unknown. It had been thought

Knobbed adzes of various sizes were utilized in woodworking and the making of dugout canoes. Found primarily in Koens-Crispin habitation sites. (Photo by the author.)

these crescent and butterfly-shaped stones, with holes drilled through their centers, were worn as emblems of authority, hence the name bannerstone. We now know they were actually used as a counter balance weight in conjunction with the atlatl, or spear-thrower.

A number of these bannerstones were known to have found their way into the pockets of workmen at the Koens-Crispin site. Even then, their monetary value to collectors and dealers was well established.

The excavators in 1938 were puzzled by the presence of large projectile points found in association with numerous shaft-smoothers having worn grooves of 3/8 inch diameter. They had thought these slabs of sandstone were used in the smoothing of arrowshafts, but the diameter of the grooves in the shaft-smoother indicated a shaft too thin to support these large projectile points. It has been theorized that the shaft-smoothers were actually used to smooth the socketed foreshaft of the atlatl to which the bannerstone was fastened. This is a logical assumption, given that the diameter of the hole in the bannerstone corresponds to the groove in the shaft-smoother.

Numerous sites of the Koens-Crispin Complex are in the Medford area and surrounding counties, all of which reveal some or all of the identical assemblage of artifacts. Due to the excellent work of archaeologist Richard A. Regensburg in excavating the Savich Farm site in Marlton, we now know a great deal more about these Koens-Crispin people. Carbon 14 tests performed by the University of Pennsylvania on charcoal samples at the Savich Farm revealed an age of more than 4,000 years B.P.

For many years, the author surface-collected several Koens-Crispin type sites in Medford, Marlton, Voorhees, and Cherry Hill on farmland that is now covered over with asphalt, cement, or housing developments. Hundreds of projectile points and related tool assemblages that were found are identical to those found at the Savich Farm and Koens-Crispin sites. Many other Koens-Crispin–type sites are located in Burlington, Monmouth, Gloucester, and Camden counties, thus attesting to the widespread wanderings of these particular people.

E. W. Hawkes was known to have performed additional work after his completion of the Koens-Crispin site in 1916. He did not file any written reports on other sites, although he did send many letters to his superior, Dr.

G. B. Gordon, Director of the University Museum in Philadelphia. While staying at Locust Farm in Medford, owned by A. P. Stackhouse, July 2, 1916, Hawkes mentions excavating a large number of argillite points, hammerstones, and celts. He expected to finish there at the end of that week. He visited a site in Indian Mills that was part of an old Indian burial ground.

Polished celts from the late Archaic Period. Hafted in wooden handles and used for various woodworking chores. (Photo by the author.)

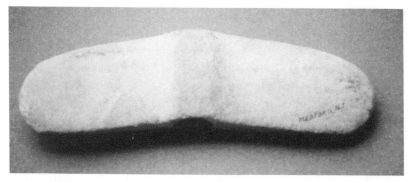

A wing-type bannerstone was used as a counter balance weight on the atlatl, or throwing stick. Prized by archaeologists and collectors alike. (Photo by the author.)

Excavation at the Savich Farm site in June 1968, from left to right: John Lukenda, George Flemming (the author), and Don Cassidy. (Photo courtesy of the author.)

There was also a modern schoolhouse nearby. Hawkes reported that the man who owned a portion of the property had given him permission to dig. He records finding some skeletal material and pieces of pottery. He said this material was deposited with the burials but does not give any further description. Hawkes commented about a local amateur removing a skeleton from the schoolhouse grounds and being taken to court, apparently because he did not have permission to dig.

Hawkes's next letter was from Locust Farm dated July 7, 1916. He intended to go to Indian Mills that Sunday to start work on the old cemetery site there. He describes it as a desolate place, seven miles from the nearest railroad station. He did not expect to stay there long unless the excavation was to turn out well. There is no mention of his partner Linton or having any help in the digging at these additional sites. He complains frequently about his expenses and not getting paid for his work. He records that his next address would be Indian Mills, care of Mr. Jacob Waters. This home still stands, long vacant and in a dilapidated condition, near the corner of Schoolhouse Lane and Stokes Road. It was owned by Jacob Waters in 1916, but has had a succession of owners ever since.

Jacob Waters's House is located on Stokes Road and is in near ruin. Nearby is a prehistoric habitation site and burial ground. (Photo by the author.)

Hawkes's next letter to Dr. Gordon dated July 10, 1916, advised he was starting work on the cemetery site that same day. Apparently he did not spend much time at the site. His next letter was from Tuckerton, New Jersey, dated July 24, 1916, where he had begun work and was shipping the items excavated at Indian Mills that day. He considered the Indian Mills site as a halfway station of the Indians living along the Rancocas Creek when they migrated to the shore in the summer. He also felt they followed the old trail across the state. The cemetery site is directly on this trail known as the Shamong Trail or Stokes Road.

Hawkes visited the Armstrong Farm located on Atsion Road near Indian Mills and apparently did some digging there as well, because he describes finding charcoal and bones, also argillite specimens underlying the more modern Lenape material on top. Mr. Armstrong had told him that in plowing deep he had uncovered many argillite ceremonial points and axes. He also described two remarkably shaped hoes, one heart-shaped and the other a disc. Hawkes felt that they were possibly ceremonial objects and not hoes. He believed the evidence from the Armstrong Farm was as conclusive as that from the Locust Farm site at Medford. All of this was being shipped to the University Museum. Hawkes again complained that he had not received reimbursement for his expenses for the month of June. His next letter was dated September 1916 from 3911 Pine St., Philadelphia when he advised Dr. Gordon he had secured a position at the Wanamaker Store. Apparently his lack of prompt pay for his efforts and expenses proved too slow in coming and he moved on to more lucrative endeavors.

The skeletal material Hawkes excavated near the Jacob Waters house was most likely prehistoric and should not be confused with the burial ground of the reservation Indians that was located a short distance away.

Toward the end of the Archaic Period approximately 4,000 years ago, flat-bottomed cooking vessels were fashioned out of steatite, also known as soapstone. One large quarry for this material lies in Lancaster County, Pennsylvania, just west of the village of Atglen. It has also been known as Christiana. The area is still being farmed and very few traces of this quarry remain. A soapstone bowl was once plowed out in Indian Mills and was prized by a local collector.

Projectile points of various sizes and shapes were used over a span of 8,000 to 10,000 years of Early Man's flint-knapping capabilities. (Photo by the author.)

Small pendants worn as decoration. Top example undrilled with groove for hanging. Bottom row displays three pendants that are drilled. Bottom left made of petrified cypress wood and very unusual. (Photo by the author.)

Early Man traveled great distances to procure many of the raw materials needed for his tools and implements. Eventually these same types of cooking pots were fashioned out of local stream clay and many were tempered with crushed steatite fragments, apparently from stone bowls that were no longer serviceable. In time these bowls were shaped into a more conical style with round bottoms instead of flat. Aboriginal pottery was never glazed and is easily distinguished from modern pottery. Fragments of both steatite and pottery bowls are frequently found on the surface of prehistoric sites.

Projectile points were still being utilized at the end of spears, although the Koens-Crispin points eventually disappeared and were replaced with smaller variations. At the same time much more slender projectile points were also being utilized. This variation could have occurred from an influx of migrating bands of hunters who settled in this area for a time, or simply through communication and trade with others from various areas.

It is interesting to note that many projectile point styles are either identical or very similar over a distance of hundreds of miles or more. This

Triangular points. Most of the smaller ones were used on the tip of arrowshafts; the larger ones were used in all periods on thrusting and throwing spears. (Photo by the author.)

Roller type pestles were utilized in grinding and crushing corn and grains in wooden and stone mortars. (Photo by the author.)

17

seems to establish the constant nomadic wanderings of these early prehistoric people.

THE WOODLAND PERIOD

Man, the hunter, continued his quest for game animals armed with the traditional spear. This period emerged from the end of the Archaic Period some 3,000 years ago and lasted until approximately 1,000 years ago. The projectile points were noticeably smaller, although many were extremely well made. Trading and communication with other bands of people from hundreds of miles away seemed to occur more frequently. This interaction led to the adoption of many new point styles as well as very unusual stone tools and ornamental artifacts.

Pottery became much more elaborate and highly decorated. The wet clay was impressed with fish netting, woven mats, and a cord wound stick. Sharpened sticks or bone awls were used to incise the wet clay. Pendants worn about the neck were fashioned out of flat stones and occasionally decorated. The author has many such pendants, including one made of petrified cypress wood found near Lumberton.

Flaking batons were used by man, the tool-maker, in flaking various knives, blades, and projectile points. (Photo by the author.)

Many aboriginal sites in the area of Indian Mills reflect extensive use of the Brotherton Reservation lands in prehistoric times. There is no demonstrable evidence that the natives were occupying this land at the time of the reservation founding.

Toward the end of the Woodland Period, about 1,000 years ago, the bow and arrow came into use. Projectile points radically changed and became even smaller. The most common shape was triangular.

Man, the hunter, became more domesticated and sedentary. Bands of people became larger, possibly consisting of many families. Villages of bark lodges eventually populated the major creeks and rivers of South Jersey and along Delaware Bay. Many of these villages became permanent in nature. The campsites along the lesser streams and tributaries were, for the most part, only temporary in nature, primarily used on hunting and fishing excursions.

CHAPTER 2
European Colonization

When the Europeans arrived in the early 17th century the Delaware Valley was occupied by native villages of perhaps 200 to 300 inhabitants each. They called themselves Lenape (pronounced Le-nah-pay), which very simply means "men." They were a loose confederation of clans and family groups, each with its own leader or elder. There was no supreme head of all the various clans or family groups. Their separate villages were usually named after geographical locations. Along the present Rancocas Creek were the Rancocas Indians. Rancocas means "sloping." Robert Evelyn's map of 1634 shows this village near the present town of Centerton. The chief's name was Ramcock, and he is described as having 100 warriors. The Indian population at that time was quite small.

One might surmise that the native population was immense owing to the large number of artifacts that are continuously being unearthed throughout New Jersey. Yet the aboriginal population, as can best be estimated, never exceeded 10,000 persons throughout the entire state. The most logical explanation of the vast number of artifacts the natives left behind is simply that they were living in the area for more than 12,000 years, constantly moving from one place to another, and consequently leaving many traces of their culture behind. The majority of their hunting implements were made of stone and therefore were not perishable, as were other items made of wood and bone, of which very few have survived.

At the time of initial European contact, the area now known as Shamong Township was a wilderness. It is doubtful there were any contemporary sites of Early Man with the exception of scattered and temporary hunting camps. The majority of the permanent villages were along the Delaware River, the Atlantic Coast, and the Delaware Bay and their main tributaries.

Many aboriginal campsites that remain in the area of Shamong Township reflect extensive use of the land that eventually became the Brotherton Reservation. The area has been sorely lacking in archaeological work. Much remains to be done in this respect. Many questions plague historians and archaeologists as to why this particular area, known as Edgepillock, or "place of pure water," by the natives, was chosen for the location of their reservation. Did they have some say in choosing this location or was it chosen for them? Had they been located there in any kind of permanence since the arrival of the Europeans? Had traditions passed down through the generations bestowed some special significance on the area? Was it just an area that was so remote and sparsely settled that they could live in peace without interference? Or was it simply chosen by members of the colonial government as an ideal place to isolate the peaceful natives from the more warlike Indians to the north and west of New Jersey? By choosing this spot, the government may also have desired to keep the native population from interacting with the white settlers whose population far exceeded that of the natives. The records remain unclear. Wherever the true facts lie, the evidence to date does not indicate any habitation of the reservation area at the time of first European contact.

In 1524, the Florentine, Giovanni da Verrazano, sailing on behalf of France, very briefly had contact with the native Indians in New Jersey. It was not until the early 1600s that more extensive contact began with the natives by Dutch, English, and Swedish traders.

The Lenape Indians were then mainly concentrated in villages along the main waterways emptying into the Delaware River and Bay, and along the Atlantic Coastal areas. They were still a primitive people living entirely in a Stone Age environment. When trade began with these strangers from Europe, the natives became utterly fascinated with objects made of metal. In a very short time the Indians began to lose their desire to fashion tools and arrowpoints out of stone. Instead they preferred anything and everything made of metal. Arrowpoints were being fashioned out of parts of metal pots and barrel hoops. Pottery bowls were being discarded in favor of brass and iron cooking kettles. All manner of household goods were traded to the Indians. The slow process of eliminating their culture and identity had begun.

Before long the natives became almost totally dependent on bartered goods from Europeans. The demand for beaver and otter fur by the

Europeans caused the natives to forget their old habits of conservation. They hunted and trapped the fur-bearing mammals almost to extinction. Before the White man came, the natives only hunted and trapped what they needed to survive. Now all this had changed.

Settlements in the early 1600s by the Dutch and Swedes became more frequent along the Delaware River. The natives called themselves Lenape, however the Dutch and Swedes called them "Renape." The Lenape speech is considered part of the Algonquian language family and is shared by many Indian tribes in the eastern United States. There were several dialects of this language spoken in New Jersey, and the dialects varied considerably from one section of the state to the other.

The Dutch and Swedish settlers had fairly amicable relations with the natives, with few exceptions, and some purchases of land were made mostly with trade goods. The early deeds reflect no exchange of money. The Indians' insatiable desire for European trade goods caused them to sell their lands away for household goods, bolts of cloth, ornaments, various and sundry trinkets, and, worst of all, rum and brandy.

The Indians' concept of land ownership totally differed from that of the Europeans. They allowed the settlers to build homes on land they had purchased, but still felt they could hunt, fish, and trap on the same property. In other words, in their minds, they had not bargained these rights away. There were many land disputes and boundary disagreements between the settlers and the natives. This was caused in part by how the land was originally obtained. Indians would often sell tracts of land that were also claimed by several other Indian families. Boundaries were cited by vague physical locations, stumps of trees, streams, rocks, and hills. The Lenape did not feel any sale was final. Their creator had given them such things as the land. This concept of land ownership became even more complicated when the English eventually took possession and control of New Jersey in 1664. The British Lords of Trade had instructed the Proprietors of East and West Jersey to make it a matter of policy to buy Indian lands in every case to prevent any hostility.

The English were not content in merely small purchases of land, but rather negotiated with the Indians for vast tracts, which they were intent on colonizing with thousands of settlers. The fact that the natives still felt they could use the land for hunting led to conflict and confusion. One group of natives would enter into a land deed for a large area, and then another group of natives would come along at a later date asserting their hunting and fishing rights to the same property.

As a consequence of this confusion of land ownership it is estimated there were upward of 800 or more deeds made with the Indians to secure most of the land in the Delaware River Valley, and elsewhere in the state.

A typical Indian deed for land between the Assinpink and Rancocas Creeks reads:

> One Conveyance or Deed bearing date the 10th of October 1677 made by Ahtahkones, Okanickhon, Weskeakitt, Pecheatus, Kekroppamant, Indian Sackamackers of the one pte to Joseph Hemsley, Robert Stacy, William Emley, Thomas Folke, Thomas Olive, Daniell Wills, John Pennford & Benjamin Scott of the other pte, that Tract of Land lying along the River Dellaware from & between the midstream of Rankokus Creeke to the southward & the midstream of Sent Pinck Creek at the falls to the northward, and bounded to the eastward by a Right Lyne & extending along the countrey from the uppermost head of Rancocas Creeke to the Partition Lyne of Sr. George Carteretts Right against the uppermost head of St Pinck Creeke for the considerations of Forty six fadome of Duffields, Thirty blankets, one hundred & fifty pound of powder, Thirty Gunns, Thirty kettles & Thirty kettles more instead of Wampam, Thirty Axes, Thirty Howes, Thirty aules, Thirty needles, Thirty looking glasses, Thirty pair of stockings, Seaven anchors of Brandy or Rum, Thirty knives, Thirty barres of lead, Thirty six rings, Thirty Jews harps, Thirty combs, Thirty braseletts, Thirty bells, Thirty tobacco toungs or Steeles, Thirty pair of Sissrs, Twelve tobacco boxes, Thirty flints, Tenn spoonfuls of red paint, one hundred of fish hooks, one gross of tobacco pipes, and thirty shirts to them paid.

Witnessed & executed before Henricus Jacobs, Marmaduke Rosendale, Mathew Smith, Alex Watts, Tuckahoppenick, Attarrumhah.

One of the Indian kings or sachems mentioned in this deed was Ockanickon, who lived in the vicinity of Burlington. He had befriended the Quaker colonists from the time of their arrival in August 1677 and remained an ally until his death in 1681. He was converted to the Quaker faith and interred with considerable ceremony at the Friends Burial Ground in Burlington.

The Grave of Chief Ockanickon. A great and good man to White and Indian alike. He lies buried in the Friends Burial Ground in Burlington, NJ.
(Photo by the author.)

Members of the Religious Society of Friends, more commonly known as the Quakers, were the most prominent of the early English settlers. Their friendly relationships with the natives were exceptional. The tenets of their faith respected the dignity of every man regardless of his station in life. The Indians recognized the peaceful, nonviolent nature of these early colonists and welcomed them. As time went on however, the colonists multiplied by the hundreds and then by the thousands. Along with this explosion in population, not only by Quakers, but other English settlers, the Indians' numbers decreased dramatically.

Thousands succumbed to the ravages of smallpox, which could not be cured by their herbal remedies or sweat lodges. Trading with the colonists frequently involved the Indians' lust for rum to the point where abuse of alcohol also devastated them. Many of the natives fled across the Delaware River into Pennsylvania and points westward, often carrying contagious diseases with them.

Moravian missionaries met with some success in areas of Eastern Pennsylvania in the early 1700s, along the Susquehanna and Lehigh rivers. The Lenape Indians were then more frequently referred to as the Jersey Indians or simply the Jerseys. These Indians were peaceful and friendly to the settlers in central and southern New Jersey. The area north of the Raritan River was inhabited by the Munsee Delaware, a warlike people who were involved in several tragic incidents of murder and destruction with the settlers there, when they sided with the French during the French and Indian War.

By the year 1745 the non-native population of New Jersey approached 60,000 persons while the Indian population had suffered a devastating loss, not only from smallpox and alcohol abuse, but also due to forced migration westward. Their numbers had decreased to less than one thousand, only a tenth of what it had been when the first Europeans arrived.

The rapid demise of the native population caused the religious community to take particular notice of what had been occurring. This was the age of what is known as the Great Awakening, a period of "fire-and-brimstone" evangelistic preaching. One of the chief architects of this period was the Presbyterian minister, Reverend Jonathan Edwards, of Massachusetts. He is one of the most significant figures in American history. Edwards was born in 1703 and died of smallpox in 1758. During his life he was of the aristocratic class. At his death at the age of 54, he was president of the College of New Jersey, which later became Princeton University. His importance to this story lies in the fact that he was the mentor of the devoted missionaries David and John Brainerd and many others.

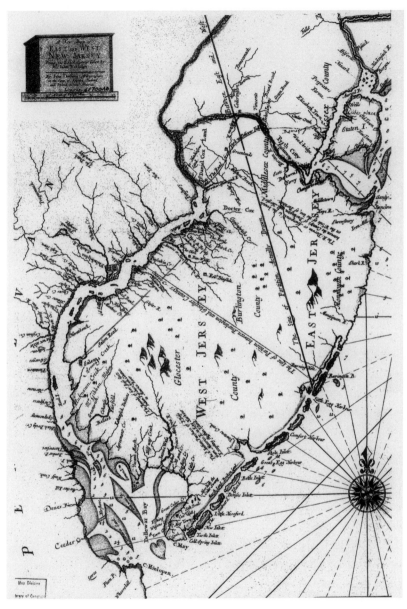

A map of New Jersey showing the division of East and West Jersey in 1700.
(Courtesy of Map Division, Library of Congress.)

CHAPTER 3

Bethel and Crosswicks

The village of Crosswicks in Burlington County is located along the southern bank of Crosswicks Creek. It is a quaint village developed today primarily along one main street, much as it must have appeared more than 300 years ago when it was known as Crossweeksung, meaning "divided waters" or "place of separation" by the Indians.

Town of Crosswicks as it appears today going down the main street.
(Photo by the author.)

The first Friends Meeting House was built in 1693 and was a small frame building. This was replaced in 1707 by a larger brick one, and again by another brick meeting house in 1776. This building is still standing today in a prominent part of the village and bears a cannonball embedded in the north wall as a mute reminder of the skirmish that occurred here during the Revolutionary War.

Crosswicks Friends Meeting House erected in 1776 on the site of an earlier meeting-house where many conferences took place with the Lenape. (Photo by the author.)

In the early part of the 1700s there was an Indian encampment on the north side of the Crosswicks Creek opposite the village. It was here that the Presbyterian missionary Reverend David Brainerd first preached to the Indians in New Jersey.

David Brainerd was born April 20, 1718, in Haddam, Connecticut. He was the son of well-to-do New England parents, Hezekiah and Dorothy Brainerd. Losing his parents at a very tender age complicated his youth. He was only 9 when his father died, and his mother passed away when he was 14. He then moved across the Connecticut River to live with his married sister, Jersuha. When he was 19, he inherited a farm where he lived for a year or more.

David Brainerd managed to enter Yale College in September 1739. Even at this young age he exhibited signs of poor health, described as being a very pale and sickly person. While in his first year at Yale he began spitting up blood. His health was so poor that he had to leave school for a year and did not return to Yale until November 1740.

Brainerd had a burning passion to become a minister, but was hardly a good candidate for the mission field. He was greatly influenced by Rev. Jonathan Edwards, the brilliant evangelist of his day. Brainerd became deeply involved in a cult at Yale called the "New Light." He also had publicly ridiculed one of his professors named Chauncey Whittelsey, saying, "he had no more grace than a chair and he wondered why the Rector did not drop dead for firing students for their evangelical zeal." Such was the climate of the Great Awakening. David Brainerd was expelled from Yale in 1742 after he refused to apologize for his actions. Confused and depressed, he turned to Rev. Jonathan Edwards who encouraged him to seek out other avenues for his restless spirit and overwhelming desire to become a missionary. He completed his studies for the ministry privately and became licensed by the Association of Ministers at Danbury, Connecticut, on July 29, 1742. He was approved as a missionary for The Society in Scotland for Propagating Christian Knowledge on November 25, 1742.

David Brainerd initially labored among the Housatonic Indians some 20 miles northeast of Stockbridge, Massachusetts, where he remained from April 1743 to March 1744. The Presbyterian Church in Newark, New Jersey, ordained him on June 11, 1744, and slowly he began his mission work among the Lenape at the Forks of the Delaware near Easton, Pennsylvania. He had very little success there, and then visited other villages on the Susquehanna River in Pennsylvania where again his results were not particularly to his liking. The native men were especially distrustful of him.

Brainerd's life as a missionary was one of hardship and suffering. Brainerd was frequently exposed to cold and hunger, often sleeping on bare ground in all kinds of weather. He had periods of frequent depression. In spite of his failing health, however, he continued to persist. He was determined to win over the confidence of the heathen Indians and convert them to Christianity.

He journeyed by horseback on June 19, 1745, to the Indian village of Crossweeksung, and it is there that he began to write in the journals he was to keep until June 19, 1746. Rev. Jonathan Edwards, who had been keeping in close contact with Brainerd, would subsequently publish them. The journals gave a detailed day-to-day account of his labors among the Indians and had a dramatic impact on those interested in pursuing a career as a missionary. Even today these journals continue to provide an inspiration for those interested in the mission field.

David Brainerd's initial contact with the Indians at Crosswicks was disappointing. He had heard there were many natives living there, but when he arrived he found only a few families comprised mostly of women and children. Others were scattered over a wide range of the countryside from five to 15 miles away, and as much as 30 miles distant. By June 22 the number of Indians had increased to 30, including a number of men. The news of his arrival was spreading.

In July 1745 Brainerd returned from a visit to the Forks of the Delaware and was able to baptize his Indian interpreter, whom he called Moses Tunda Tanta, about 50 years of age, and his wife. He had initially employed him as an interpreter in the summer of 1744. This interpreter became known in history as Moses Tatamy, and he was actually an Indian from New Jersey who claimed an interest in lands near Allentown at the 1758 Peace Conferences. Tatamy, who had migrated to Pennsylvania many years prior to his first contact with Brainerd, was a skilled interpreter having had previous contact with Moravian missionaries. He had become a great friend to the colonists and frequently acted as an intermediary between his people and the early settlers. Moses Tatamy would eventually play an important role in the fate of his New Jersey brethren.

By March 24, 1746, Brainerd writes that the Indians at Crosswicks numbered 130, both old and young. His triumphs at Crosswicks, however, were not without a price. He struggled with relentless and recurring bouts of depression. His ministry was a very emotional one, and he writes that the Indians "were universally praying and crying for mercy in every part of the house and many out of doors."

Brainerd's brand of religion did not sit too well with the Quaker inhabitants of Crosswicks. Tensions continued to increase between the two groups. The Quakers disapproved of Brainerd's evangelical style. The Quaker meetings were basically conducted in reverent silence where they very simply relied on God's inner light to guide them.

Quakers eschewed the emotional methods so central to Brainerd's "fire-and-brimstone" philosophy.

Problems were not only developing in a secular way, but White settlers were constantly taunting the Indians. The natives were frequently demoralized by alcohol-induced public displays of inappropriate behavior. Brainerd complained that local settlers were giving his Indian converts alcohol, and that caused them to lose their moral values and Christian ways of life. In addition, the fields they had in cultivation had lost their fertility and were not producing sufficient crops. Brainerd had to pay some of the Indians' debts out of his own pocket. Excessive drinking was the chief contributor to their indebtedness to the settlers.

The time had come to move to more fertile lands near Cranbury, some 15 miles from Crosswicks, on territory allegedly still owned by the Indians. They began clearing the land there for cultivation and also to erect cabins. Cranbury was the nearest town to this land, and the Indians later became identified with that name and called the Cranbury Indians. It had been David Brainerd's dream to someday have a self-contained, self-sufficient community for his Indian mission. His dream was about to come true.

BETHEL

David Brainerd named his new community Bethel, a Hebrew word meaning "House of God." On May 4, 1746, he writes in his journal "my people now removed to their lands." He writes he was obliged to board with an English family in Cranbury, June 19, 1746, exactly one year since he came to preach at Crosswicks. On September 27, 1746, he writes, "I was able to ride over to my people every day, and take some care of those who were at work erecting a small house for me to reside in among the Indians." During the subsequent winter, Brainerd said, "I have often been obliged to preach in their houses in cold and windy weather, when they have been full of smoke and cinders, as well as unspeakably filthy, which has thrown me many times into violent sick headaches." These horrific conditions, coupled with tuberculosis, hastened the final days of his life. John Brainerd had been appointed by the Scottish Society to replace his brother.

John Brainerd arrived at Bethel on April 15, 1747, and found the fulfillment of his brother's dream. The settlement was on 80 acres of cleared woodland and had developed into a self-sustaining community and a flourishing cabin town that included a schoolhouse and a home for the pastor.

David Brainerd was facing his last days. His illness combined with the harsh conditions he was forced to live in had taken their toll. He left Bethel on horseback April 21, 1747, never to return. After staying for a time at the home of friends in Haddam, Connecticut, he made his way to the home of his beloved mentor, Rev. Jonathan Edwards in Northampton, Massachusetts, arriving there May 28, 1747. He struggled daily with depression and physical discomfort. During the last months of his life Jerusha Edwards was his constant companion. She was the daughter of Rev. Edwards. Then only 17, she was also David's fiancée.

David Brainerd died of tuberculosis, in his 30th year, October 9, 1747. Jerusha Edwards died February 14, 1748, also of tuberculosis, which she may have contracted from David. They are buried next to one another in Northampton, Massachusetts. The Reverend Jonathan Edwards wrote, concerning his daughter Jerusha,

> She was a person of much the same spirit with Brainerd. She had constantly taken care of him and attended him in his sickness for nineteen weeks before his death, devoting herself to it with great delight, because she looked upon him as an eminent servant of Jesus Christ. In this time he had much conversation with her on the things of religion; and in his dying state often expressed to us, her parents, his great confidence that he should meet her in heaven; and his high opinion of her, not only as a true Christian, but a very eminent saint, one, whose soul was uncommonly fed and entertained with things which appertain to the most spiritual, experimental, and distinguishing parts of religion; and one, who by the temper of her mind, was fitted to deny herself from God, and to do good beyond any young woman whatsoever, whom she knew. She had manifested a heart uncommonly devoted to God, in the course of her life, many years before her death; and said on her death-bed, that

"she had not seen one minute for several years, wherein she
desired to live one minute longer, for the sake of any other good
in life, but doing good; living to God and doing what might be
for his Glory."

Rev. Edwards was an aristocrat by birth with a Puritan heritage. He was
one of the chief proponents of the Great Awakening of the 18th century.
He had published a biography of David Brainerd along with his journals.
This became a best-selling text in 19th-century America and was known to
encourage countless Christians to seek careers in missionary service. He
died at the age of 54. He had been president of the College of New Jersey
at Princeton.

*The wooded area of Thompson Park just outside Jamesburg, NJ,
where the village of Bethel once was located.* (Photo by the author.)

John Brainerd, the younger brother of David, succeeded him in the work
of evangelizing the Indians. He was born in Haddam, Connecticut,
February 28, 1720. He entered Yale College in 1742 and graduated in 1746
without incident. On April 13, 1747, he was examined by the New York

Presbytery in Elizabethtown, New Jersey, and was appointed by the Scottish Society to assist his brother David at Bethel.

John Brainerd arrived at Bethel on April 15, 1747, and joined his brother there. David acquainted his brother with the community and the Indians welcomed him joyfully. At that time they numbered over 120, 78 of whom had been baptized. David then left the care of his beloved Indians to his brother John and began the slow and tedious final journey back to New England. It must have been a sad day for all concerned. David was leaving his life's work after only three years in the mission field. His life had been abruptly ended by illness. It has been said he became a martyr for his beliefs and his overwhelming dedication to the poor Indian natives wherever he found them.

John Brainerd had entered his mission field with some apprehension at the enormity of the work that lay ahead of him. He was comforted however in the progress he was making in such a short time as evidenced by a letter he wrote to Rev. Ebenezer Pemberton in New York dated June 23, 1747, from Bethel. It reads, in part,

> There are now belonging to the society of Indians something upward of one hundred and sixty persons, old and young, who I think may properly be called inhabitants of the town. Out of the number first mentioned there are about thirty persons who came to this place since my arrival here, which was the 15th of April last. The next thing I shall mention is the school that consists of fifty-three children who properly belong to and generally attend upon it. The Indians have upwards of forty acres of English grain in the ground and about so much Indian corn, and they do, I think, in general follow their secular business as well as can be expected considering they have all their days been used to sloth and idleness.

Brainerd's optimism seems to have been short-lived as he later records, "About this time a mortal sickness prevailed among the Indians, and carried off a considerable number, and especially those who had been religiously wrought upon, which made some infidels say, that it was because they had forsaken the old Indian ways and become Christians." There is no mention of the actual sickness but it quite possibly could have been smallpox, a European disease that was recurrent and deadly to the natives.

John Brainerd was ordained a Presbyterian minister at Newark in 1748. He felt fulfilled and happy at his accomplishments in the mission field. This period of time, though, was not without adversity. He was now confronted with possible eviction from the farmland and cabin community at Bethel. As early as 1746 there had been rumors that some of the local surrounding farmers were apprehensive about such a large number of Indians settling so near to them. The Royal Governors Council had received these complaints on April 9, 1746, stating that for the past six years only two Indians, Andrew and Peter, had lived on these lands. They were fearful that a larger number of Indians would possibly steal or kill their livestock. This did not happen and the Indians continued to prosper at Bethel.

In 1748 a visitor, named Job Strong, noted "the diligent attention of the children in school and their proficiency in reading and writing and catechisms of divers sorts." On October 30, 1749, the Royal Governor Jonathan Belcher and his lady walked through the town of Bethel to visit the Indians and see their town and dwellings. Perhaps the governor's visit was just a prelude to further complications with respect to the land titles for Bethel. Prior to the governor's visit the Chief Justice of New Jersey, Robert Hunter Morris, sued the Indians on June 20, 1749. Morris was known as a professed deist absent of any religious faith or sentiments of humanity. He claimed title to these lands at Bethel under pretext of a will made by the Indians' former king that was undoubtedly forged. Justice Morris had aristocratic connections and eventually was victorious in evicting the Indians from their homes at Bethel. He was a shrewd land speculator and eventually produced deeds that predated the establishment of Bethel—not only his own deeds but also deeds from his aristocratic friends. They had also made purchases from the proprietors.

Apparently Ebeneezer Heywood, the Indian schoolmaster, had died, as John Brainerd advertised in the New York Gazette in 1750, for all bills against the estate of which he was the executor.

In 1755 the Indians were required to leave their homes. Brainerd had wanted to keep them together in one community but now this was not possible, and so they scattered. There was utter confusion. Some of the Indians went back to the Crosswicks area and some stayed in the wilderness area of Bethel.

Before the actual eviction at Bethel, John Brainerd had been attending the College of New Jersey nearby, later to become Princeton University, where he received his master's degree. He had been traveling great distances and continued to spend as much time as possible with the Indians at Bethel. On November 1, 1752, he married Experience Lyon of New Haven, Connecticut. Their first child, Sophia, was born August 11, 1753, probably at Bethel. Their second child, Mary, was born July 18, 1755. Shortly after Mary was born, John Brainerd obtained a pastorate at the First Presbyterian Church in Newark. During his repeated absence from his beloved Indians, he enlisted the help of the Reverend William Tennent of Freehold who visited the Indians at least once a week. It was very difficult to gather them all together as they had scattered throughout the area, but he did the best he could. These were very unsettled times and the French and Indian War was just about to commence.

On December 3, 1755, the Indians at Bethel and Cranbury sent a petition to Royal Governor Jonathan Belcher setting forth the danger they were in from either being destroyed by the English, or by Indians on the side of the French. They asked the governor for protection. Books were distributed throughout the state to various justices of the peace who had to list the names of Indians and obtain a solemn declaration from them that they were loyal to the English Majesty. The Indians had to be registered as one of his Majesty's good subjects. They in turn would be given a certificate and a red ribbon to be worn upon their head so they would not be mistaken as a spy or enemy of the English.

In December 1755 the General Assembly named Charles Read, Richard Salter, and Samuel Smith as commissioners to deal with some grievances of the Indians, who were now widely scattered rather than contained at Bethel. They held their first conference at the Friends Meeting House in Crosswicks on January 8, 1756, where they met with representatives of the

Indians. In March 1757 an act was adopted that prohibited the use of steel traps weighing more than 3-1/2 lbs., declared that an Indian could not be imprisoned for debt, and placed rigid restrictions on the sale of liquor to the Indians. The act also strictly rendered the sales or leases of land void unless they were obtained as directed by the act.

A second meeting was held at Crosswicks from February 20 to February 23, 1758. The commissioners present were Andrew Johnston and Richard Salter, Esquires of the Council, and Charles Read, John Stevens, William Foster, and Jacob Spicer, Esquires. The Indians were Teedyuscunk (also spelled Teedyuskung), king of the Delawares, and George Hopayock from the Susquehannah. Crosswicks Indians present included Andrew Wooley, George Wheelwright, Peepy, Joseph Cuish, William Loulax, Gabriel Mitop, Zeb Conchee, Bill News, and John Pombelus. A ledger of John Imlay dated 1757 provides ample evidence that the Indians were still maintaining residence in nearby Crosswicks. Imlay's store was on the Southeast corner of Park & Farnsworth Streets in Bordentown. One of the entries in the ledger is for John Pombelus, who was at the Crosswicks Conference, and whose Indian name was Matanoo. He had traded six fox skins, five raccoon skins, and 41 deer skins as credit for one felt hat, three saws, one knife, four pounds of shot, a half gallon of molasses, two pounds of powder, one quart of rum, one dozen pipes, one jug, and one paper of tobacco.

Also in attendance at this conference were mountain Indians named Moses Tatamy and Phillip, and a Raritan Indian named Tom Evans. Ancocas Indians were Robert Kekott, Jacob Mullis, and Samuel Gosling. The Indians from Cranbury were the most numerous and included Thomas Store, Steven Calvin, John Pompshire, Benjamin Claus, Joseph Wooley, Josiah Store, Isaac Still, James Calvin, Peter Calvin, Dirick Quaquay, Ebeneezer Wooley, and Sarah Stores, widow of Quaquahela. Abraham Loques and Isaac Swanela represented the southern Indians. John Pompshire served as the interpreter.

The Indians were brought together to settle any claims they had in regard to lands in the colony. Their claims were all for lands south of the Raritan River. The tracts of land in question were very numerous and included large areas of land in central and southern New Jersey that the

Indians felt they had never been paid. Several tracts need to be cited as they have a bearing on information contained in the forthcoming chapter on Wepink, "the other Indian town." Jacob Mullis claimed the pinelands on Edge Pillock Branch and Goshen Neck, where Benjamin Springer and George Marpole's Mills stand, and all the land between the head branches of those creeks to where the waters join or meet. The Indians collectively claimed their settlements near Cranbury, on Menalopen River, and in Falkner's Tract where many of the Indians now live. They also claimed a few acres below the plantation of Robert Pearsons, on the north side of Crosswicks Creek.

After the Indians had delivered these claims to the commissioners, they executed a power of attorney and appointed Indians Tom Store, Moses Tatamy, Steven Calvin, Isaac Still, and John Pompshire to transact all future land business for them with the government. Most of the Indians were well acquainted with John Brainerd. Many had adopted biblical names as well as the last name Calvin, which was so prominent in the Presbyterian faith.

Sometimes working behind the scenes and other times quite openly, Brainerd had been trying to obtain a reservation for his Indians. In 1754 he attempted to obtain a tract of 4,000 acres through the Society for Propagating Christian Knowledge but had failed. In another instance in April 1757, Burlington County Quakers formed the New Jersey Association for Helping the Indians, but this too never materialized. Their efforts seemed to have encouraged the colonial government to take appropriate action not only to protect the White settlers from any possible harm should these Christian Indians merge with the wild Indians, in a time when the French and Indian War was raging, but also to contain the remaining natives in the colony so they could be nurtured, protected, and made useful citizens. At least that was the plan.

John Brainerd continued to serve as pastor at his church in Newark, and his life was still one of happiness until hardship and sadness struck. His third child, named David after his brother, was born April 11, 1757. On September 17, 1757, his wife, Experience Brainerd, died. Brainerd made the following tender and affectionate notes,

My dear wife after a long and painful sickness departed the 17th of September 1757, and the greatest loss I ever sustained, the most sorrowful day my eyes ever saw. May God sanctify the heavy stroke to me and my little babes. Support me under it and make up the great loss to us in spiritual and divine Blessings. Dust thou are and Dust thou shalt return- having a desire to depart and be with Christ which is far better. She has exchanged a vale of tears for a Crown of Glory. Blessed are the Dead that die in the Lord. They rest from their labours and their works will follow them.

As if the pain and suffering he endured on the death of his wife was not enough, more tragedy was to follow. His first-born, Sophia, in her sixth year, died September 5, 1758. His son David, in his second year, died nine days later on September 14, 1758. Both are buried in the graveyard of the First Presbyterian Church in Newark. Brainerd's only surviving child, Mary, now

A plaque in Thompson Park commemorating the noble
experiment of the Brainerd brothers. (Photo by the author.)

41

age three, accompanied him further into his destined future as missionary to the last remaining Indians in New Jersey.

The Indian town of Bethel was now just the sad memory of a mission that had prospered and then failed. In 1841 Alexander Redmond purchased the area of land that included the Bethel property. He found many cellars in the fields where the Indian cabins had been. He retained many of the stones that were used as hearths and also many Indian relics. There were numerous apple and cherry trees on the property still bearing fruit. Today this land once occupied by the "Cranbury Indians" lies just south of the present village of Jamesburg. A plaque on a boulder in the forest describes what was once there. The area of Bethel is now known as Thompson Park. It is a beautiful and serene spot in a semi-wooded area. There are many trails to explore on which one may conjure up memories of what had once been, but is no more.

A never-ending spring of pure clean water is still on the property and was doubtless used by the natives when they lived there.

CHAPTER 4

The Founding of Brotherton

At a conference with the Delaware Indians held in Burlington on August 9, 1758, a proposition was received from the Indians present requesting that a tract of land, in the possession of Benjamin Springer, should be purchased for the Indians living south of the Raritan River. This land was known as Edgepillock, meaning "place of pure clear water." The Indians agreed to release all their rights to land south of the Raritan River excepting the claim of Moses Tatamy and those of some who held property under English rights. In particular, a tract of land called Wepink, formerly secured to the family of King Charles (or Mahamickwon by his Indian name) is cited. The natives also referred to this tract as Coaxen.

Sufficient money was appropriated to purchase the Springer property that consisted of 3,044 acres excepting a lot of 100 acres, claimed by a James Denight and family who would continue to live there. The Springer property was described as comprising a cedar swamp and saw mill adjoining many thousands of acres of poor, uninhabited land that was suitable for hunting and convenient also for fishing on the sea coast. The deed was taken in the name of the governor and commissioners, and their heirs, in trust for the use of the Indian natives who have or do reside in this colony south of the Raritan, and their successors. A clause, provided that it would not be in the power of the Indians, their successors, or anyone else to lease or sell any part thereof of the land; and any person (Indian excepted) attempting to settle there, would be removed by warrant from a justice of the peace; no timber to be cut but by the Indians, under penalty of 40 shillings fine for every tree.

On August 15, 1758, Charles Read, one of the Indian Commissioners, wrote a letter to Israel Pemberton, which reads in part,

> We have purchased an tract of Land for the Indians extremely Convenient for them abt. 2000 or 2500 acres & have

this day sent a Surveyor to Survey a parcel of Wild natural meadow near the place where they can cutt their Hay & directed him to take up 500 acres of it. They can in a day come

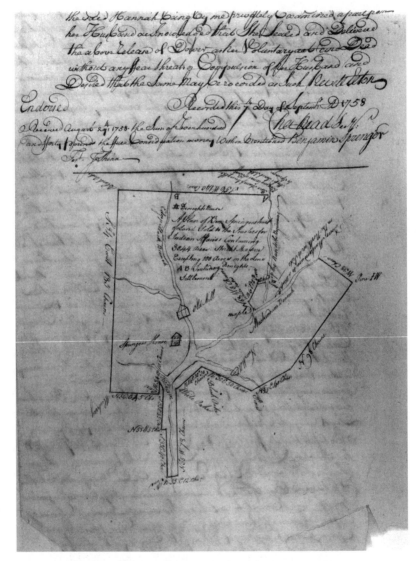

Map of the land the Indian Commissioners purchased from Benjamin Springer for use as a reservation by the peaceful Lenape. (Courtesy of the New Jersey State Archives.)

from the sea within 5 miles of this place with Clams & oysters. There are 300 bearing apple trees on it & 24 Acres of good Indian Corn wch we propose to lay down with Rye & this will be their first Years provisions on their removal.

A second conference was held at the Forks in Easton, Pennsylvania, on October 8, 1758, and did not conclude until October 26, 1758. There were 507 Indians present representing the various tribes of Northern New Jersey and New York, as well as representatives of the Six Nations Iroquois. There were also the royal governors of Pennsylvania and New Jersey, Governor Denny and Governor Francis Bernard respectively, as well as Indian dignitaries in the presence of King Teedyuskung, Moses Tatamy and Stephen Calvin, who also served as interpreters, as well as various chiefs of the Six Nations. Many belts of wampum were exchanged and many eloquent speeches were given over the course of nearly three weeks. There was also much drinking and rancor but perhaps not an unusual occurrence at such a large gathering held over such an extended time. Postponements, often several days, caused the conference to drag on so long and were usually blamed on the Indians' drunkenness. Conclusions were finally reached, however, and the purchase of land for a reservation to be utilized by the Indians south of the Raritan was approved.

The lands in northern New Jersey and claims attached to them were also settled and approved at the same meeting. At a time when the French and Indian War was still raging on the frontier, Governor Bernard found it imperative that peace come within the borders of the Colony of New Jersey.

Rev. John Brainerd had been pastor of the First Presbyterian Church in Newark, but had taken leave to accept a position as a chaplain in the British Army, serving in the area of Lake George, New York. In March 1759 he states,

> I was requested by Mr. Bernard, governor of this province, at a joint meeting at Perth Amboy, again to resume my mission to the Indians. I took their proposals under consideration and in May following laid the matter before the Synod at Philadelphia; and with the unanimous advice of that venerable body, gave up

my charge at Newark, and embarked once more in the cause of the poor Indians. About this time I made the Indians a visit at their new settlement and procured some supplies for them by order of the Synod during my absence in the Army; and upon my return the November following fixed myself down among them where I have steadily resided ever since.

Recalling the effects the war had on his Indians, Brainerd states,

In 1757 we lost near twenty, taken captive at Fort William Henry, and but three or four have ever returned to this day; so that our number is greatly reduced. The Indians have, ever since the commencement of the war, enlisted into the king's service far beyond their proportion, and generally more or less every campaign have died in the army.

A letter to a Reverend Wheelock is dated from Crown Point, New York, August 9, 1759. It reads in part,

It has pleased a sovereign God to bereave me of all but one dear little babe; I know he is just and righteous in giving me a bitter cup to drink, for I am worthy. But to lose such dear friends, such tender parts of ourselves, as wife and children, is hard to flesh and blood! The world can never be to me what it has been; and doubtless tis best it should not.

After considerable hesitation I thought it my duty to come into the Army again. But, alas! Dear Sir, I feel as if I did but little good. Profanity and wickedness greatly prevail, and at times my heart sinks within me, but I try after my poor manners to make a stand for God, and I desire to be very thankful. I never had so much courage in general as this year.

Brainerd mentions that he had, "left Carillon a few days ago and that the provincial chaplains were all at Carillon." The name Carillon is French meaning "chime of bells." Brainerd uses the French name for this place that was actually Fort Ticonderoga, which had been retaken by British forces in July 1759. The French were in retreat at this point and hostilities were essentially over when, in 1760, the French were defeated at Montreal and Quebec. The final conclusion was the Treaty of Paris, which was signed in 1763. The French and Indian War had severely depleted the British treasury and as a consequence taxes were increased substantially in the American colonies. This eventually led to the war for independence from British rule.

On June 15, 1759, Governor Francis Bernard sent a letter from Perth Amboy to the Lords of Trade in England to advise them what had been done to resolve any possibility of hostility in the New Jersey Colony. It reads in part,

> I went to Burlington County to lay out the Indian Town there, I have before informed your Lordships that by agreement with the Indians south of the Raritan. They released all their claims in the province, in consideration of a tract of 3,000 acres to be purchased for their use. This purchase was made and the Indians are removed to the place. It is a tract of Land Very suitable for this purpose, having soil good enough, a large hunting country and a passage by water to the sea for fishing. It is out of the way of communication with the Wild Indians and has a sawmill upon it serves to provide them with timber for their own use and to raise a little money for other purposes. To this place I went with three of the Commissioners for Indian Affairs, where we laid out the plan of a town, to which I gave the name of Brotherton & saw an house erected being one of ten that were ready prepared; and afterwards ordered lots of land to be laid for the Indians to clear & till, the land already cleared being to remain in common till they have acquired themselves separate property, by their own industry. We also made an appointment of an house & lands for a Minister, I having engaged Mr. Brainerd a Scotch Presbyterian for that purpose, for which he is most peculiarly suited. The next day I had a conference with the chiefs, at which they expressed great satisfaction at what had

been done for them and I assured them that the same care of them should be continued and exhorted them to order, sobriety and industry. The whole Number of them at present does not amount to 200 and when we have gathered together all in the province they will not be 300. If I can but keep them from being supplied with rum, for when there are laws strict enough, I shall hope to make them orderly and useful subjects.

The Indians in the Northern parts of the province have entirely quitted it and are gone to the Susquehanna, where they live in peace with the English. There has not been the least disorder committed near our frontier since the Treaty of Easton. I have disbanded the frontier guard and the country is in great tranquility.

William Foster, one of the Indian Commissioners, advanced a considerable sum of his own money in settling the Indians during their first year at Brotherton. On December 7, 1760, the colonial governor enacted a formal bill stating that, "it shall be lawful for the said William Foster to use the saw-mill on the said Indians' Land together with the necessary timber until the same shall repay him for the sums so advanced." In a similar bill the Reverend William Tennent was paid the sum of three pounds for his trouble and service in assisting to remove the Indians to Brotherton.

Brainerd had been living at Brotherton since November 1759, occasionally tending to business at the College of New Jersey at Princeton where he was a Trustee and also attending meetings of the Synod in Philadelphia. His daily activities were maintained at a grueling pace with his only means of transportation by horseback.

Brainerd very shortly seemed to be gloomy and depressed at his new mission. In a letter to the Scottish Society in Edinburgh, he writes, in part,

I had repeated promises from Governor Bernard of a comfortable, decent house for the place of my residence, as also a house for the public worship of God. But promises were all I could get towards either; and, when I came to think of moving

48

here, was obliged to sell almost all my household furniture, because I had no place to put it in. And the loss I hereby sustained, together with the losses and expenses in my several removes, was about 150 pounds damage to my estate, besides all the fatigue and trouble that attended the same.

A much clearer picture of his circumstances is presented in a letter written from Brotherton on August 24, 1761, to a close friend, Mrs. Elizabeth Smith of Wethersfield, Connecticut.

Madam, according to my promise, I here send an account of the Indian mission in this province, which for some years has been the object of my care. On this spot, which is a fine, tract of land, and very commodiously situated for their settlement, there is something upward of an hundred, old and young.

About twelve miles distant there is a small settlement of them, perhaps near forty. About seventeen miles farther there is a third, containing possibly near as many more; and there are yet some few scattering ones still about Crossweeksung. And if all were collected, they might possibly make two hundred. I spend something more than half my Sabbaths here at Brotherton; the rest are divided. At this place I have but few white people: the reason is because this is near central between Delaware and the sea, and the English settlements are chiefly on them. The other places are in the midst of the inhabitants, and, whenever I preach there, I have a large number of white people that meet to attend divine service. But besides these, I have preached at eight different places on Lord's days and near twenty on other days of the week, and never fail of a considerable congregation so large and extensive is this vacancy.

Two large counties, and a considerable part of two more, almost wholly destitute of a preached gospel (except what the Quakers do in their way), and many of the people but one remove from a state of heathenism.

As to the success that has attended my labors, I can say but little: it is a time wherein the influences of the Divine Spirit are mournfully withheld. I think, however, I have ground to hope that some good has been done among both Indians and white people, and the prospects of further usefulness are very considerable if proper means could be used. But such is the state of the country, there is such a mixture of Quakers and other denominations, and so many that have no concern about religion in any shape, that very little can at present be expected towards the support of the gospel. On my own part, I have never thought proper to take one single farthing yet in all my excursions, fearing that it might prejudice the minds of some and so, in a measure, frustrate the design.

At this place, where most of the Indians are settled, we greatly want a school for the children. When I built the meeting-house last year, I provided some materials for a schoolhouse, and in the fall addressed the legislature of this province for some assistance, not only for the support of a school, but for the erecting of a small grist-mill, a blacksmith's shop, and a small trading store to furnish the Indians with necessaries in exchange for their produce, and so prevent their running twelve or fifteen miles to the inhabitants for every thing they want; whereby they not only consume much time, but often fall into the temptation of calling at dram-houses (too frequent in the country), where they intoxicate themselves with spirituous liquors, and after some days, perhaps, instead of hours, return home wholly unfit for anything relating either to this or a future world.

The Governor, the Council, the Speaker of the House of Assembly, and several of the other members, thought well of the motion, and recommended it; but the Quakers, and others in that interest, made opposition, and, being the greater part of the house, it finally went against us. If the same could be done some other way, it would be the best step towards the end proposed, and be the most likely to invite not only the Indians at these other small settlements above mentioned, but those also who live in more distant parts of the country.

Thus I have touched upon the most material things relative to this mission, and, I fear, tired your patience with my long epistle. And now, that all needed provision may be made for the promotion and perfecting of this good work among the Indians, and you, among others, be made an happy instrument of the same; that many faithful laborers may be thrust forth, and all vacant parts of the harvest be supplied; that this wilderness in particular may be turned into a fruitful field, and even the whole earth be filled with the knowledge of the Lord, is the fervent prayer of,

Madam, your most obedient, humble servant,

John Brainerd.

P.S. Since my settlement here, I have been obliged to advance above 200 pounds for the building of the meetinghouse, for some necessary repairs of an old piece of a house that was on the spot, and for my support and other necessary expenses.

Not all was a bed of roses for the fledging missionary, but he persevered, even to the point of spending his own money, when the government that appointed him should have provided funds.

CHAPTER 5

The Brainerd Years
1758–1781

The new Royal Governor, Josiah Hardy, officially appointed Reverend John Brainerd as Superintendent and Guardian of the Indians at Brotherton, March 22, 1762. Brainerd had already been acting in that capacity under the term of Governor Francis Bernard, and perhaps it was an oversight that this appointment had not been made officially.

Rev. Brainerd kept daily journals of his life as a missionary; unfortunately, none of these have survived with the exception of slightly less than two years, from January 1761 to October 1762. The journal gives considerable insight into his daily life. It shows the extent of his mission field not just at Brotherton but also throughout southern New Jersey. He even made occasional trips into Pennsylvania. Brainerd's missionary labors were not only confined to Indians. They were his main concern, to be sure, but it becomes increasingly apparent that his efforts were directed to the white settlers as well.

> In my late journey to Penn's Neck & Salem which was by Presbyterial appointment I suffered much, by reason of the severity of the season; took a great cold, and after my Return, was in a poor state of Body for several Weeks, but not confined to the House; and thro' divine goodness, able, in some Part, to perform the Duties of the Mission.
>
> Thursday Jan. 15, 1761 Rode several Miles to a Cedar Swamp, to visit an afflicted Family; they having one child lying dead in the House & the Mother in a very weak and low state.

It is obvious from his journal that he was a minister to all, wherever he was needed.

Lord's Day, Jan. 18, 1761 Performed divine worship twice with the Indians and others that attended. And spent some Time the ensuing week in visiting them at their Houses.

It was not uncommon for Brainerd to preach to assemblies of Indians and Whites alike.

Toward the latter end of the week I went to Great Egg Harbor about 40 miles hence.

Lord's Day Jan. 18, 1761 Rode fifteen miles and preached twice at the House of William Reed on the seashore, to a numerous congregation. Rode ten miles the next day eastward and preached a lecture at Chestnut Neck; and after stayed the principal members of the congregation to discourse about building a meetinghouse. And the same evening rode about 25 miles homeward. The next day I passed by my own dwelling and rode to Bridgetown [now Mount Holly], being called to meet The Trustees of the College at Princeton the next day at eleven o'clock. Accordingly I set out very early in the Morning, and arrived there about twelve, having ridden near thirty miles.

Brainerd was constantly riding by horseback many miles, almost daily, in pursuit of his pastoral duties. It can be exhausting even to read about his daily travels under such adverse conditions.

Lords Day March 1, 1761 Spent the Sabbath with the Indians and performed divine service both Parts of the Day in the usual manner. And on Thursday evening, convened the Indians again and attended the Worship of God.

Spent some time this Week with the Indians about their Temporal Business; Particular with Regard to preparing their ground for corn and other seed.

Brainerd worked very hard attempting to teach the Indians to be self-sufficient in raising their own crops.

He was then called to preach at Neshaminy, some 45 miles away in Pennsylvania, and the next day in Abington on his way to Philadelphia. He became ill from a cold and had to spend a few days in his home at Brotherton.

> On March 18th I gathered the Indians together, in the evening, and gave them a discourse upon Industry; pointing out the great evil of Idleness, and exhorting them to honest, diligent Industry as being friendly both to their temporal and spiritual good.

Brainerd frequently chastised the Indians for their idleness, which in some instances was caused by their excessive use of alcohol. The natives were many times tempted by settlers in the vicinity to forget their Christian teachings and piety.

> Lords Day April 26, 1761. Kept Sabbath at home, and performed divine service twice. Preaching two short discourses, one for the Indians, the other for the White people at each exercise.
> Lord's Day June 14, 1761 spent the Sabbath again with the Indians, and attended two religious exercises as usual. This week I took a journey to Cohansey [near Bridgeton], about 50 miles. Preached three Lectures, and returned on Saturday evening.

It has been suggested by some writers that his visits to Cohansey were to visit his only child, Mary, now age six, and apparently being cared for by family friends during his many calls away from home.

> Lords Day July 12. Kept Sabbath home again, and performed divine services both Parts of the Day as usual. This week I rode to Cohansey upon some personal Business and returned by Woodbury where I spent the next Sabbath. The next day I preached a lecture at Timber Creek [now Blackwood] and came

fifteen miles homeward, but was prevented coming any further by a heavy thunderstorm. Spent part of the Week visiting the Indians at their respective Habitations. And the next Lord's Day convened the Indians at their several settlements in these Parts, at Bridgetown and attended their religious exercise, one peculiarly calculated for the Indians, a very considerable number of whom were present, and gave devout attention to divine service.

The next morning Brainerd set out for New England but because of rain, he got no farther than New York. He did not return to Brotherton until mid-August after visiting many churches in New England.

Lord's Day Aug. 30th. Kept Sabbath at Bordentown to accommodate a small number of Indians who reside opposite to this town in Pennsylvania [near Pennsbury, the former home of William Penn]. I had likewise a View to the White People who are destitute of the Gospel Ministry in these Parts. Performed an Exercise for the Indians, and another for the English.

Brainerd visited this group again on October 4, but this time at the "Place where the Indians reside and then crossed the River and preached an evening sermon at Bordentown." Brainerd was constantly traveling by horseback over lengthy distances, spreading the gospel to Indians and Whites alike. In one week alone, he traveled from Bordentown to Wading River, the Forks of Little Egg Harbor, Manahawkin, Mays Landing, Beesleys Point, and to Cold Spring in Cape May County.

Lords Day Sept. 6, 1761 spent the Sabbath at home, and attended two religious exercises; and at the close of the latter administered the Ordinance of Baptism to an English child, the Parents residing near this Indian settlement. The next day I rode to Cohansey and returned the Thursday following. And the next Day preached a Lecture at the Forks of Little Egg Harbor [now Pleasant Mills] about 15 miles from home.

> Lords Day Dec. 6, 1761 rode this Morning about 14 miles to Wepinck, the old Indian Town, and attended divine Worship there; accommodating myself to the Indians, and likewise to the White People, a number of whom were present. In the afternoon preached at Bridgetown [now Mount Holly] to a crowded Assembly.

This is the first mention of Wepink in Brainerd's journal. The location of this "old Indian town" was approximately 1.5 miles west of present day Vincentown and will be discussed in detail in a later chapter.

On December 7, Brainerd spent a short time at the college in Princeton where he was a Trustee, transacting some business relative to his mission with the Indians. He then rode to Perth Amboy to pay his respects to Joshua Hardy, "a Gentleman lately arrived with the King's Commission to take the Seat of Government in the Province."

> Lords Day Jan. 10, 1762 rode to Wepinck and officiated to a mixed Congregation of Indians and White People, in the Forenoon; in the afternoon at Bridgetown. The next Day I preached a Lecture at Julitown [Juliustown] about 7 miles from Bridgetown, to a very considerable congregation, and the next Thursday Evening at the Indian Town.

The Indian Town Brainerd refers to may not have been Wepink or Brotherton but actually a small settlement of Indians still living in the vicinity of Juliustown.

> Lords Day Jan. 24, 1762 preached in the Forenoon at Wepinck, to a large congregation; in the Afternoon at Bridgetown. The next Day at Julitown again to a much larger Congregation than before.

Brainerd spent most of the following week in Bridgetown tending to ministerial duties of a more private nature. He is known to have purchased considerable property in Mount Holly as early as 1761 and additional parcels in the years that followed. Although Brainerd received his living expenses from the Presbytery and other mission sources, he also had money that he had accumulated from his family estate in New England. He was never a particularly wealthy man but did have independent means of support.

> Monday April 12, 1762 spent some time with a company who were clearing land. Took care that they had not too much Strong Drink. The rest of the Day I spent in bodily Labour; and the Evening in settling Differences between a Man and his wife. Spent the next two succeeding Days about my Garden preparing for seed and other Spring work. And in the Evening convened the Indians and attended divine Worship in the usual manner.

On April 20, Brainerd preached a lecture to a number of people working at a cedar swamp three miles away and the next day preached at a place called Goshen. This too was about three miles distant from Brotherton and was a small settlement near the Goshen Sawmill that was owned by James Inskeep.

> Lords Day May 9, Preached in the Forenoon at home; then rode about 17 miles and officiated to a very considerable Congregation in a Dutch neighborhood; returned home again and performed divine Service, in the usual manner, with the Indians. Spent a good part of the succeeding Days at Labour in the Field; planting Corn, etc.

Brainerd continued to spend many days traveling throughout South Jersey but always returning to Brotherton, Wepink, and Bridgetown where he would apparently preach all in the same day. He never seemed to tire of his mission to raise up the Indians.

> Lords Day October 27, 1762. Convened the Indians, and attended a religious Exercise in the Evening according to our usual method. Also visited a number of the Indians at their Houses.

On September 22, 1762, the Indians at Brotherton petitioned the General Assembly with grievances they had, saying, "that their Provisions, Clothing, and Nails for building the first year they came to Brotherton, amounted to 106 pounds; which they are still in Debt for; and that their Mill is lately burnt which renders them utterly unable to pay their said Debt; and praying that the Province will pay the same, as they have had some Reason to expect." Later in 1763 William Foster was paid 106 pounds for the use of the Indians at Brotherton, to discharge some expectations for-merly given the Indians by the Commissioners of Indian Affairs, his receipt was to be a discharge of the said Treasurers for said sum of money.

Stephen Calvin, a Crosswicks Indian who had been an interpreter at both the Crosswicks Conferences and the Treaty at Easton, held a promi-nent place among his people at Brotherton. He served as the reservation schoolmaster and was considered an elder. His son, Bartholemew S. Calvin, would eventually succeed him but was now just a lad of eight years of age. He was most likely born at the closing of Bethel in 1755.

The noted historian, Samuel Allinson, delivered an address to the New Jersey Historical Society on January 21, 1875. He commented in part, "My grandfather, Samuel Allinson, frequently visited Brotherton and considered Stephen Calvin to be an excellent teacher. He collected money from his neighbors to purchase books for the school."

After the gristmill burned in 1762 the Indians appeared to encounter many difficulties in trying to embrace a lifestyle that was contrary to their native spirit. They found it difficult to adapt themselves to the white man's agricultural ways and instead became increasingly idle with a diminishing desire to conform to the teachings of Rev. Brainerd. Perhaps if Brainerd had spent all his time at the reservation instead of preaching the gospel through-out South Jersey, and sometimes even in Pennsylvania, his mission at Brotherton would have been more successful.

ARCHAEOLOGICAL DISCOVERIES

It was difficult to imagine exactly what life was like in those primitive times until a startling discovery was made in the early 1990s by professional archaeologists. Not in all the years since the reservation days ended had there ever been an Indian habitation site found that was coexistent with Brotherton. In 1990 R. Alan Mounier was conducting an archaeological investigation some two miles north of the Brotherton Reservation boundary. This was being done in preparation for the widening of a road in that vicinity. There were a number of sites identified where signs of Indian habitation were present, but all appeared to be prehistoric in nature.

Another contract archaeological firm, MAAR Associates, Inc. of Newark, Delaware, was engaged to conduct an additional investigation. Archaeologists Ronald A. Thomas, the owner of MAAR, and his employee Betty Cosans-Zebooker were assigned to this project. What they found has greatly enhanced our knowledge of the Indian natives at Brotherton.

An exploratory trench was dug at the site identified, 3 feet wide and 25 feet long to a depth of 3.5 feet. MAAR Associates reported a total of 1,313 artifacts dating from the years 1745 to 1765 in an undisturbed midden deposit within a pit feature.

They had determined the pit feature to be a mid-18th-century residential site that had been occupied by an Indian male and female based on the nature and type of the artifacts excavated. The dwelling had been roughly 10 feet square and estimated to be lightly framed with saplings, and part wattle and daub. It extended partially underground and there was little evidence of any interior finishing of the floor or walls. Most pit-houses of this type utilized bark for a roof covering. Prior to erecting more substantial dwellings or cabins, early colonists had constructed similar dwellings.

The artifacts recovered clearly indicated an aboriginal presence. Fire-cracked hearthstones, Late Woodland incised pottery, jasper, quartz, and chert waste flakes indicative of stone toolmaking, as well as two triangular arrowpoints were found. Two antler tools were also excavated that could have been utilized in flint-knapping processes.

Many fragments of red earthenware, English slipware, green bottle glass, numerous clay-pipe stems and bowls, brass buttons and cuff links, candle holders, spoons, iron nails, lead shot, gun flints, buckles, and an English copper half penny minted between 1727 and 1760 were recovered in the excavation. This clearly indicated frequent trading with the European colonists.

The skeletal remains of numerous wild animals were found, which provided a glimpse at what this male and female subsisted on: white-tailed deer, elk, bear, squirrels, rabbits, fish, clams, oyster shells, birds, and turtles. There was no evidence of any domesticated animals except the numerous pig bones that were found.

The excavators felt that no children were living in the household because none of the artifacts recovered reflected their presence. One cannot read the complete report of the archaeologists' findings without wondering how many other contact period sites remain to be discovered and excavated in the area of the Brotherton Reservation.

In 1766 John Brainerd was remarried to a widow named Elizabeth Price of Philadelphia. Brainerd had purchased considerable property in Mount Holly as early as 1761 in the vicinity of what was then known as New Street (later to be named Brainerd Street, in honor of John Brainerd). He was known to have erected a small Presbyterian church there in 1762. Later he erected a modest one-story frame house east of the church and near the end of the street. There is a one-story brick schoolhouse, the oldest of its kind in New

Oldest schoolhouse in New Jersey, erected privately in 1759 on Brainerd Street (then New Street) in Mt. Holly. John Brainerd lived close by and may have taught there occasionally. (Photo by the author.)

Jersey, erected in 1759 by a group of concerned citizens. For many years it was erroneously called the Brainerd School. John Brainerd did not build this school although he may have possibly taught there on occasion.

Within a short time after his marriage to Elizabeth Price, they moved from Brotherton to Mount Holly in 1768. His daughter Mary, who had been living in Cohansey, most likely returned and lived with them. She was now 13 years of age.

The large brick Quaker Meeting House still standing on Garden Street was erected in 1775 to the rear of Brainerd's home. He had sold the Quakers two lots of land that formed a portion of the church property before it was built.

Friends Meeting House at High and Garden Streets, Mt. Holly, erected in 1775 on land purchased from John Brainerd. (Photo by the author.)

Brainerd no doubt continued his missionary work among the Indians at Wepink and Brotherton as before, but he seemed to have become somewhat distracted from his mission to the Indians. He is shown as one of the incorporators of the Bridgetown Library in 1765 and by that time had accumulated considerable property in Mount Holly.

Some vague signs of disenchantment on the part of the Brotherton Indians and others came in the spring of 1767. Joseph Peepy, a Delaware Indian interpreter, originally from Crosswicks, was then living in Ohio with a large group of Delawares who had moved there after the end of the French and Indian War. The Ohio group was upset that some of their people continued to live in New Jersey and possibly many, in fact, were related. Joseph Peepy was their spokesman and he had been chosen to visit the Brotherton Reservation to extend an invitation to the residents to join the Ohio group.

In a lengthy and emotional letter of reply the offer of the Ohio group was declined. Those who signed the response were Thomas Store, Joseph Meely, Stephen Calvin, Isaac Still, and Jacob Skekit. They informed the Ohio Delawares of all the benefits they had at Brotherton. "We have here a good house for the worship of God, another for our children to go to school in, besides our dwelling houses and many comfortable accommodations, all of which we shall lose if we remove." This was somewhat a stretch of the truth. For, in fact, the Brotherton band was deteriorating either by some leaving the reservation to assimilate into the White man's world or else to migrate westward to join family members elsewhere. Not all the natives chose to stay within the reservation boundaries, nor did the law require them to. Their residence on the reservation was voluntary and could account for various fluctuations in the known population of Brotherton.

Brainerd was doing his best under the circumstances and even encouraged and promoted higher education for his Indians by sending them off to college. He was influential in placing many of them. The fact that he was a Trustee at Princeton College may have helped gain entrance for some. In particular, Peter Tatamy, (son of Moses Tatamy), Jacob Wooley, Bartholomew Calvin (son of the Brotherton schoolmaster Stephen Calvin), and many others attended. The tuition was paid by the Scottish Society; however these funds ceased at the outbreak of the Revolutionary War.

Nothing further seemed to develop in respect to the proposed move to Ohio until May 1771 when one of the Ohio Delaware elders, John Killbuck Jr., met with William Franklin, Benjamin Franklin's illegitimate son, then colonial governor of New Jersey. Apparently Killbuck had been in communication with Stephen Calvin at Brotherton, again encouraging him to come to Ohio. The stumbling block as reported by Killbuck to Governor Franklin was that the Brotherton Indians needed money to make the move. The governor replied he could not act without a petition from the Indians at Brotherton saying that the majority of them desired to leave the reservation at Brotherton.

Stephen Calvin and a number of the Brotherton Indians met with the governor's council in June 1771. Many of the Indians testified that they had never seen the petition about leaving to go to Ohio. Calvin later admitted that he had signed for them because he wanted the reservation lands to be sold so they could all move whether the majority desired to or not. Members of the governor's council described Calvin as being under the influence of alcohol and acting in an erratic manner.

The entire petition was disregarded once the government officials determined only two individuals knew anything about this effort to move. Some decided to move to Ohio with their brethren but the majority preferred to remain at Brotherton.

Brainerd was still living in Mount Holly with his wife and daughter Mary, and continued his preaching activities throughout his mission field. There is no indication in the records that his pattern of missionary work to the Indians and Whites alike had changed. What did change his life drastically, and that of his wife and daughter, was the impending outbreak of the Revolutionary War in 1775. He at that point may have begun to visit Brotherton and Wepink less frequently. Phillip Vickers Fithian, a Presbyterian minister from Greenwich, records in his journal February 13, 1775, that "the day was snowy. Preached at the Indian Reservation. I preached but once. I rode up to Brotherton and preached to Mr. Brainerd's Indians. Present were about 30 and as many white people, by appointment up to Brotherton."

Rev. John Brainerd was an ardent patriot and known to be a staunch supporter of the war against Britain. He would go from town to town as always, preaching his religious doctrines, but now he was also encouraging the churchgoers and others to be loyal to the American cause, in their fight for liberty and freedom from unbearable taxation.

Brainerd moved his family back to his home at Brotherton in 1775 as Mount Holly was in too much turmoil due to the war. His return to his former home among the Indians was not a particularly pleasant transition for him. He had become accustomed to more comfortable surroundings, as evidenced in a letter he sent to the Mission Board dated February 9, 1775. It reads, in part,

> The Mission house at Brotherton, which I believe is near about 30 pounds in my Debt, has no more done to it than was necessary to make it Some how tolerable for Worship, is very cold and uncomfortable in Winter, and has only a wooden foundation, or in other words is suspended with wooden blocks, stone being not to be had without Some Expense, having now stood more than 15 years, Stands in need of some other repairs. The dwelling house, which is a Parsonage, is so ruinous as not to be habitable in the Winter Season, and dangerous in every high wind at any other time. This obliges us to move every fall with very considerable Trouble and Loss, besides the Detriment to the Mission.

In 1776 Brainerd preached to a Presbyterian congregation in Blackwoodtown, Gloucester County. The reference for his patriotic sermon was Psalm 144, "Blessed be the Lord my strength, which teacheth my hands to war, and my fingers to fight." This was one of many such sermons he preached in the early years of the war. Apparently Tory sympathizers reported these patriotic sermons to the British military commanders. Between June 20th and June 22nd 1778, British troops entered Mount Holly. First they destroyed the iron works on Pine Street, and then proceeded to Brainerd's church, which they initially used as a stable for their horses, before burning it to the ground. This was in retaliation for his fiery patriotic sermons. Some historians have reported that the British also burned Brainerd's home, but this is not true. His home did survive. In 1778 a William Chew advertised that he had opened a general store in the house formerly occupied by Rev. Brainerd near the Friends new meetinghouse. The house was later occupied by a Harding Murrell and in 1844 by John

Gibson. The late Judge William A. Slaughter, who wrote an extensive history of Mount Holly, recorded that in 1895 the house was removed in sections and rebuilt north of the Tomlinson property, on a side street of West Washington Street. He recalled in 1930 that the house had been so altered and enlarged that little of the original structure remained.

The effects of the war were devastating to the Indians at Brotherton and probably to the small group living at Wepink as well. There was no longer any governmental support and the reservation Indians were basically left to fend for themselves.

Brainerd had begun helping a Reverend Enoch Green at his Presbyterian Church in Deerfield, Cumberland County. Reverend Green had been pastor there since June 9, 1767, but was in failing health. Brainerd baptized Green's son, Charles, at Deerfield on March 27, 1776. Pastor Green became gravely ill and died on December 2, 1776, at the age of 41.

John Brainerd was called to become pastor of the Deerfield Presbyterian Church shortly after Enoch Green's death and arrived there to stay in early 1777. His wife accompanied him, although his daughter Mary may have already moved elsewhere.

Deerfield Presbyterian Church in Cumberland County where Rev. John Brainerd spent his declining years until his death in 1781. (Photo by the author.)

In the Brainerd Family Bible, it is recorded that Mary Brainerd was married August 8, 1778, at Egg Harbor to John Ross. He was born at Mount Holly March 2, 1752. He enlisted in the patriot army in 1776. On February 9, 1777, he was commissioned a captain. By 1779 he had attained the rank of Major of the Second Regiment. He had been wounded once but was able to serve until the end of the war. He later became a physician. It should be noted that the place of their marriage, Egg Harbor, was not the town that is known by that name today, but present day Tuckerton.

When Brainerd and his wife moved to Deerfield, they brought with them an Indian woman, known as Becky. She had been in their service as a housekeeper for many years. She was apparently a very pious woman who washed clothes and bed linens, helped keep the house, and spent her leisure hours making baskets. It has been said that when her female friends visited her from Brotherton they were upset at having to sleep on a feather bed, which was a radical change for them considering the more primitive arrangements on the reservation.

After Brainerd became pastor at Deerfield, he seemed to confine his preaching mainly to that location, although he tried to return to Brotherton at least once every other week.

At about this same time, a ministering Quaker of Evesham, New Jersey, John Hunt, began visiting the Indians at Brotherton. In all likelihood his actions were one of benevolence, rather than an effort to interfere with Brainerd's mission responsibilities. Hunt kept a private diary from July 1770 to May 1800, and it seems ironic that his first recorded visit to Brotherton took place at about the same time John Brainerd moved to Deerfield. John Hunt records,

> Ye lst. Mo., 1777, I went with my Friend Josh Evans to See the poor Indians at Edgepillock and wee found them in very Low Circumstance as to food and Raiment Joshua Tok them a Considerable parcel of old Cloaths with which the poor Nakid Children Seemd Exceedingly Pleasd. Joshua had been under Some Concern for these poor Creatures & proposed to them that if they Could get Some money he would try to get some Blancets for them and So Mentiond the Case amongst friends

and collected a parcel of Blancets for them gratis and So made them pay for them at a moderate price and when he had got their money he Laid it out in Corn for them, Not Leting them know what he Intended to do with their money till after he Deliverd the Blancets. This he did because these poor things are too apt to Lay out their money in Strong Drink.... there was one Indian woman that had a Child just three weeks old that morning and She was so well that it Seemd as if nothing had ailed her at all—this I could but Remark because her Cabbin was so open/ not so tite and worm as our Stables are in Common...which under a Consideration of the weaklyness of our women at Such times Caused me to Conclude that the more tenderly wee Cept and Nursed our Selves & Children the more tender and weakly we were.

During the ensuing year there was considerable military activity in South Jersey and no further entries were made in Hunt's journal until the following year. Then, John Hunt writes,

Ye lst mo., 1778 Joshua Evans &I went up to Edgpiluck to See the Indians and we found them in a very poor Sufering Condition as to food and Raimant....many of the white people ....were afflicted and Disquieted in mind because of the great destruction there was in the Land at this time.

On January 20, he writes,

Joshua Evans and I went up to Indian town to Carry Some blankets & old Cloaths which our friends of Chester [now Moorestown] had bestowed to the Indians and the poor nakid Creatures Seemd to Receive them with Abundance of thankfulness & Some Was affected with tenderness to see friends kindness and Seemd Desirous to Make Some Little Retaliation for the kindness they had Recevd.

On June 8, 1779, he records, "I mad one plow for the Indian Mary Colvin this afternoon." The spelling in his diary is anything but perfection. Perhaps this Indian woman's last name was actually Calvin as this was a very prominent name among the reservation Indians. It is interesting to note that the male Indian seldom engaged in agricultural duties following their age-old traditions. The man's role was still as a hunter with farming chores left to the women.

On March 18, 1781, John Brainerd died at Deerfield at 61 years of age. He had been in failing health for several years and reportedly died of a pulmonary ailment. It could have been tuberculosis, which had afflicted his brother David, but this is only supposition. His remains were initially buried beneath the brick floor of the broad aisle in his church at Deerfield. In

The grave of Rev. John Brainerd, located just outside the Deerfield Church walls. (Photo by the author.)

1907, owing to the need for space to install a new heater, Brainerd's grave was transferred to a new location alongside the memorial walk in the churchyard, where it may still be seen today.

Brainerd had apparently sensed that his end was near, as he had made his will on March 21, 1780, a year before his actual death. It reads, in part,

> John Brainerd of Cumberland Co., Minister of the Gospel. First, I give and bequeath to my dear, well beloved, and faithful wife Elizabeth Brainerd, and all that part of my estate that was hers before we were married. Second, I put all the rest of my estate into her hands, as money or cash, bills, bonds, certificates, cattle, horses, and every other part and parcel of my estate except what will by and by be mentioned, not to be aliened or given away, but which may be sold for her comfortable support during her state of widowhood; then to become the property of my dear, well beloved, and dutiful daughter Mary Ross, wife of Major John Ross. Third, I do now give and bequeath unto my only daughter and child all and every individual thing that came to me by her mother, as also the bed I had before I was married, all the plates marked E. L., together with a mustard pot and pepper box not marked at all, as also a three year old heifer and yearling heifer. My horses I leave with my wife and daughter, to be disposed of as they shall agree and think proper; and they have free liberty to sell any number of them as they shall choose.

Brainerd appointed his son-in-law Major John Ross as executor.

Following his death, Elizabeth Brainerd went to live with her stepdaughter Mary and her husband Major John Ross in Mount Holly. Mary Brainerd Ross died January 1, 1792, after a six-month illness. Elizabeth Brainerd died August 28, 1793, of yellow fever contracted by a visit to Philadelphia a week prior. Both are buried in Saint Andrews Churchyard, Mount Holly.

Major John Ross later married Miss Sarah Hilyer on May 10, 1794; however, the marriage was short lived. He expired on September 7, 1796, and was laid to rest next to his first wife, Mary, in Mount Holly.

CHAPTER 6

Decline, Exodus, and Aftermath

Following John Brainerd's death in 1781 the Indian mission at Brotherton began a steady decline. In 1783 an ordained Indian minister was appointed by the Presbyterian Synod to preach there, but was soon suspended for immorality. All support from the Synod ceased at this time, and there had been no support from the government since before the war.

The native Indians at Brotherton were left without any religious guidance or compassion for their deplorable circumstances with the exception of the benevolent Quakers John Hunt and Joshua Evans. Even these two paid less attention to the Indians than they had in the past, possibly due to the war that had been raging, and perhaps due to their own personal limitations and availability.

John Hunt records in his journal the hard cold winter of 1780. Hundreds of cattle and other creatures had perished for want of food. The winter grass had been destroyed. He states, "The want of Bread more and more appeared & the Crys of the poor began to be heard in our once plentiful & peaceful land. The winter has been so hard that it has killed many fruit trees." He complains of soldiers burning barns and stacks of hay. Also a very dry summer had caused fire in the barren lands and destroyed a great part of the cedar swamp.

On June 3, 1780, he records,

> I went with Wm. Rogers & John Moxel to See some poor women & other poor people in ye Baron Lands & Some Indians who with their children were very much Straightened for to get the Necessaries of Life the children had nothing to hide their Nakidness & much pinched for want of Bread in Some families of the white people. We went to about Six families & Left Something for their Sustenance at most places.

The outlook of the reservation seemed to continue in a downward spiral, as John Hunt writes on October 28, 1782, "I met some Friends at Joshua Lippincotts to Consider of Schooling Indian Children but wee Could not get forward Some hung back & opposed the work." Apparently he had been trying to find help for the Indian children and in the ensuing months met with other Friends to discuss the Indian School. On March 5, 1783, he records, "We all 5 of us went to See the Indian School at Brotherton which we found in a hopeful way Considering all things." It is quite possible this group of concerned Quakers were satisfied with the teachings of the Indian schoolmaster, Bartholomew, who had been educated at Princeton College.

Other than a brief entry dated July 26, 1783, regarding a plow Hunt made for an Indian Squaw, there is no further mention of Brotherton or the Indians there until June 8, 1798, when he writes "This afternoon 4th hour was appointed to meet at the Burial of Joshua Evans, Negrows & Indians for whom he had been a Great Advocate testified their Regard for him by their Attending of his Burial as well as the White people."

On August 25, 1799, he records, "John Simson had appointed a meeting at Edgpelik for the Indians at 10 and one for the Indians at 2." It appears the Quakers had been attempting to provide some sort of religious experience for the Indians but no further comments are made. On December 1, 1799, the Friends Meeting received a message from the Indians at Brotherton "acknowledging our kindness in visiting them & Requesting our further care of them."

As early as 1771 the Brotherton Indians had petitioned the colonial legislature for permission to lease some of their land to white farmers, but their request was denied. Obviously the reservation Indians were having difficulty adjusting to an agricultural life. Even Thomas Jefferson, America's first amateur archaeologist, took an interest in the Brotherton Reservation. Aside from his official duties as Secretary of State, he maintained an abiding interest in the aboriginal inhabitants and their languages. A document in the manuscript section of the American Philosophical Society in Philadelphia states, "A vocabulary of the Lenape language was obtained for Mr. Thomas Jefferson, in 1792 at the Village of Edgpiiliik, New Jersey."

Several historians have suggested the Indians sought other endeavors. In his book, *Early Forges & Furnaces in New Jersey*, Charles S. Boyer stated,

> During the early days of operation many of the Indians living at the Edgepillock Reservation (now Indian Mills) three miles away, found steady employment in and around the Atsion Works. These Indians were supplied with their food, tobacco, and rum from the company store, but unlike the dealings with the other workmen, a receipt was always taken from them for their purchases. Being unable to write they would make their "mark" and the transaction would be witnessed by some bystander.

There is no disrespect intended in refuting Boyer's conjecture; however, there does not appear to be any documented evidence to support these statements in any contemporary writings of the reservation period. Nor is there any indication whatsoever that the Indians were in any way desirous of the hard work involved at a forge and furnace three miles away. The Indians were living in abject poverty through most, if not all, of the reservation period.

Nathaniel R. Ewan, long known as the dean of local historians, once wrote,

> The old account books of Atsion Store given the writer several years ago are now in the Burlington County Historical Society. A number of semi-civilized Indians from the Indian Mills Reservation were employed at the furnace and much of their wages were credited to goods purchased in the store.

This author has examined all of Nathaniel Ewan's writings as well as the Atsion Store Books and ledgers and found nothing to support this statement. The only known books and ledgers of Atsion commenced from the Richards ownership of Atsion in 1825, many years after the Indians had vacated the reservation.

There is no doubt an earlier store at Atsion did exist, since the ironworks began in 1766 by Charles Read and others, but no store books of that era have ever been discovered, nor are they a part of the archives of the Burlington County Historical Society. More than likely the statements by Boyer and Ewan were supposition on their part and not based on historical fact.

On February 17, 1796, another petition was placed before the state government "on behalf of the Indian Natives residing at Brotherton who request they appoint commissioners to take charge of the Lands and Mill at Brotherton, and let or lease the same for the use and Benefit of the Indians." The commissioners were appointed to lease the land in a way beneficial to the Indians, and to pay the rent "or the value in necessaries, to those most needing aid." Joseph Salter, Josiah Foster, and Thomas Hollingshead were appointed. They were to render an account annually to the Burlington Court of Common Pleas, which was authorized to remove the commissioners on occasion and to fill vacancies.

It appears much of the Indians' income was derived from handiwork of the Indian women and not the men, who seemed to have returned to their old ways of hunting and foraging, with little attention paid to providing for their families other than putting food on the table. Samuel Mickle, an early historian, reported he had once bought baskets made by the Indians at Brotherton or Edgepillock.

At the August 1799 Term of Court, in Burlington County, there is a report of the Committee on Indian Affairs.

> The subscribers a Committee of the Court of Common Pleas appointed in the May Term 1799 to settle the accounts of the Commissioners of Indian Affairs in said county. Having met and heard the allegations of Jacob Skekit, the only Indian attending, and examined the accounts of Josiah Foster & Thomas Hollingshead, Esq. Two of the Commissioners (Joseph Salter the other commissioner not attending) Do report that it appears to your Committee that the Indians have been for many years and now are in practice of leasing their lands and receiving the rents, Issues, and Profits aforesaid is in the hands of either of the Commissioners. And there is due to Josiah Foster,

Esq. for surveying said Land for his time and Expenses at
Trenton and for Cash expended for the use of said Indians the
sum of forty eight dollars and ninety three cents and to Thomas
Hollingshead here for his attending at Trenton and dividing the
Lands the sum of twelve dollars, Mt. Holly, Aug. 13, 1799.
Signed Isaac Cowgill, Wm. Russell, Thomas Adams.

The Indian, Jacob Skekit, mentioned here, is the same man who had
signed the reply to the Ohio Delaware in 1767.

Professor Christian Feest of Frankfurt, Germany, made an unusual discovery in the 1990s. He had found the text of a book published in 1795 by
C. E. Bonn in Hamburg, Germany, entitled *Description of a Short Walking
Tour in the Province of New Jersey*. The author was a young German lad
named Johann Ferdinand H. Autenrieth. Professor Feest then conferred
with Henry Kammler of J. W. Goethe University in Frankfurt who published an article about the Brotherton Reservation including some of the
Autenreith text. Kammler's article relates that Johann Autenrieth, born
October 20, 1772, had accompanied his wealthy father Jacob, a college professor, on a tour of the Middle Atlantic States. His brother August also
made the trip. They toured New Jersey from November 1794 to April 1795.
Jakob Autenrieth was contemplating the possibility of moving his family to
America due to an uncertain situation in Europe. This apparently never
occurred.

Johann Ferdinand Autenrieth, only age 22 at the time, kept a vivid
detailed diary of his tour. In particular is the text describing his visit to the
Indian Reservation at Brotherton. It provides a startling eyewitness account
of the reservation during a period of time when other documentaries are
nonexistent. The text, in part, states,

> The land already belonged to the Indians and was less sandy
> and of better quality than that we had seen up to this point.
> Nice winding paths like in an English park led to the individual
> residences of the Indians. On a tilled, fenced-in field, just like
> the loghouse standing on it, was entirely European-American in

manner, even having fruit trees, resided their leader, whose name was Skiket.

Although this traditional bark-covered home was used by the Lenape, it was apparently not used on the reservation at Brotherton. (Photo by the author.)

In him, we found a tall, well proportioned, old man with black hair, small blackish-brown eyes, and with a complexion that was not coppery-red (as seldom as was the case with some Iroquois I had the chance to see in Philadelphia) but yellow or mulatto colored, but not having the blackish shade present among those. He had some red of old age on his cheeks. His physiognomy did not deviate much from the European one, his cranium was large, the thick brow of his forehead was protruded strongly and therefore made the not so large nose appear indented at its beginning. His wife was of the same height. She might have been approximately 40 years old or more. She too, had the same complexion, but without the slightest red on her cheeks, shiny black hair, small black eyes; her forehead narrowed upwardly, her cheekbones were prominent and, through this and through her chin, her face in a way had a quadrangular appearance. This Asiatic trace struck me all the more, as I already had noticed it in the skull of a Wabash Indian woman. Men never have this feature, but always a more rounded, bigger, more strongly projected in the middle of the sides and in the back of their skulls.

Soon afterwards, in another house in the neighborhood we saw a boy of about 13 years, this one had the same yellow complexion without red color, black hair, a broad face, small black eyes, with distinctly slanting, close-set eyes, consequently like among North America's almost adjacent neighbors, the Asiatic peoples. In addition, in the boy's house we saw two old women of much darker, as if smoked, complexion. In this same house, were two young Indian women, who hid themselves upon our arrival, so we couldn't set eyes on them. All those Indians we saw were dressed like white Americans. Even the old man no longer tore his beard out and had begun to shave his still growing beard in European fashion. We conversed with this principal person, who spoke English as all of them did. Their own language is pronounced entirely through the throat, like the German of the Swiss, and is very rough; this one they use still among themselves, by the way. Although he was able to read and write and seemed to be a reasonable man, his conversation was very poor, though he spoke slowly and only a little, and when not asked, he was sat there as if in deep contemplation.

Already having been far removed from their natural ways of living for many years, all activity seemed to have died away among these Indians, still cultivated too little, and not out of idleness (like among the old Germans, which the woods people of North America resemble so closely and, who knows, also will resemble in their later history) began to scorn agriculture, they often lease their land for cultivation; at best they weave baskets and make brooms which they carry to the market in

Philadelphia. They have entirely forgotten their old occupations; they do not even wield the tomahawk anymore. This lack
of mental stimulation and their totally inactive way of life is
probably the main reason that their numbers are obviously
dwindling. Only about nine families are said to remain, among
which there is also a family of a New England Indian, whose
tongue they themselves do not understand and with whom they
have to speak English.

The Whites living at some distance and who no longer see
as many Indians as before, maintain their younger people desert
to the warring Indians of the backlands. Out of envy for their
possessions, on the whole, they have a treacherous spite against
this remainder of rightful owners. The land transferred to them
for their settlement is called Edgepillock and is said to comprise
3,000 acres. Except for not being allowed to sell it, they have
complete command over it; they can sell lumber and even lease
the land, if they so choose. It does not seem as if they have
divided the land into certain allotments among themselves.

The common authorities judge their quarrels with Whites.
Their own disputes they do not sue for, and none takes them
into account. Many people remember that some years ago an
Indian, whose father had been murdered, took revenge in a
manner that was law among them. All of a sudden he took a
knife and stabbed his enemy, with whom he was drinking in a
local pub, pursued him as he escaped and knocked his brain out
with a stone.

They are all nominally Christians. They have a wooden
chapel where an itinerant preacher still preached to them a
year ago.

We started out again after our Indian and his wife had
drunken up the greater part of the bottle of rum with as much
indifference as others would have done with a glass of water. I
would have liked receiving anything special of some kind from
him, but neither a stone axe nor a chisel nor any other kind of

antiquity was possible to obtain among these people. Neither songs nor even their former war chant did this headman know? I only found a trace of an old tradition of their sacrifices with him. At the change of moon, it is said, a long hut was constructed and three deer were slaughtered around which the people danced.

The leader of the Brotherton band named Skiket, in the Autenrieth's narrative, was also mentioned in the 1799 Court of Common Pleas, and previously in the reply to the Ohio Delawares in 1767 as Jacob Skeket. He appears to have been the leader of the Brothertons at this time or at the very least one of their headmen or elders.

In 1801 the Brotherton Indians received an invitation from a group of Mahicans who by then were known as the Stockbridge Indians, residing near Oneida Lake, New York. The original document has disappeared, but in 1832, the noted historian Samuel Allinson recalled that he had seen a copy of it. He recollects the Mahicans urged the Brothertons to "pack up their mat and come eat out of their dish," they said it was large enough for them all and that, "their necks were stretched in looking toward the fireside of their grandfathers till they were as long as cranes."

The Indians at Brotherton were pleased with the offer and may also have been influenced by a Mahican family living with them. C. A. Weslager had suspected the possible influence of Mahicans when he wrote his superb *The Delaware Indians, A History* in 1971, but he did not have the benefit of Autenrieth's narrative, which tends to prove his supposition in that "a family of New England Mahicans was living among the Brothertons." The Brotherton Indians again petitioned the Legislature requesting they sell the reservation lands for them and use the proceeds to transport them to Oneida Lake, New York.

An act was passed December 3, 1801, appointing William Salter, William Stockton, and Enoch Evans as Commissioners. They were to divide the reservation tract into separate lots of not more than 100 acres, and to sell them at a public sale provided that three fourths of the Indians at Brotherton consented. Two men, James Ewing and John Beatty, were appointed to go to the Brotherton Reservation to determine exactly how many of the Indians wanted to leave. On January 15, 1802, they visited Brotherton and found only 46 adults present out of the 63 adult Indians who had rights in the tract. Thirty-eight voluntarily signed the petition to sell and move. Eight others signed when they met Ewing and Beatty in Trenton on March 20, 1802, at which time they reported their findings to Governor Bloomfield. Even though 46 Indians who signed the petition were slightly less than the three fourths necessary, the governor accepted the petition.

On March 29, 1802, the governor appointed Abraham Stockton, William Stockton, and Charles Ellis as Commissioners in place of William Salter and Enoch Evans who had resigned. Josiah Foster, the son of William Foster, one of the original commissioners who purchased the reservation lands for the Indians in 1758, was chosen to survey, run out, and divide the Brotherton Reservation into 100-acre lots. It was actually found to contain 3,284 acres instead of the original 3, 044 acres surveyed in 1758. An advertisement was placed in the *Trenton Federalist* newspaper dated March 31, 1802.

> To be Sold. Agreeable to an Act of the Legislature of the State of New Jersey passed the third of December, 1801 appointing commissioners to sell and convey for the benefit of the Indians a certain tract of land called Brotherton in the township of Evesham and county of Burlington containing about 3,000 acres and near several noted Iron Works. A great part of this land is in timber of different kinds of wood as pine, maple, hickory, white and red oak and cedar. There are several streams of water and a good saw mill in good repair on the premises: likewise another good seat where a mill has formerly been, the dam chiefly entire, a quantity of cedar swamp on the tract, several farms are cleared theron which are chiefly fenced with cedar rails, several valuable apple orchards, together with peach and other fruit trees. A number of houses are built on said tract; the land is very suitable for Indian corn, rye, and other grain. A great part of the land is uncultivated and that improved is of a good loamy soil, very suitable for the cultivation of red clover and

other grasses, separate from which it is supposed a quantity of meadow may be made, the above to be sold in 100 acre lots, the sale to begin on the 10th day of May next, and to continue from day to day until the whole is sold.

The terms of payment will be made easy and attendance given by William Stockton, Abraham Stockton, and Charles Ellis, Commissioners.

N.B. Any person wishing to view said land may apply to William Salter Esq. at Atsion Works, near the premises who will show the same.

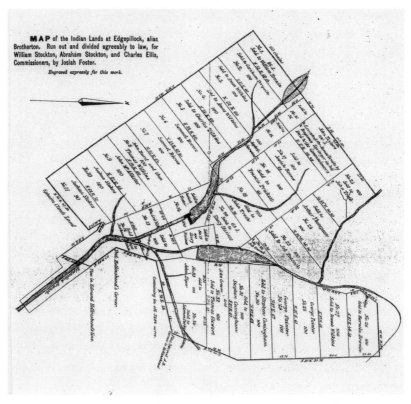

This map depicts the division of the Brotherton Reservation as it appeared in Woodward & Hageman's History of Burlington and Mercer Co. *in 1883.*

Another advertisement appeared in the *Trenton Federalist* on August 24, 1802. It reads,

> About 1500 acres of land, the remainder of a tract of land called Brotherton situated in the town of Evesham and County of Burlington. Part of said land, in timber of different kinds, part thereof cleared and fenced. There are on the premises several apple orchards and other fruit trees. Chief of the land is loamy soil, suitable for Indian corn, rye, and clover. There is also a good mill seat on said tract and a dam entire. The sale to begin in the 4th day of October next at the house of John Piper in said township where attendance will be given and conditions known by William Stockton, Abraham Stockton, and Charles Ellis commissioners.

The "house of John Piper" mentioned in the advertisement was actually Piper's, known as the Sign of the Buck, located on the present day northeast corner of Oak Shade and Atsion Roads. At that time Oak Shade Road came to a dead end at Atsion Road heading south.

The reservation property of Edgepillock was sold to 25 different persons at prices of $2 to $5 per acre. Josiah Foster, who had surveyed and divided out the lots for the Indian Commissioners, was also the purchaser of Lot #14, which included the original Indian sawmill, and also the sawmill pond and surrounding land. He paid 255 pounds for the 100-acre property on May 10, 1802. A Samuel Reeves had bought 200 acres adjoining in Lots #6 and #7. In 1803 Josiah Foster sold Lot #14, to Samuel Reeves for $775, making a handsome profit. Samuel Reeves operated the sawmill for many years thereafter.

Age-old traditions recall an ancient mulberry tree in a wooded area of the Gardner Farm. This is known locally as the Treaty Tree. The tradition has persisted in the Gardner family for many generations since Congressman John James Gardner purchased his farm in January 1902. The story was told to him by many of the older residents of the area that this particular tree was a gathering place of the reservation Indians and the place where their treaties were signed.

The Treaty Tree that once stood on the Gardner Farm now lies on the forest floor.
Tradition recalls that it was once a gathering place for the reservation Indians.
(Photo circa 1950s, courtesy of the Gardner family.)

There is no actual written documentation of this tradition to positively prove its validity but the very fact that this story has persisted for so many years seems to give some credence to its authenticity. Assuming that such is the case, there is one recorded instance where a document was presented to the Indians at their place of habitation. You may recall this occurred when the governor's representatives James Ewing and John Beatty went to Brotherton to obtain the Indians' signatures on a petition for removal to New York State.

Is it not logical to assume that the signatures were obtained at this traditional gathering place? This is the only recorded instance where the Indians at the reservation signed any document. Although this document was not a treaty of any sort, it could have been the source of the treaty tree tradition.

Today this ancient mulberry tree with a trunk diameter of 6 feet lies decaying on the forest floor, its gnarled and twisted branches only mute reminders of its former majesty. To pause for a moment at this peaceful spot conjures up visions of former times when this area was a virtual wilderness and its inhabitants the earliest Americans.

A short distance from the treaty tree lies a small area of disturbed ground, which tradition identifies as the location of the chief's cabin. The area clamors for the spade and sifting screen of the archaeologist.

The Indian Mills Historical Society erected an historical marker on Willow Grove Road near these sites. The marker is visible, but permission to view the actual site needs to be obtained from the owner of the property, as these sites are not visible from the road.

Once the final lots of the reservation were sold the proceeds were used to hire drivers and wagons to transport the last 83 inhabitants of Brotherton to their new home at New Stockbridge near Oneida Lake, New York. The old and infirm rode in the wagons with their belongings while those that were able walked the 275 miles to their new home. The three commissioners who held the auction proceedings accompanied them on their journey. On their return the commissioners reported they were presented with five strings of white wampum beads by the New Stockbridge Indians as a pledge of friendship and security for land and privileges they were giving to the Delaware Tribe.

In Thomas Brainerd's biography of his ancestor, he quotes a letter from the Honorable Pomeroy Jones of Westmoreland, Oneida County, New York.

> When the Delawares emigrated to Oneida in 1802 they passed my residence in Westmoreland. They had twelve wagons for their baggage and those too feeble to journey on foot. The next day, when on their return to New Jersey, the wagons again passed my house. I presume they had been hired for the occasion.
>
> The Delawares were completely amalgamated with the Oneidas and inducted into their habits, and soon were around amongst the white inhabitants selling their commodities, split brooms and baskets. In 1830, I was appointed by the Commission of the Land Office, one of the Commissioners to appraise seventeen hundred acres of land sold by the Oneidas the previous winter to the State. As the land was partially settled, a number of families residing on it, it led to quite an

intimacy with them; and I found a portion of them were of the Delaware tribe, but possessed of all rights of Oneidas to the soil they occupied.

On September 23, 1823, at nearby Vernon, New York, the elders of the Delaware tribe, Bartholomew Calvin, Jonathan C. Johnston, and Charles Tanseye, entered into an agreement with the Mahican or Mahheconnuck tribe whereby they granted the Brotherton Indians and "their scattered brethren in New Jersey" an equal right and interest in their tribe. This also included the lands that had been purchased near Green Bay, Shaweno County, Wisconsin, where they subsequently moved in 1824. Their descendants may still be found in Wisconsin today, far from the lands of their forefathers, and their identity totally merged with the Mahican tribe.

This agreement clearly indicated that even after the move to New York State there were still some Lenapes living in New Jersey, which would seem to somewhat substantiate numerous accounts of those living here today claiming some Lenape ancestry, the author's wife included. Subsequent chapters will discuss this in more detail.

In 1832 Bartholomew S. Calvin, the Princeton-educated former schoolmaster at Brotherton, appeared before the New Jersey Legislature. His Indian name was Shawuskukhkung, which means "Wilted Grass." He was now 76 years of age, white haired, and an eloquent spokesman for the Delaware tribe now removed to Wisconsin. He addressed the Assembly in part by saying,

> My brethren, I am old, and weak and poor, and therefore a fit representative of my people. You are young, and strong, and rich, and therefore fit representatives of your people. But let me beg you for a moment to lay aside the recollections of your strength and our weakness that your minds may be prepared to examine with candor the subject of our claims.
>
> Our tradition informs us, and I believe it corresponds with your records, that the right of fishing in all the rivers and bays south of the Raritan, and of hunting in all unenclosed lands,

was never relinquished, but on the contrary was expressly reserved in our last treaty, held at Crosswicks, in 1758.

The Honorable Samuel L. Southard spoke in support of Calvin's petition by saying,

> That it was a proud fact in the history of New Jersey, that every foot of her soil had been obtained from the Indians by fair and voluntary purchase and transfer, a fact that no other state of the union, not even the land which bears the name of Penn, can boast of.

The Legislature acted accordingly by authorizing the sum of $2,000 to be paid to Calvin as he had requested in his petition. This was more an act of kindness and compassion than any legal obligation.

On March 12, 1832, at the State House in Trenton, the venerable and humble leader of his people delivered the following address.

> Bartholomew S. Calvin takes this method to return his thanks to both houses of the state legislature, and especially to their committees for their very respectful attention to, and candid examination of the Indian claims which he was delegated to present.
>
> The final act of official intercourse between the state of New Jersey and the Delaware Indians, who once owned nearly the whole of its territory, has now been consummated, and in a manner which must redound to the honor of this growing state. And, in all probability, to the prolongation of a wasted, yet grateful people. Upon this parting occasion, I feel it to be an incumbent duty to bear the feeble tribute of my praise to the high toned justice which, in this instance, and so far as I am acquainted, in all former times, has actuated the councils of this commonwealth in dealing with the aboriginal inhabitants.
>
> Not a drop of our blood have you spilled in battle, not an acre of land have you taken but by our consent. These facts speak for themselves, and need no comment. They place the

Character of New Jersey in bold relief and bright example to those states within whose territorial limits our brethren still remain. Nothing save benisons can fall upon her from the lips of a Lenni Lenappi.

There may be some who would despise an Indian benediction; but when I return to my people, and make known to them the result of my mission, the ear of the great Sovereign of the Universe, which is still open to our cry, will be penetrated with our invocation of blessing upon the generous sons of New Jersey.

The entire Legislature rose to shouts of acclamation, and thus ended all official connection the Delawares had with the State of New Jersey. A once powerful, yet kindly nation of people were now scattered into numerous enclaves with other tribes, in various parts of the United States and Canada.

In June 1861 Reverend Thomas Brainerd, the biographer, and Reverend Samuel Miller of Mount Holly paid a visit to Brotherton, now known as Indian Mills. Brainerd writes,

A morning drive of fifteen miles, with a light buggy and two horses, through a well cultivated country and on a good road, brought us to the ancient farm of Stephen Calvin, father of Hezekiah and Bartholomew Calvin [Brainerd's pupils] about noon. Stephen Calvin was a substantial farmer, and an elder in John Brainerd's church. One hundred years ago his dwelling was the home of genuine Indian hospitality; but dwarf pines and scrub oaks have so reclaimed their occupancy of the soil, that Mr. Miller and myself found only an open orchard of ancient trees to indicate the existence of former cultivation. We measured some of these apple trees and found them more than six feet in circumference. Having taken our field repast under the most ancient tree, and possessed ourselves of a living limb as a relic, we proceeded to Brotherton, one mile distant. There the stump of a mammoth oak indicated the spot where stood the ancient Indian sanctuary, a depression in the earth, the remains of a former cellar, told us the spot of Brainerd's own dwelling. A modern mill occupies the very place and bears the name of the mill erected by Brainerd's Indians a century gone by. We found traditions rife there of the piety and labors of the good missionary; and aged persons told us they remembered the final departure of the Indians for their new home in Western New York.

Thus has been told the story of one of the oldest and greatest nations in American Indian history and a story of the first and only authentic Indian reservation in New Jersey. The Delawares have become a people of the past, but a people that will live on in history, and never will be forgotten.

CHAPTER 7

Wepink—The Other Indian Town

Wepink, also spelled Weepinck, Weekpink, and Wepinck, was the name of an historic Indian village approximately 1.5 miles west of present-day Vincentown. Early English settlers gave it this name after the small run of water that flows on the edge of the village into the south branch of the Rancocas Creek.

The actual history of Wepink begins with the first mention of this Indian village by another name in 1703. Franklin M. Earl, a well-known and respected surveyor who lived four miles east of Wepink, wrote a letter to Reverend Samuel Miller of Mount Holly. He writes in part on April 14, 1880,

> In a deed in my possession, made by the Indian Chiefs the 28th day of April, 1703 this town was then called by the Indian name of Okokathseeme, and is represented as being west by south, or thereabouts, from the land on which I now live, and my deed was given by the chiefs for a consideration, as a relinquishment of the Indian claim upon said land. The three chiefs who signed the deed, Amearthtoth, Hockakemock, and Keetawawa, and witnessed by many Indians such as Efendway, Mitopp, and others, prominent amongst the Indians.

Gabriel Mitopp was one of the Indian elders from the Crosswicks band present at the Conference held at Crosswicks February 1758.

Earl's letter further describes the location of this village as being in 1880,

> on the farm that now belongs to William J. Irick, and near where the two roads separate, the one leading to Eayrestown, [now Village Lane and the other leading to Medford [Church

Road]. There is on said farm and near the garden attached to the Mansion House, an old Indian graveyard, and some years ago, while there, the marks of very many graves were plainly to be seen. Between the graveyard and the Eayrestown Road runs a small stream of water that is known as WEPINK. There can be little doubt the Indian town of Wepink was located near that place. For many years, I remember the graveyard was surrounded by a fence, but no one feeling an interest for its protection, it has gone down, and the graveyard is now out of sight, having been ploughed and cultivated; but its location can readily be found.

The William Irick Homestead farm still stands on the Dolan Farm along Church Road near Vincentown. Tradition and eyewitness accounts recall that the Indians of Wepink buried their dead somewhere close to the rear of this house. (Photo by the author.)

In a subsequent letter to Reverend Allen H. Brown of Camden, New Jersey, May 7, 1880, Earl writes,

King Charles was or claimed to be the head Chief over all the Indians, both at Brotherton and Wepink. His Indian name was Himmickson or King Charles. I have three or four deeds from King Charles and one other chief Welongomit for lands between Brotherton and Wepink, large tracts of land. There were several chiefs at Brotherton and Wepink, such as Sisowheto and Allomoogos. The present owner of the farm, William J. Irick, traces his title back to the chief or chiefs, who devised the same to Josiah Foster.

The farm, on which the Indian graveyard is, was devised by the Indians by will to Josiah Foster, one of the Commissioners appointed to take charge of the Indian lands by Act of the Legislature, to rent and work the same for the benefit of the Indians. I have not examined the records but Tradition says that the will was contested in Court and Foster came out victorious, by confirming said will, showing the Indians had a good title in fee.

Several of Franklin Earl's statements in his letter to Reverend Brown are not historically accurate as will be demonstrated throughout this chapter. The King Charles mentioned as having the Indian name Himmickson was actually Mahamickwon, also known as Mahamecun and Mehemickon, depending on the recorders. The early colonists gave him the English name Charles. This was to denote a person of great wealth and prestige, particularly in Burlington County. The English King Charles II was in power from 1660 to 1685. Mahamickwon, alias King Charles, an Indian sachem, most likely claimed vast tracts of land in the 1600s and early 1700s and must have died sometime before the relinquishment of all Indian claims at the Crosswicks Conference in 1758. His son Moonis, alias Jacob Mullis or Moolis, is mentioned as being an Ancocas Indian. He had claimed the pinelands at Edgepillock Branch and Goshen Neck where Benjamin Springer and George Marpole's mills stand and all the land between the real branches of the creeks to where the waters form or meet.

The Council of Proprietors for West Jersey held a meeting at Burlington on June 28, 1703. Mahamickwon made an application to the council concerning the bounds of two Indian purchases formerly made. The one was a deed for land between Assunpink and Rancocas Creeks dated October 10, 1677, and the other for lands between Rancocas and Big Timber Creeks dated September 10, 1677. He claimed the bounds of the tracts were in error due to a misunderstanding between the interpreter and the English. New bounds had been run out afterward. His application was to have all the original bounds rules null and void and the council agreed that the new bounds should be accepted and approved.

In the Burlington County Quarter Sessions Court dated March 16, 1705, in the 3rd year Reign of Sovereign Lady Anne, Queen of England,

> Indian King Charles complains to the bench against the wife of Mons. Coxs for cheating him of four pounds it being money shee had of him in the street at Philadelphia. The bench satis-fied the Indian that he shall be heard before my Lord.

That Mahamickwon, alias King Charles, was a chief of some regional importance seems quite obvious when he was the apparent spokesman for many other chiefs who had previously negotiated their purchases many years before.

A survey was made in 1691 for 400 acres of land for Thomas Evans at the Indian Town of Quaexin on one of the branches of Ancocas River. The Indian name for the present day Little Creek was Quoexing or Coaxing. The name has been corrupted many times over and mainly comes down to us as Coaxen. An Indian village existed in historic times on the banks of Little Creek to the rear of the present day Roberts farm. As was the custom of the Indians, they frequently moved from one land setting to another on a seasonal basis. The village of Wepink, on the small run of water by that name, was merely a continuation of the same habitation site at Coaxen. In later land deeds, this entire property, spreading over portions of several farms, became known as the Coaxen Tract.

Soon after the arrival of the Quaker settlers in Burlington, they formed the Proprietors of West Jersey. In turn they appointed commissioners to pur-chase land from the Indian inhabitants. One of these commissioners was Dr. Daniel Wills, who eventually owned large tracts of land in the vicinity of Rancocas Creek. When he died in 1698, his son, John Wills, inherited the

*Partial view of the Coaxen Tract to the rear of the Roberts Farm
at Church and Eayrestown Roads. (Photo by the author.)*

farm on the north side of the Rancocas and also 624 acres lying near the
forks of the river. John Wills died in 1746, but before he died he devised a
242-acre tract of land to a family of Indians. The exact reason for his doing
this is not reflected in the records. Possibly as part of his kindly and benevolent nature as a Quaker he felt the Indians would have nowhere to live if
all their land was sold to the colonists.

He therefore sold 242 acres of his father's estate, which is recorded in
West Jersey Deeds, Book E-F, page 76, and reads in part,

> This indenture made the 8th day of Oct. 1740 in the
> 14th year of our sovereign Lord, George 2nd, over Great Britain,
> France and Ireland, King, between John Wills of the township
> of Northampton in the County of Burlington and Province of
> New Jersey (Gentlemen), of the one part and the children of
> the late Indian King Osollowhen, late of the township of
> Northampton, in the County and Province aforesaid, deceased,

and to his two brothers, called by the names of Teannis and Moonis, Indians and natives of the westerly division of the Province of New Jersey of the other part; Witnesseth, that the said John Wills for and in Consideration of the sum of four shillings Current money of the aforesaid Province of New Jersey, to him in hand paid by the said Children of the said Indian King, and Teannis and Moonis, his two brothers, at or before the ensealing and delivery of the presents, the receipt whereof, he the said John Wills doth hereby own and acknowledge, and thereof and of every part and parcel thereof doth hereby acquit, release and discharge the said Children of the said Indian King, and the said Teannis and Moonis, and every of them forever by these presents, and also for and in Consideration of the good will that he has to the children of Osollowhen and his two brothers Teannis and Moonis, that they might have perpetual habitation for their generations, offspring, stock, or kindred forever; has given, granted, bargained, sold, aliened, enfeoffed, released, conveyed and confirmed, and doth by these presents, fully, clearly, and absolutely give, grant, bargain, sell, alien, enfeoff, release, Convey and Confirm unto the Children of Osollowhen and his two brothers Teannis and Moonis, and their progeny forever; All that tract of land and plantation, situated in the forks of the Rancocas River in the Township of Northampton, in the County of Burlington and Province of New Jersey, and by the survey thereof lyeth thus bounded. Beginning at a Maple, marked with the letters BVRR, standing on the south side of the middle branch of Rancocas, commonly called Ayres Mill Creek, and at the mouth of a small run of water, then by the land of John Burr to a black oak by the head of said run, thence still by said Burr's land to a dead black oak with a living white oak by the side of it, Marked for a corner, thence by said Burr's to a large white oak tree on the east side of Coaxen run, thence by the land of Daniel Wills, thence to place of beginning containing 242 acres of land with allowances for highways.

The deed concludes, after much verbage of meets and bounds and much redundant recitation, with these words: "the said land may descend according to the custom among the Indians, so long as the water runs in the river Delaware and Rancocas or Northampton rivers."

The land described above has long been known as the Coaxen Tract that contained the Indian villages of Coaxen and Wepink. In 1740 the primary means of travel was by water in a canoe or barge, or overland by walking or on horseback on various Indian paths through the area. There were no roads mentioned that would exist today. In 1740 the land was still a pristine wilderness with some land that had been cleared for farming with only paths made from one farm to another.

The names of the children of the deceased King Osollowhen are not mentioned, only his brothers Teannis and Moonis. John Wills signed the deed, and also in the presence of one of his Majesties, the King's Council for

A view of Wepink as it appears today on the Dolan Farm off Village Lane near Vincentown. (Photo by the author.)

95

the Province of New Jersey named Richard Smith. Also present were Isaac Pearson, Caleb Roper, and Isaac Delso. John Wills appeared to take great pains and precautions to be sure this transaction was authentic, valid, and beyond any challenges in later years, especially when he only received the mere sum of four shillings lawful English money from the Indians for a 242-acre plantation. There is also no mention or reference to Mahamickwon, alias King Charles, who was now deceased as noted in the following deed of sale found in West Jersey Deeds, Book I-K, Page 71, from the Indian Teanish (also spelled Teannis) to John Burr dated September 19, 1745.

To All Christian People, to whom these presents shall come greeting, Whereas John Burr of Burlington Co. in New Jersey, Yeoman, became seized in fee of several shares of Proprietary Rights to land in West Jersey by virtue of which and pursuant to an Act of Assembly of the Province of New Jersey he the said John Burr obtained a license from the governor and Commander in Chief of the said Province to purchase of and from the Indian Native owners of land in West Jersey the quantity of two thousand two hundred and twenty acres of land aforesaid. Now know ye that Indian Teanish native owner of Lands Between the Swimming River and Ancocas Creek in the county aforesaid which remains unsold by my Father Mehemickon alias King Charles and my brother Osolowhenia Late of the County aforesaid doth sell to John Burr several tracts and parcels of Cedar Swamp situate in the county aforesaid and on the Branches of the Swimming River (to with) all that Cedar Swamp called Bards Swamp and the Lower end of what is called Fosters Swamp and all that Cedar Swamp called the Unknown Swamp with the Branches thereof and also all the lower end of a Cedar Swamp called Ettomsqueoung up to John Haines survey and containing in the whole of said Cedar Swamp about 250 acres. These words for myself and my heirs being interjoined before signing his mark X Indian Teanish.

John Burr had paid eight pounds 10 shillings for 250 acres of cedar swamp. It is made quite clear in this deed that the Indian Mahamickwon, alias King Charles, was the father of Teanish, Moonis, and Osolowhenia, also known as King Osollowhen in the prior deed, and that Osolowhenia and Mahamickwon, alias King Charles, were now both deceased. The Swimming River mentioned in the deed was an old name for the current Batsto River. Bards Swamp is still a large cedar swamp off Bards Run, which is a branch of the Batsto River. Unknown Swamp was located west of Ongs Hat near what is today known as Cedar Run, a tributary of Friendship Creek that flows into the south branch of the Rancocas. Foster's Swamp is not shown on any of the older maps researched, however, the name of the cedar swamp called Ettomsquaoung (also spelled Ettomsqueong) is an earlier name for the Nescochague Creek, a branch of the Mullica near present day Pleasant Mills. Nathaniel Cripps owned (or so he thought) Edgeackick Swamp in 1728 and Samuel Cripps dammed the creek for a sawmill as early as 1740.

Where Teanish, alias Teannis, lived after this sale is unknown. His brother Moonis, alias Moolis, is not mentioned in the John Burr deed. Teanish may have moved elsewhere or simply remained on the Coaxen Tract at Wepink with the rest of the band.

The Burlington Court Book dated December 14, 1749, records,

> the Necessity of a further division to be made betwixt the Township of Northampton and Eversham. We therefore do agree that the said Division do begin where the former record leaves off and thence to the forking of the said South Branch and the beginning just at the said fork and thence going to a certain bridge over a creek called Mill Creek or Thomas Evans Run near the Indian Town called Coerxing and along the same to the head therof.

This appears to be near the same Indian town of Quaexin surveyed for Thomas Evans in 1691 for 400 acres of land. Little else is known of the Indians of Coaxen or Wepink until Reverend John Brainerd recorded entries in his journal.

> Sun. Dec. 6, 1761. Rode this morning abt. 14 miles to
> Wepinck the old Indian Town and attended divine Worship
> there; accomadating myself to the Indians, and likewise to the
> White People, a number of whom were present.

He preached again there to a mixed congregation of Indians and White people on January 10 and 24, 1762. On March 7, 1762, he,

> performed divine Services in the Forenoon near Wepinck in the
> dwelling house of a White Man more commodious than any of
> the Indians. After service I used some endeavor to have a meet-
> inghouse built to accommodate both the Indians and White
> people and got upwards of twenty pounds subscribed for that
> Purpose. April 18th Preached in the Forenoon at Wepinck. The
> next day I rode out to take care of the Indians Lands, having
> been informed that People cut off the Timber, as also some
> other affairs of a temporal nature relating to the Indians. Friday
> April 23rd. Rode to Bridgetown to consult the Law respecting
> the Indian Lands at Wepinck, and what should be done to pre-
> vent the White People cutting off the Timber and returned
> home next day. May 2nd Rode to Wepinck performed Divine
> Service. A number of Indians and a large Congregation of
> White People attending. June 13, 1762 Rode to Wepinck the
> other Indian Town and officiated to a mixed Congregation of
> Indians and White People.

On June 30, July 4, and July 8, Brainerd writes he continued to preach to large gatherings of Indians and White people at Wepink.

During late July 1762, Brainerd took an extended trip to visit the Indian camps on the Susquehanna near Lancaster. The chiefs were not willing to attend to any instruction respecting Christianity. He left Lancaster, Pennsylvania, on August 22. He stayed in Philadelphia overnight and left by horseback early in the morning. He rode some 20 miles to Bridgetown where he officiated in the Forenoon. Then he rode to a house near Wepink where he found a large number of people consisting of English and Indians.

Tuesday September 7, 1762 Attended Evening Meeting with the Indians at Wepinck; a large number of White People also, were present. After service we consulted further about the meetinghouse which we are endeavoring to build for these Indians and the adjacent People.

This was the last entry in Brainerd's journal concerning Wepink. He was obviously enthusiastic in trying to work with both Indians and Whites in trying to build a meetinghouse for all. One was eventually erected made of logs, and Brainerd gives a vivid description of it in a letter he wrote nearly 13 years later, to the Mission Board, on February 9, 1775.

At Wepinck, the other Indian place, about 12 miles from Brotherton; we have put up with meetings for Divine Worship in a poor Indian Hut, after the bigger part of the Congregation out of Doors, till about Summer, when we attempted to raise a Meetinghouse, and proceeded so far as to get it enclosed, with three glass Windows and the under Floor laid. Some boards that were left laid on Blocks Serve us for Seats. The neighboring White People have Subscribed and Paid something toward it.

The place of worship became known as the Coaxen Meeting House for Indians and Whites alike.

It is again mentioned in Book A of Road Returns at the Burlington County Courthouse, which describes the building of a road from Vincentown to Coaxen Meeting House in 1794.

Beginning at a post in Vincentown Street about the middle thereof and running thence to a post near a hickory, a little to the westward of Joseph Burr's Gristmill, thence to a post on the west side of a run of water called Wepink, thence to the Great Road leading from Eayrestown to Little Egg Harbor, a little to the westward of said meetinghouse which said road to be 3 1/2 rods in width to be opened Nov. 1794.

*Shinn Log Cabin of 1712 stands today in a parking lot of the
Burlington County Courthouse. The Coaxen Meeting House
most likely resembled a structure of this sort.* (Photo by the author.)

The Great Road mentioned is the present day Red Lion–Eayrestown
Road. The road described in the return was for many years known as the
Vincentown–Eayrestown Road, which is now known as Church Road
where it forks left at Landing Street and just after the Irick Mansion bears
to the right to become present day Village Lane. The road originally ran all
the way through to the Great Road, which made sense in those days. In the
late 1950s, this unpaved road still skirted the farmland out to Eayrestown
Road.

The Coaxen Meeting House remained at its original location for many
years. In the late 1800s the Honorable Henry J. Irick of Vincentown, a state
senator, recalled,

> Brainerd's meeting house stood on the southeast corner of the
> crossroads at John P. Lippincott's house. The burying ground was
> located on the farm of William J. Irick, and I can show you the
> exact spot, and well remember when it was fenced in.

It should be pointed out that John P. Lippincott once lived on a rise of ground on the west side of Eayrestown Road, just beyond where Village Lane once intersected with the Great Road. After Brainerd's death in 1781, history does not record who preached to the Indians at Wepink. They had a meetinghouse built, but their numbers were dwindling until there appeared to be only a small group remaining. The records are very few concerning these Indians with the exception of two estates that were probated in Burlington County.

The first will was recorded June 15, 1783, and was the Last Will and Testament of Jacob Moonis of Quoickson, an Indian, of Northampton Township, Burlington County.

> Wife Hannah shall live on my plantation and be maintained by my children Mary, Charles, and Hannah. My plantation which I had by deed Oct. 6, 1740, Book EF page 76. The executors named were Charles, Mary, and Hannah. Witnesses, Thomas Bond, Anthony Charmely, Edmund Harris, and Derick Quickquies. The will was proved Sept. 8, 1803.

Note that this same individual was the brother of Osollowhen and Teanish, and the son of Mahamickwon, alias King Charles. Although instead of just calling himself Moonis, he had also taken the biblical first name of Jacob. He must have previously used his full name Mullis, as he is also listed as Jacob Mullis, or Moolis, an Ancocas Indian at the Crosswicks Conference in 1758. One of the witnesses to the will was also an Indian by the name of Derick Quickquies, who had also been present at the Crosswicks Conference in February 1758, identified as a Cranbury Indian named Dirick Quaquay.

The second will filed was that of Charles Mooless of Northampton Township, Burlington County.

> To my housekeeper, Barshabee Pombeles, my young horse and cart and household goods, also 1/3 of the grain with pasture for horse and cow and the privilege of house where I now live with one acre of ground during her life. Friend Henery Armstrong, 10 acres of land to be laid off for him during his life,

my brother-in-law John Hays, 5 acres of land to be laid off for him during his life, Friend Josiah Foster, residue of real and personal estate and sole executor. Witnesses Phineas Kirkbride, David Joyce, and William Joyce. Proved April 29, 1802.

The Indian known in the will as Charles Mooless was actually the son of Jacob Moonis (also known as Mullis, or Moolis), and the grandson of Mahamickwon, alias King Charles. It is interesting to note that Charles Moolis had also assumed the pseudonym of King Charles. Many older residents of the Vincentown area in the mid-1800s remember these Indians at the turn of that century when only a handful remained and were recalled as King Charles Moolis and Bathsheba his wife. One historian, Alfred Heston, wrote in 1880, "There are yet persons in Vincentown who recalled these Indians before they wholly passed away either by death or removal."

The individual named Barshabee Pombeless, the housekeeper, may well have been the legendary Queen Bathsheba Moolis, who late 19th-century historians record making annual visits to the seashore with her entourage and coming from the Medford area. A John Pombelus, alias Matanoo, was a chief of the Crosswicks band in 1758 and may have been a relative.

Charles Moolis makes no mention of his sisters Hannah and Mary and possibly they were deceased. He does name his brother-in-law John Hays who may have been married to one of his sisters and was a non-Indian. There were no subsequent land transactions recorded for John Hays or Henery Armstrong.

Friend Josiah Foster, the former Quaker Commissioner and surveyor of the Indian lands at Brotherton in 1796, was named as sole executor and inherited all the rest of the estate of Charles Moolis. He was the son of a prominent Burlington County judge named William Foster, who had been one of the original Commissioners of Indian Affairs in 1758. The area of Fostertown in Lumberton Township was named after this family. Both father and son had played a major part in the various stages of the Brotherton Reservation and also the final stages of the other Indian town of Wepink.

Josiah Foster was born on the family farm in Evesham (now Lumberton Township) on May 20, 1743. Their home was a scant two miles from

Wepink and no doubt his involvement with the Indians at Brotherton had also caused him to have friendship with the Wepink natives. He was a local justice of the peace, a noted surveyor, and a prominent member of the Evesham Friends Meeting, now located in Mount Laurel. He apparently was also a close friend and confidante of Charles Moolis, who had entrusted almost his entire estate to him.

Problems did occur for Foster when he had to appear in Burlington County Orphans Court on August 14, 1798, concerning the Will of Charles Moolis.

> The surrogate having reported to the court the will instrument exhibited into his office by Josiah Foster for probate and Testament and last will of Charles Moolis late of the county of Burlington deceased wherein the said Josiah Foster is named executor and having also reported a paper filed in his office purporting to be a caveat against the probate of the said instrument. It is ordered that the said instrument called the will of the said Charles Moolis and the court thereto be filed at the courthouse in Mt. Holly on Tuesday, 11th of Sept. 1798.

The Burlington County Orphans Court again met at the appointed time and reported,

> The court having heard and duly considered the Testimony and agreements of council in the above cause are of opinion and do decree that the said instrument of writing exhibited by Josiah Foster as the Testament and last will of Charles Moolis deceased for probate is not proved to be his testament. And last will and that Letters Testamentary therein ought not to be granted. Whereupon the council on behalf of the said Josiah Foster Executor, and did instantly appeal from the said decree to the Governors ordinary and it is allowed.

The will was proved April 29, 1802.

As Franklin Earl had once written "the court had challenged the will of Charles Moolis but Foster came out victorious." At about this same time, Josiah Foster was deeply involved in the final days of the Brotherton Reservation and is named as executor of many wills of fellow Quakers in the area.

Josiah Foster was the son of William Foster and Hannah Core. His father died November 1, 1778, and his mother November 11, 1778. Both are buried at the Evesham Friends Meeting burial ground in Mount Laurel. Josiah had married Rachel Burr, November 5, 1764. They had five daughters. She was the daughter of Henry Burr, a prominent Quaker in the area. They had lived for a while on the family farm, now known as Fostertown, near the intersection of Mount Holly–Lumberton Road and Fostertown Road.

In further testimony to the fact that not all of the Indians had left Brotherton and Wepink in 1802 is the following Legislative Act dated March 13, 1806, in which commissioners were appointed naming Joseph Budd Esq. and Phineas Kirkbride to take charge of the Coaxen lands in the county of Burlington. The act was in response to a petition filed by the Coaxen Indians. Their names are not given. Their petition advised that they claimed right to a tract of land in said county, of which they and their ancestors had been in possession upward of 60 years, and that they were incapable of managing the same to the best advantage. They authorized these commissioners to take full charge of all the Coaxen lands and to put out the same on improving leases. It provided nevertheless that nothing in this act should be construed so as to validate or in anywise affect the title, claim, or demand of any person whatever, claiming title to, or interest in the said Coaxen lands or any part thereof.

A law was enacted that the commissioners prosecute all actions or suits at law for the recovery of any debt or debts due and owing from any person or persons, to any *or either of said Indians* or any trespass committed on the said lands. It also stated that all leases or grants, which shall hereafter be made by any of the said Coaxen Indians, to any person or persons whatever, without the consent of the commissioners shall be null and void.

Nothing further is recorded concerning the petition. It is interesting to note that the act refers to "either of said Indians," implying there were only two Indians at Coaxen. The act does not distinguish whether these two were male or female, nor is there any mention of Josiah Foster's involvement with the property. The two could have been Barshabee Pombeless and another family member. Curiously one of the commissioners named in this act was also a witness to the will of Charles Moolis in September 1797.

The fate of the Coaxen Tract and Wepink was near at hand. By law Josiah Foster was the legal owner of the Coaxen Tract with the exception of possibly an acre retained by Barshabee Pombeless, alias Queen Bathsheba, five acres to John Hays, and 10 acres of land willed to Henery Armstrong. The original Coaxen Tract was almost equivalent to a gift when John Wills sold the tract to the children of King Osollowhen and his brothers Teannis and Moonis in 1740. Barring any other deletions from the tract of land, the bequests made by Charles Moolis would have reduced the tract down to 224 acres.

What transpired further concerns none other than Josiah Foster, the Quaker Friend of Charles Moolis. Foster's wife, Rachel, died April 2, 1813. Sometime in the ensuing years, Foster moved to Haddonfield, which was then in Gloucester County. In the Burlington County Deed Book K-2, on page 316 dated September 29, 1819, Josiah Foster of Haddonfield transferred the Coaxen Tract over to David Jones of Philadelphia and Burr Woolman of Burlington City with instructions to them that they should sell this land as consisting of 259 acres as soon as convenient and for a fair price, and further, that the proceeds should be paid over to Richard S. Core, his executor and administrator, $1,500, and that Jones and Woolman were to be paid $1,000 for their trouble and expenses. The land had passed out of the hands of the Coaxen Indians forever. Possibly, by this time, they had all died, or may have left the area, which delayed Foster's sale of the property if they were still occupying it. There is no further mention of Barshabee Pombeless, John Hays, or Henery Armstrong in any county or state records. They seem to have vanished.

Josiah Foster must have been aware of his impending death. Four months later, on January 15, 1820, he died in Haddonfield. Records of the Surrogate's Office in Woodbury, Gloucester County, show that he died intestate (without a will). Letters of Administration were filed May 23,

1820, appointing David Jones Administrator of Foster's estate. An inventory of the goods and chattels of Josiah Foster, late of Haddonfield, were taken and appraised by John Gill and Thomas Redman of Haddonfield and the only item listed was a Bond against a Benjamin Dugan for $637.95. Nothing further was shown in his estate. Essentially he had divested almost all his assets before his death.

On April 10, 1824, David Jones of Philadelphia and Burr Woolman of Burlington sold the Coaxen Tract to William Newbold of Springfield Township Burlington County. This was recorded in Deed Book Q-2 on page 418. The deed records that a survey had been done on the property in 1820. In the deed it recites that "Josiah Foster, late of Haddonfield in Gloucester County in his lifetime was seized in his demise as of fee simple this particular tract of land of 259 acres." The tract sold for $4,500. It again advised that the proceeds of the sale were to be paid over to Richard S. Core. He may possibly have been a relative, as Josiah Foster's mother was the former Hannah Core, daughter of Enoch Core.

William Newbold apparently never moved from Springfield Township. His will was dated September 1, 1828, and a division of his entire estate was done on January 9, 1832, and divided the Coaxen Tract between his two daughters, Rachel Newbold Pancoast and Hannah Newbold. Rachel N. Pancoast then bought out her sister Hannah. In turn, they also sold 25 acres of the tract to a James Lippincott, further reducing the Coaxen Tract to 234 acres.

On December 20, 1835, Rachel Newbold Pancoast and her husband Samuel A. Pancoast sold the Coaxen Tract to William Irick for $13,500. It appears he may have had the home that is still standing on the farm around that time. The farm remained in the Irick family for many years and passed to his son William J. Irick, who also continued to live there until he expired in 1939. The farm, then known as Quaxin Farm, had seen many changes, additions, and deletions of the acreage over the years.

On March 9, 1945, Monroe Smith and Maud A. Smith purchased the farm from Quaxin Farms, Inc. In February 1949 Maud A. Smith sold the farm to Allen S. Hatcher and Lena W. Hatcher, his wife, where it remained in their hands for many years; however, various tracts had been divided and subdivided until the farm now only contained 121.8 acres of the original Coaxen Tract. Allen Hatcher died in 1964. His widow Lena did not pass until 1990. Subsequently, the Hatcher Estate was sold by the heirs to Michael and Theresa Dolan of Moorestown on April 6, 1994, the current owners as of this writing.

The original Irick mansion house is still standing along the banks of the south branch of the Rancocas. The Indian burial ground to the rear of the mansion is most likely still intact, although its exact location has not been definitely established. The historic village of Wepink is on the western end of the Dolan property alongside the run of water by that name, still swiftly flowing as it has for centuries. Not only has this farm been the site of Wepink, but also the habitat of Native American people for more than 4,000 years, and possibly longer. The 40-acre portion of the farm containing the village of Wepink is in danger of destruction. The owners of the property have applied to the local planning board for permission to build 12 luxury homes on the site. Thus far their request has been denied until they comply with existing ordinances and environmental concerns. There is also archeological recovery work that has yet to be done. An alternative to the development has also been discussed with the possibility that this farm may be preserved as open space. Hopefully this site will be protected for future generations, and archaeologists will be able to fully evaluate and preserve its historic and prehistoric significance. In addition to the cultural treasures of this farm, the banks of the Rancocas that border the farm also contain rare plant species and paleontological remains of considerable age, and should be preserved. It is a beautiful location and quite understandable that the owners want to develop the property, but at what cost? Time will tell.

After Brainerd's death and the demise of the remaining Coaxen Indians at Wepink, the old log meetinghouse that had become known as Coaxen Meeting House was taken apart and moved into the center of Vincentown near where the railroad station had been. It then became known as the "Free Meeting House" and was open to all Protestant denominations. It was known to have been used by the Methodists and also the Baptists until they built their own churches in 1830 and 1835 respectively. The Quakers had their own meetinghouse, originally built of logs, in 1782. A brick meetinghouse was built on the same site in the year 1813, and parts of the walls were from the log meetinghouse. It was later changed to a two-story Grange Hall, and stucco was placed over the bricks; however, the date stone of 1813 was retained over the entrance. The building still stands today on South Main Street.

In 1957 Walter Daniel Joyce of Collingswood told a story of Brainerd's log meetinghouse to Nathaniel R. Ewan. Ewan recorded that Joyce said,

> The old log church used by Brainerd for his Indians and later moved into Vincentown was once again moved down the road from Eayrestown to Red Lion and reconstructed on the north side of Prickett Town Road and some distance back from the intersection. It was then known as New Freedom School. Around 1860, the old log school was taken apart again and moved across the road to the back of a lot on the corner where

The Friends Meeting House of 1813 still stands on Main Street in Vincentown although considerably altered and now used as a Grange Hall.
(Photo courtesy of Everett F. Mickle.)

S. Prickett owned the land and he used it for a barn. Eventually Ely Joyce, uncle of Walter Joyce, tore it down about 1916.

His entire narrative is somewhat inaccurate, but eyewitness recollections are priceless.

The old log barn as I remember it was about 16 ft. wide and 20 ft. long, one story high with a gable roof and a door in the end of the gable. The barn was made of large oak logs squared on both the out and insides and dovetailed together at the corners that made it easy to take apart whenever they wanted to move it.

Thus ends the story of Wepink, the other Indian Town, and the Coaxen Indians. But perhaps not. There may yet come to light further information about possible descendants of the natives who may have intermarried with the early settlers or were otherwise assimilated into the White man's world.

CHAPTER 8

Indian Ann— Last of the Delawares

Ann Roberts, more commonly known as Indian Ann, has been the subject of countless anecdotes over the years, but much of what has been written about her has been grossly distorted and is misleading. For the most part, these writings should be relegated to the realm of entertaining folklore, not history.

For many years the author has pondered the true identity and authenticity of this woman known as Indian Ann, reputed to be the last full-blooded Delaware Indian to survive in New Jersey. Was she in fact a living person or just another fanciful myth of the Pine Barrens?

The following account is an attempt to record the true story of Ann Roberts. The author had previously published much of this chapter in an article in the Central Record, Medford, New Jersey, on February 14, 1974, but this expanded version includes new documented evidence that, to the author's knowledge, has never before appeared in print.

Ann Ashatama was born about 1805 on the John Woolman Farm near the Forks of the Rancocas Creek. She was the daughter of Elisha Ashatama, a full-blooded Lenape Indian who had previously resided on the Brotherton Reservation at Edgepillock, now Indian Mills. The identity of Indian Ann's mother, a much discussed subject, remains unknown. The author had considerable correspondence with the late Nathaniel R. Ewan in 1957 and 1958 regarding the parentage of Indian Ann. Mr. Ewan has long been revered as the dean of Burlington County historians. In one of his letters he writes,

> I doubt if there is any provable evidence whatever to show Elisha Ashatama's subsequent career or in particular what woman became his wife or consort. Indian Ann, his daughter, was certainly by features and habits a full-blooded Indian, but

who her mother was is problematical. Many fragments of the story need to be brought in alignment that it is impossible to more than guess the actual facts.

Mr. Ewan wrote this letter from the Burlington County Masonic Home in February 1958, shortly before his death.

Elisha Ashatama had resided on the Brotherton Reservation and went to New York State with the rest of the band in 1802. He tired of it there and returned to New Jersey and went to live on the Woolman Farm at the Forks of the Rancocas. Traditions passed down in the Woolman family relate that Elisha Ashatama lived in a log cabin on the Woolman Farm, down by the river, and following his death was buried in the nearby grave-yard of the Rancocas Friends Meeting graveyard along Centerton Road. He lies in an unmarked grave and is one of many Indians supposedly buried there. Ann doubtless spent her childhood on the Woolman Farm but any further information of her early years and young adult life remains shrouded in mystery.

She is known to have subsequently married a black man named John Roberts, although no actual record of this marriage has been found to date. John and Ann Roberts were the parents of seven children. The census for Washington Township, taken June 1, 1850, lists John Roberts as born in Virginia, age 52, which would indicate a birth year of 1798. Ann, his wife, age 47 and born about 1804, John Jr., age 21, placing the year of his birth about 1829, Richard, age 15, Maria, age 14, Peter, age 13, Hester, age 4, and Lydia, age 1. They also had a son Samuel. Perhaps he was away from home at the time of the census. They lived in a small cabin in a hamlet known as Dingletown, in Shamong Township. This was a small settlement of cabins and shanty dwellings in a densely wooded area.

Ann and her husband were instrumental in founding an African Methodist-Episcopal Church nearby on Carranza Road. It was destroyed by fire in 1935. All that remains of it today is the graveyard that contains, among others, the headstone and grave of a Civil War soldier named George H. Eares, Co. E. 25th Regiment, New Jersey Volunteers, age 64.

On June 15, 1945, Mr. Ewan received a letter regarding the Civil War records of John Roberts Jr. from the National Archives in Washington, D.C.

*African Methodist-Episcopal Church that once stood on Carranza Road
Ann Roberts is said to have been instrumental in its founding.
It was demolished in 1936. A graveyard survives and contains
the remains of a Civil War soldier. (Photo courtesy of Burlington
County Historical Society, N. R. Ewan Collection.)*

Records indicate he had served in Company A, 22nd Regiment, U.S. Colored Troops. He was shown as being the son of John and Ann Roberts of near Indian Mills, Burlington County, New Jersey. John Roberts Jr. enlisted December 9, 1863, in Philadelphia to serve for a period of three years. He died of pneumonia at the Post Hospital, Yorktown, Virginia, less than three months after his enlistment.

The next documented evidence found is that of a deed dated April 8, 1865, in which Peter Roberts, Ann Roberts's son, purchased a tract of 20 acres of land near a Bears Hole Corner on Dingletown Road in Shamong Township. The purchase was made from William and Mary Cotton for $50. Another deed recorded shows that Peter Roberts then sold this same 20 acres of land to his mother, Ann Roberts, on June 30, 1868, for a sum of $150. It appears that Peter had realized a handsome profit in the short space of three years from none other than his own mother. Ann Roberts was shown as living in Shamong Township at the time of this sale, in a small cabin a short distance away from this property. There is no record of any prior property owned either by her or her husband, John Roberts Sr.

The author also obtained information from the National Archives that provides much additional information regarding the application process and what had transpired in trying to obtain it.

On June 28, 1880, Ann Roberts made application for a pension in regard to her deceased soldier son John Roberts Jr. Her age then appeared as 75 years indicating a birth year of 1805 whereas the census records of 1850 would indicate 1804. The application shows her husband, John Roberts, died in the Burlington County Alms House, New Lisbon, New Jersey, on July 15, 1852. Several historians have reported that her husband was a Civil War veteran and this is incorrect.

It took a number of years before her pension was actually granted due to miscommunication. Her son was confused with another John Roberts, born in Indiana, who died in Texas in 1865. There was also a curious letter in the paperwork from William A. Woolman to the Adjutant General's Office on November 9, 1885, asking him to look after the pension case of Ann Roberts, mother of John A. Roberts, and to call on George C. Lemon for the papers in the case. All correspondence for Ann Roberts was to be sent to William A. Woolman, her lawful attorney in care of the Atsion post office.

Ann Roberts was unable to read or write, but she did have Thomas Cotton write the following letter of affidavit:

> State of New Jersey, Burlington County Personally appeared before me the Subscriber, one of the Justices of the Peace in and from said county, Ann Roberts who being by me duley affirmed on her affirmation said that she never gave William A Woolman any Power of Attorney to do her business or to get her a pension that the said William A. Woolman went so far as to take full control of her papers and letters in her pension case so much so to even change my post office address from Indian Mills, N.J. to Atsion on business to this affirment. Also said he

wanted one half the whole of it. I gave Thomas Cotton fifteen dollars to pay said Woolman but he refused it then I told said Cotton to offer him twenty-five dollars and he refused it and the said Woolman and the said Woolman's wife have abused me on several occasions on account of my refusing to pay him what he demands. Ann Roberts X Her Mark. Affirmed and Subscribed Before Me this the 17th Day of September AD 1887, Thos. Cotton, Justice of the Peace

In another affidavit, written by Edward T. Thompson and William Cotton, it is stated that Ann Roberts attested that she was a full-blooded Indian woman. At the time of her son John's death, all her children had reached their majority and had left home. He was her only means of support before he enlisted in the Army. She couldn't say exactly what his age was other than that he was over 21. She was ignorant of writing and had no record of the births of any of her children. She described her son John "as being about 5 ft. 6 inches in height and weighing about 150 lbs. He was a light or bright colored Negro with dark eyes and hair."

In another letter sent out by these same gentlemen to the Department of the Interior, Pension Office, they attest that they had known Ann Roberts for more than 30 years and that she had lived with her son and that he had been employed by each of them at various times before he enlisted. He had provided for her before his enlistment in December 1863. At that time she had no property of any kind save a small supply of clothing and a few of the plainest household goods and furniture not worth more than $50, and that she now had a small cabin and lot of ground, which she occupies and where she is supported mainly by the charity of sympathizing neighbors.

Her pension was finally granted and she began receiving $8 monthly, which was increased to $12 monthly in 1886, thanks to the kindness and efforts of Edward T. Thompson and William Cotton.

Indian Ann was most remembered during her declining years. She was a frequent visitor on surrounding farms and in the neighboring towns where she sold hand-woven baskets, brooms, and berries in an effort to supplement her Civil War pension. Many farmers and others in the area have baskets in their possession attributed to this industrious soul.

Basket made by Indian Ann Roberts circa 1880. (Photo by N. R. Ewan, Nov. 21, 1946. Basket was then in possession of Howard Weeks of Indian Mills. Photo courtesy of Everett F. Mickle.)

Ann Roberts frequently walked some 12 miles to the railroad station in Vincentown where she would take the train into Mount Holly to sell her baskets and other trinkets she had made. At times she was so exhausted she was unable to make the long walk home. Frank Wright, a former telegraph operator and station agent, once recalled he would allow her to sleep in the waiting room until she was rested enough to continue her journey home the next morning.

Many tales have been told and retold through the years regarding Ann's wanderings and adventures, and some are quite entertaining. Florrie Zimmerman, a lifelong resident, recalls hearing tales about Indian Ann when she was a young girl. Her grandmother, Selena Doughty, often gave Indian Ann some of her homemade bread. Her grandfather, Samuel Doughty, built Indian Ann's home. Florrie said,

Vincentown Railroad Station near the turn of the 19th century.
Ann Roberts would frequently sleep overnight here before leaving to walk home.
(Photo courtesy of Everett F. Mickle.)

Her hair was jet black and so long she could sit on it. Many times she would start out on one of her jaunts to Vincentown or Mount Holly, to sell her baskets. She would leave out a sort of war whoop and off she would go down the road.

An eyewitness account of Ann Roberts, which best describes her in her later years, was written by Nelson Burr Gaskill, in 1956.

As I recall her, she was short, thick set, with a skin more brown than red, and long stringy black hair. She usually wore a man's black felt hat and a man's coat with man's brogan shoes. She was a strange exotic figure to us small boys. Ann was not a neat dresser. She wore so many skirts that nothing seemed to move inside them. She was frowsy and Mother insisted that she was something that rhymes with it but begins with "L" so we were ordered to keep a sanitary distance away from her. I remember that she brought little baskets woven of sweet grass and filled with teaberries.

Mr. Gaskill was reminiscing about his early boyhood years in Mount Holly before 1900.

With what meager savings she had accumulated, Ann was able to have a small two-story frame house built on the 20-acre tract she had acquired from her son Peter. Up until the time she had this home built, she had been living on what was then known as Dingletown Road (now Forked Neck Road) in a one-room log cabin on the west side of the road a short distance from her new home. Samuel L. Doughty, a carpenter by trade, built her new home. He had lived just a short distance from her cabin home on the opposite side of the Dingletown Road. He and his wife, Selena Doughty, along with his brother Aaron and his wife, Rachel Doughty, extended her a mortgage on the property in the amount of $450. It was recorded on August 29, 1887, which indicates approximately when this home was built. The mortgage was discharged October 30, 1895, some 10 months after her death. The

Indian Ann Roberts's home that once stood on Dingletown Road. (Photo courtesy of Rutgers University, Alexander Library, William Augustine Collection.)

Doughty family had built many of the older homes in the Pines. Florrie Zimmerman was also told that her grandfather, Samuel Doughty, had gone to Philadelphia to buy Ann Roberts furniture for her new home.

Indian Ann had lived in her new home seven years when she died on December 10, 1894. She must have enjoyed all the comforts of this new home, comforts she had done without for so many years in her small cabin. The following article appeared in the *New Jersey Mirror* on Wednesday, December 19, 1894.

> Ann Roberts, last of the Brotherton Tribe of Indians, died at her Home on the Dingletown Road, Indian Mills, New Jersey, on December 10, 1894. Her remains were taken to the Tabernacle Methodist-Episcopal Church for Memorial Services, and then buried in the Tabernacle cemetery on December 13, 1894 in an unmarked grave. She was described as being a very gentle and inoffensive old Lady and very kind to all that knew her. She was also very proud that she was a full-blooded Indian of the Delawares.

Gravestone of Ann Roberts that lies in Tabernacle Cemetery.
Nathaniel R. Ewan located her unmarked grave and was instrumental
in having this marker placed. (Photo by the author.)

Mr. Nathaniel R. Ewan accidentally found the gravedigger's chart for the cemetery and was able to locate Indian Ann's grave. He persuaded the Burlington County Historical Society to place a modest marker there, and so it remains today.

The Surrogate's Office of Burlington County records her Last Will and Testament.

> In the name of God, Amen. I, Ann Roberts of the township of Shamong in the county of Burlington; Being of sound mind, memory and understanding; for which blessing I thank God; do hereby make and publish my last Will and Testament in manner following that is to Say;
>
> First it is my will, and I do order that all my just debts and funeral Expenses be duly Paid and Satisfied as soon an conveniently can be after my decease;
>
> ITEM 1. I give unto my Son Peter Roberts four Dollars; I give unto my son Samuel Roberts four Dollars; I give unto my son Richard Roberts four Dollars;
>
> ITEM2. I give unto my Daughter Lydia Spencer four Dollars; I give unto my Daughter Hester Ann Arland four Dollars;
>
> ITEM 3. I give unto my daughter Maria Marshall all my Right Title and interest in and all the land and Real Estate, House and land where I now Reside situated in the township of Shamong; to be and Remain her Property;
>
> I also give unto my Daughter Maria Marshall all my personal Property whatsoever situated to be and remain her property;
>
> Lastly I hereby appoint my trusty and well Beloved friend James Wills executor of this my last will and testament;
>
> Dated this the 7th Day of August in the year of our Lord A.D. 1894
>
> Ann X Roberts
> her mark
>
> Signed, published and declared by the said Ann Roberts to be her last will in the presence of us who were present at the

same time and subscribed our names as witness in the presence of the testator. James J. Wills, Franklin D. Cotton & Thomas Cotton.

It would appear from the terms of this will that Ann Roberts's daughter, Maria Marshall, was living with her in her later years as will be further indicated in the petition of James Wills to the Surrogate's Court.

> To Charles B. Ballinger, Surrogate of the County of Burlington, N.J. in the matter of the probate of the Last Will and Testament of Ann Roberts, deceased. The petition of James Wills of Indian Mills, Burl. Co., N.J. respectfully showeth that he is the Executor named in the Last Will and Testament of Ann Roberts dated the Seventh day of August A.D. 1894. That said Ann Roberts departed this life at Indian Mills the County of Burlington and State of New Jersey on Wednesday the Tenth day of December A.D. 1894 leaving her surviving as her heirs at law and next of kin the following persons, to wit; Peter Roberts, Son, Moorestown, N.J. Samuel Roberts, Son, Address Unknown; Richard Roberts, Son, Address Unknown; Lydia Spencer, Daughter, Address Unknown; Hester Ann Arland, Daughter, Address Unknown; Maria Marshall, Daughter, Indian Mills, N.J.

An appraisal of Ann Roberts's estate was made by Thomas Cotton and Benjamin W. Small, described as two disinterested freeholders, on December 29, 1894, at the request of the executor James Wills. The inventory lists wearing apparel, one settee, one feather bed, one clock, one wash boiler, one lounge, six chairs, one rocking chair, one bureau, one small stand, one flour barrel and flour, one small stove, one cook stove, stove pipe and kittle, one dining table, and one bed stead, valued at a total of $18.65.

Ann Roberts's personal belongings were quite meager and could easily fit into the small two-story home where she lived, with room to spare. She had nothing but the bare essentials in the way of furnishings. No livestock or farming equipment is shown in the inventory, also an indication of the impoverished conditions in which she spent the last years of her life.

A number of years prior to Indian Ann's death, articles appeared in local newspapers concerning her son-in-law, John Marshall, who had been living with her.

The late Frank W. H. Convery, local historian, shared these articles with the author. One appeared in the *New Jersey Mirror* on Wednesday, March 25, 1890, which reported,

> Mysterious disappearance of John Marshall, colored man of Indian Mills, N.J. who has not been seen since March 9, 1890 when a law suit was going on at "Smalls Hotel." All politicians and many others were present and there was considerable drinking.
>
> As night drew on John Nutt, a friend of Marshall, went home, leaving Marshall at the hotel. It was getting dark and Mr. Small, Proprietor of the Hotel, went out to do a chore and told Marshall not to leave until he came back as Marshall was very intoxicated, but Marshall left in the absence of Mr. Small.
>
> He was next seen on the farm of Joseph Jones near Flyatt Rd. by Mr. Jones son who assisted him to his feet as he fell down. Young Jones told him to come into his father's barn and sleep it off, but he said he was going home and would be all right. Young Jones then walked with him to Naylor's Corner where Marshall turned the corner home. This was the last seen of Marshall. It was then raining hard and lasted until about midnight.
>
> On Wednesday, Mrs. Marshall and John Nutt notified the neighbors of his disappearance and a large group of people turned out and searched the vicinity, woods and swamps, but no trace of him. His hat and handkerchief were found about 200 yards from Flyatt. His hat was in a ditch and handkerchief on a fence and the ground and brush around were disheveled indicating he had fallen or stumbled. Many neighbors believe foul play.

On Sunday, Constable Miller and a search party made a thorough search of his residence from garret to cellar but failed to find anything to shed light on the man's whereabouts.

Marshall is the son-in-law of Indian Ann Roberts and resides with her, with his wife, and two children. He was somewhat prominent in political matters and was a member of the Hagerthey faction of the Democrats.

A subsequent article appeared in the *New Jersey Mirror* on Wednesday, December 6, 1893.

Another Mystery Cleared Up. The whitened bones of the colored man, John Marshall, whose disappearance caused such a sensation in Shamong, in March 1890, were discovered near an open road by a boy, on Saturday, Dec. 2nd and another Burlington Co. murder has been cleared up. The skeleton was found in a ditch off McKendimen Rd. near the old Tuckerton Stage Rd. Marshall was at Small's Hotel, on the night of his disappearance, which was on the eve of the Spring elections, and had been drinking heavily. When he started for home he was very drunk and it was suggested that he had better remain at the Hotel for the rest of the night. He would not however, and started off for home. He evidently fell into a stupor and lay down by the roadside. It was a cold rainy night, and exposure must have caused his death. The bleached skeleton was partly clothed when discovered, and in the pockets were found his watch, and a flask, containing a small amount of whiskey. When Marshall first disappeared there was strong suspicion that he had met with foul play, and other circumstances brought to light at that time, and as this belief grew, searching parties were formed, and the pine regions were thoroughly scoured for miles around, without a single clue being found, and it finally became settled in the belief that he had been murdered, and body buried. Now that the remains have been found, the mystery is explained. Marshall was the son-in-law of old Indian Ann Roberts, a native Indian.

Another brief article appeared in the *New Jersey Mirror* on August 29, 1890, concerning Indian Ann's son, Peter, who was living in Moorestown, N.J.

> Peter Roberts. Called "Indian Peter" son of old Indian Ann Roberts of Indian Mills, N.J. was put in Jail at Moorestown on Monday Aug. 18th 1890 for drunkenness and resisting Arrest, He bit a Policeman on the Hand.

Maria Marshall continued to live in the little frame home on Dingletown Road until her death on January 31, 1908. She lies buried in the same Tabernacle cemetery as her mother. She must have existed in sheer poverty, apparently not inheriting the resourcefulness of her mother.

A petition filed in the Surrogates Court of Burlington County, August 18, 1909, supplies the following:

> To William P. Lippincott, Surrogate of the County of Burlington.N.J. In the Matter of Goods, Chattels, and Credits of Maria Marshall, Deceased.
>
> The petition of William I. Reily of Medford in the County of Burlington and State of New Jersey respectfully showeth that Maria Marshall of Indian Mills departed this life intestate at Indian Mills in the County of Burl. And State of N.J. on the thirty-first day of January A.D. 1908. That said Maria Marshall left her surviving the following named heirs and next of kin to wit; Hester Ann Dickson, Sister, 84 Belvidere St., Trenton, N.J.; Richard Roberts alias Dick Bird, Brother, Bridgeton, N.J.
>
> That said interstate was possessed of goods, chattels, rights, and credits to the value of $50. as near as can be ascertained. Therefore the said William I. Reily respectfully applies for letters of administration upon the goods, chattels, rights, and credits of which said Maria Marshall died possessed.

On November 11, 1909, William I. Reily petitioned the Orphans Court of Burlington County requesting permission to have at public sale the real estate of Maria Marshall, advising the court that her estate was not sufficient to pay her debts. The amount of her estate was shown as $3, consisting of sundry articles of household furniture. The amount of her debts was shown as $223, consisting of debt due William I. Reily undertaker of $73 and $150 for commissions and estimated expenses, leaving a deficit of $220. There is no further explanation in the records as to what these commissions and estimated expenses actually were.

In William I. Reily's petition, he also describes the property he wishes to sell as being a 20-acre tract of land containing a small farm having thereon a small two-story frame house and pump house and no other buildings, which said land and real estate are probably worth the sum of $250.

His petition was subsequently granted and an advertisement appeared in the *New Jersey Mirror* during the month of February 1910.

> Administrator's Sale of Real Estate. By virtue of an order of the Orphans Court of Burlington Co., Jan. 20, 1910 the subscriber, administrator of Maria Marshall deceased will sell at public venue, at the hotel of Charles Braddock in Medford, N.J. on Thursday, the 17th Day of March, 1910 at 2 o'clock in the afternoon. All that certain tract of land situate between Indian Mills and Tabernacle in the township of Shamong, County of Burlington, State of New Jersey, being lot No. 18 on a survey of lots sold by the executors of Samuel S. Haines deceased bounded as follows:
>
> Beginning at a point old corner to lot No. 17, thence (1) by said lot No. 17 North seventy degrees West twenty-three chains and thirty links to a survey corner to lo No. 19 thence (2) along said line South nineteen degrees and fifteen minutes East eighteen chains and fifty links to a pine lettered "S.H." and an old corner to the survey and is called "The Bears Hole Corner" thence (3) along the boundary line of the survey North fifty-seven degrees and fifteen minutes East nineteen chains and seventy links to the place of beginning containing

twenty acres of land more or less. William I. Reily, Administrator, G. M. Hillman, Proctor.

A deed recorded April 15, 1910, shows that William I. Reily sold the property of Maria Marshall deceased to George M. Hillman of Chester, Burlington County, on March 17, 1910 for the sum of $160. This is the same G. M. Hillman who was the proctor at the public sale in Medford. As the records will indicate, these various proceedings appear to have been handled in a legal fashion, but one cannot help wonder the true circumstances of this estate. Whether the brother Richard Roberts or the sister Hester Ann were ever contacted regarding the disposal of this property is questionable.

The home that had stood for so many years was burned to the ground during the 1956 hunting season. Ironically, the brothers George and Frank Crummel were the last to live in the Roberts home and may have been lineal descendants of Ann Roberts. Frank died September 12, 1959, age 82. His brother George Crummel died at New Lisbon April 11, 1964, at an advanced age. George Henry Crummel was known in the Pines as the Indian collier. Both he and his brother Frank worked for Stanley Giberson of Indian Mills, making charcoal. They were the last of a dying breed in the Pines.

According to some research done by Frank Convery in 1973, he had interviewed a woman named Annie Smith Crummel who claimed to be the illegitimate daughter of Hester Ann Roberts. Annie claimed she was born on St. Patricks Day, 1876. Her true father was George John Smith but he died before she was born and before Hester Ann and George Smith were married. Annie Smith later married a Frank Crummel, and they were the parents of the Frank and George Crummel who lived in the old home of Indian Ann. Ann would have been their great-grandmother.

It is impossible to say whether this information is reliable. Research done by Railey T. Cruse of Trenton, grandson of Hester Ann, and a great-grandson of Ann Roberts, disclosed that Hester Ann was originally married to a man named Arland or Arnold and later to a man named Albert Dickerson. Hester Ann Dickerson died in Trenton, December 13, 1936. Cruse makes no mention of Annie Smith or the Crummel family.

George Crummel, once known as the "Indian Collier," owned and lived in Ann Roberts's home for many years. His grandmother was said to be a reservation Indian. (Photo courtesy of Rutgers University, Alexander Library, William Augustine Collection.)

On October 26, 1958, at the author's suggestion, the Archaeological Society of New Jersey unveiled a commemorative marker in observance of the 200th anniversary of the Brotherton Reservation, which had been established in 1758 by the Provincial Legislature. At this celebration some

91 descendants of Indian Ann Roberts attended, all descended from her daughter Hester Ann Dickerson. Among the 91 were six grandchildren, 14 great-grandchildren, 40 great-great-grandchildren, and 31 great-great-great-grandchildren. As the author recalls, the Indian features were quite noticeable in many of those who attended.

A historic marker was placed at the site of Indian Ann Roberts's former home, which is now just a grassy plot. Even the depression and cellar hole of the ruins are no longer visible, but one must wonder what treasures lay beneath it for future archaeologists to discover.

CHAPTER 9
The Founding of Shamong

After the demise of Brotherton and Wepink, most traces of an Indian presence in the area were gone. There were still those who remained in the area besides Ann Roberts, but they were most likely of mixed blood. One such individual, mentioned in Dr. James Still's autobiography, was Job Moore, also known as "Indian Job."

As early as 1717 there was a sawmill in operation on the site where the Indian Gristmill was built at Brotherton. Micajah Willetts was known to have been the first settler in the area and may possibly have operated this mill. The millpond at the site of this sawmill was formed by damming the Mekendom, a branch of the Batsto River, and was so named in various spellings for more than a century. This stream eventually became known as Muskingum Brook, and the millpond is now known as Indian Mills Lake. The name Mekendom is perpetuated by McKendimen Road, which ends near where the old Mckendom Bridge crosses the Tuckerton Stage Road. Micajah Willetts shortly migrated East to Cedar Run, near Little Egg Harbor, where many members of his family settled and also operated a sawmill in 1744. The Willetts family became prominent in the area of Little Egg Harbor Township and throughout Burlington County. Little Egg Harbor Township was part of Burlington County until 1891. It is now part of Ocean County.

In 1802, the year the Brotherton band left the area, a new township was set off from old Evesham, as well as parts of Northampton and Little Egg Harbor Townships. It was called Washington Township, and included most of present day Shamong Township. A survey done at the time mentions Muskingum Bridge, located on the old Tuckerton Stage Road where it crosses Muskingum Brook. The reservation area, Tabernacle, and Atsion were all part of Washington Township for more than 50 years.

In 1852 Shamong Township came into being by taking parts of Washington Township, Medford Township, and Southampton Township. The name Shamong, severely corrupted from the original Indian name of

The results of one of the many deer hunting clubs in Shamong. Truly Shamong was aptly named, meaning "place of many deer." (Photo courtesy of Rutgers University, Alexander Library, William Augustine Collection.)

chummo ong, literally means "place of many deer" or "place of the horn." Indeed it still has many deer as evidenced by the annual harvest of the numerous deer hunting clubs that remain in the area.

This history will primarily focus on the areas of the original Shamong Township of 1852. This includes the entire area of the former Brotherton Reservation, and the villages of Tabernacle and Atsion. There are numerous other locations where settlements once flourished but that now exist today as mere place names on the map. Once there were sawmills, forges, furnaces, charcoal burnings, hotels, and taverns. Today little remains to mark these areas except the tranquil wilderness that has reclaimed them. Thanks to the careful planning of the area forests by the Pinelands Commission, and the creation of the Wharton State Forest by the State of New Jersey in 1954, this wilderness has been preserved. The alternative was to see this prized area become just another example of urban sprawl, another sea of rooftops so typical of overdeveloped areas. Additional master plans of

Downtown Indian Mills at the beginning of the 20th century. Depicts the intersection of Indian Mills Road, Willow Grove Road, Forked Neck Road, and Burnt House Road. The general store is to the left, the Methodist Church to the right, and right center are the livery stables and wheelwright shops (no longer standing), where the Indian Mills Fire Station is currently located. (Photo courtesy of Frederick Miller.)

the local governments have also protected the area. Hopefully this treasure we call "the Pines" will never be lost!

Many of the industries and commercial enterprises that once flourished in old Shamong are now contained in the extensive bounds of the Wharton State Forest, while others have been totally destroyed by farming pursuits, the ravages of time, housing developers, and modern highways.

INDIAN TRAILS AND STAGE COACH ROUTES

To develop a better understanding of what has transpired here over the years, it would be well to acquaint the reader with the ancient roads that existed before the railroads came and changed everything throughout the state.

In days of old, most major roads in this area were former Indian trails primarily traversing Burlington County from the major cities to the west. The origination City of Philadelphia, settlements along the Delaware River, and Burlington City were areas that people departed from. Their destination was Egg Harbor. Not the Egg Harbor City of today, but the Egg Harbor or Little Egg Harbor of yesteryear, now known as Tuckerton. It was a major seacoast town in colonial days and once the third largest seaport on the entire East Coast. The location of the village of Washington and Sooy's Inn, built in 1773 by Nicholas Sooy, seemed to be the hub of all the stage routes running across the southern part of Burlington County. It lies a short distance north of Batsto. Today this place is marked by only a sandy trail in the Pines where many other sandy trails converge, but once it bustled with activity.

Four major stage routes ran across the state in Burlington County. One ran from Burlington City along present day Route 541 through Pine Street in Mount Holly to Eayrestown. In early deeds, the route was known locally as the Great Road to Little Egg Harbor. It proceeded through Red Lion and the site of the Red Lion Hotel down present day Carranza Road, passing the tavern at Fox Chase (where Seneca High School now stands) through Tabernacle where it intersected and became the old Tuckerton Stage Road, one-half mile past Forked Neck Road. Then it proceeded east past Hampton Gate, where, today, it becomes a sand trail that bears to the right a short half-mile before the Carranza Memorial. It then proceeds across the old New Jersey Central Railroad tracks at High Crossing and through to Washington, then straight down to the Wading River where a bridge once crossed, and then on to Tuckerton.

Another route veered off the Great Road below Eayrestown, down the main street of Vincentown, and proceeded out Retreat Road, crossing present-day Route 70 on Big Hill Road to Sooy Place, formerly known as Pine or Pine Tavern. It then proceeded past the White Horse Hotel site to Eagle Hotel and Tavern, another site, and to the Tulpehocken Road to Washington where it joins the Tuckerton Stage Road.

The earliest Tuckerton Stage Road began shortly before the Revolutionary War. It started at Coopers Ferry near Pyne Point in Camden and went east, following the Great Road almost parallel with present day Route 70 through Marlton, Medford, Indian Mills, and Tabernacle, where it is still called Tuckerton Road. This road passed by the Half Moon and

Seven Stars Tavern at Flyatt and also the Gate Tavern at Hampton Gate. For a short distance in Tabernacle it is known as Carranza Road, then it leaves the paved road just past Hampton Gate and becomes a sand trail to Washington, then continues through to Bodines and Tuckerton.

There was another route, which follows almost parallel with the present day White Horse Pike, known as the Old Egg Harbor Road, which went left oblique in Berlin (then Long-a-Coming) and became Jackson Road. It then proceeded across Route 73 where about a half mile at the curve, just before reaching the Atco Speedway, a sand trail leaves the paved road and proceeds through the pines, crossing the Mullica River near the site of Inskeep's Goshen Sawmill, where it proceeds a short distance to join the Atsion Road near where Cline's Tavern once stood. The road then runs through Atsion on Quaker Bridge Road past the site of Thompson's Tavern at Quaker Bridge, on to Crammer's Hotel near Jemima Mount, and on to Washington and Tuckerton. This route was known as the Philadelphia Stage Road before reaching Atsion Road.

Another variation of these early stage routes ran down Route 541 (Stokes Road) from Mount Holly through Lumberton, stopping at the old Indian Chief Hotel in Medford, then to Cross Keys Tavern in Fairview, bearing right on Jackson Road, then crossing Tuckerton Road and proceeding down Atsion Road, which in the section south of Medford Lakes was still a sandy trail in the early 1970s. It then proceeded on Atsion Road to Indian Mills and to the 1793 tavern of John Piper, called "Sign of the Buck." The road continued east to Ephraim Cline's Tavern and from there to Atsion and through to Washington and Tuckerton.

Another variation of this route continued out Route 541, or Stokes Road, from Medford and instead of turning onto Jackson Road it continued east on Stokes Road, crossing Route 206 through to Quaker Bridge Road and then on to Washington and Tuckerton. Stokes Road follows the path of an old Indian trail called the Shamong Trail where it passes through the Indian Mills area. This had been a portion of the Old Cape Trail from Burlington City during Indian times.

As you can see, the area of old Shamong was a very busy place and had been for more than 200 years. In the past 25 years housing developers have begun to saturate the area, and many of the sites of old have been lost and forgotten. In recent years, there has been an increasing awareness of our history and heritage, and perhaps the story that is related here will help in some small way to preserve the treasures of the past for future generations.

BROTHERTON RESERVATION LANDS

When the Brotherton Reservation property was sold at auction from May through August 1802, it was divided into 100-acre lots. Many of the purchasers were local area farmers and merchants who had already been leasing this land from the Indians for farming and timber resources.

Almost immediately the former reservation property was activated with sawmills and gristmills, farmhouses, barns, blacksmith shops, wheelwrights, stores, schools, and churches. Taverns were erected in areas surrounding the reservation property, and some of the earlier taverns had been coexistent with the Brotherton Reservation, which may have hastened the demoralization of the Indian natives.

Many of the remaining farms in the Indian Mills area follow the ancient boundaries of the 100-acre lots sold at the 1802 auction. Earthen berms, which still survive as boundaries of the reservation lands, have been observed in recent years by archaeologist Jack Cresson. Once there were boundary stones marking the corners of the reservation property. One had been located along Atsion Road near Sorden's Meadow, according to the late Fritz Miller. Another may still be located back in the swampy area to the rear of Forrest Jennings's property. Another may still be in place at the highest point of land near Oriental, sometimes referred to as Naylor's Corner, where the old Indian Mills Road intersects with Tuckerton Road.

Many of the original purchasers of the reservation land quickly resold the lots at a substantial profit, while others remained on the land for many years. The soil of the former reservation quickly responded to various fertilizers of the day and this fruitfulness has continued into the present. The farms that still survive in the open lands in the Indian Mills and Tabernacle area are some of the most productive in Burlington County.

Numerous small communities, many no more than a cluster of homes at a given location, identified their locations with specific names. The locals know many of these, while others have disappeared and been lost. Names like Flyatt, Dellett, Goshen, Taylor Town, Little Mill, Hampton Gate, Bozarth Town, Dingletown, Smalls, Piper's Corner, Deep Run, Stone Bridge, Dixontown, Willow Grove, Hartford, Oak Shade, and Eagle all denote communities that were once shown in the early record books as places of birth, death, and marriage. The only villages that survive today are Indian Mills, Atsion, and Tabernacle. Many of the others are contained within the Wharton State Forest and, were it not for their names being shown on maps of 100 to 150 years ago, would be completely forgotten. Still others have disappeared from present-day maps altogether.

Many of the roads derived their names from taverns and hotels in the area. Jackson Road did not come all the way through to Atsion Road until the early 1850s. The present Old Indian Mills Road went from a small settlement near its intersection with the Great Road to Little Egg Harbor near present-day Floral Fantasy on Route 206 and ended at Atsion Road near Piper's Inn. What today is known as Indian Mills Road was once simply the road to the Indian Town, later the Murphy Road, or road to Bedford Mills, and still later the road to Benjamin Smalls. The early road returns of 1803 also mention the sawmill of Samuel Reeves. He was one of the purchasers when the reservations lands were sold at auction. Clearly before, during, and after the Brotherton Reservation was sold, there were many roads crisscrossing the entire area. The proliferation of farmers, merchants, and settlers in the area was largely a result of the Indians leaving.

In the early 1800s substantial settlements at Hampton Furnace and Atsion Iron Works employed hundreds of workers. Today all is gone except a few scant reminders of what had once been. The peaceful farming communities of Indian Mills and Tabernacle stand alone to preserve what remains of a once vibrant region of rural America. Even the large truck farms specializing in corn and tomatoes are giving way to sod farms and soybean fields that require less care, less labor to harvest, and less loss to adverse weather conditions. Cranberry and blueberry production abounds in the area as always, and fortunately much of it is on farms that are not subject to development.

Many of the early settlers lie buried in cemeteries throughout the area at Atsion and Tabernacle, with a considerable number at the Methodist and Baptist churchyards as well as the Friends burial grounds in Medford. There are also burial plots of Shamong area residents in the churchyard of Saint Mary's of the Assumption Catholic Church near Pleasant Mills and the churchyard of the Pleasant Mills Methodist Church.

HISTORICAL REGISTRAR'S RECORDS

Reviewing the early registrar's records for Shamong Township was a tedious but rather interesting experience. Many of the death entries tell a fascinating story.

On December 21, 1854, John Gardner, married, age 94, died at Flyatt of old age. March 17, 1860, Joseph Naylor, widower, age 86, invalid, died at Flyatt. On May 6, 1864, Henry Sailor, the son of John and Mary Sailor, single, age 19, a soldier, died at the Wilderness in Virginia. Cause of death: "Shot." He was born at Flyatt. The entries clearly show what had been a settlement at Flyatt where now nothing remains but a crossroads. Numerous soldiers, many of them victims of the Civil War, are recorded. On January 21, 1864, Charles Bozearth, single, age 24, a soldier, died at a hospital of typhoid fever. He was born at Delletts Inn, the son of Isaac and Mercy Bozearth.

Thomas Dellett died January 5, 1872, of consumption. He was a hotel-keeper in Shamong, the son of Manasses and Rebecca Dellett. On May 21, 1883, Joseph Titus, single, age 45, a sawyer, died at Little Mill due to a falling limb. He was born at Atsion, January 20, 1889. James Dellett Jr., a widower and laborer, age 39, died at Indian Mills of a gunshot wound. He was born near Red Lion, the son of James and Mary Dellett. A detailed account of this death appears in a later chapter.

Numerous members of the Crain/Craine/Crane family were born, lived, and died in the Flyatt area. Records show that between 1855 and 1865 there were 13 Crain children who, under the age of 5, died mostly from dysentery.

From 1856 to 1860 records indicate that children were born to six different innkeepers. The records show the fathers' occupations and lists Daniel Joice at Flyatt as well as Andrew Bozarth at Hampton Gate, who was father to twins Richard and Anna Bozarth, both born at Willow Grove, May 6, 1858. One year later, Andrew Bozarth is shown as an innkeeper at Flyatt and John Sprow is listed as an innkeeper in Shamong in 1861.

Many members of the Dellett family are buried in the old Catholic Cemetery at Pleasant Mills. Daniel Dellett, a Civil War veteran, died March 23, 1899, age 76. He was a Corporal in the 15th Regiment of the New Jersey Volunteers. Also buried here are James McCambridge Sr., who died September 28, 1886, and his wife, Ann, who died December 27, 1855, at age 51. This family once operated the tavern at Eagle. There are many burials of Irish immigrants from County Derry and County Tyrconnell at Pleasant Mills. Members of the Kelly, McIntyre, Kane, McCambridge, and McSwiggan families who were born in the late 1700s are buried here, and the descendants of many of the old families who settled Shamong, Atsion, and Tabernacle still live in the area today.

CHAPTER 10

Early Churches and Burial Grounds

Brotherton Mission Church and Burial Ground

The earliest church in the Shamong and Tabernacle area was the log meetinghouse erected by Reverend John Brainerd and the Indians at Brotherton in 1762. There was a burial ground nearby at a slight elevation along the southern shore of the sawmill pond at Indian Mills. There are no markers and nothing remains today to commemorate the final resting place of many of the reservation Indians.

The mission church was used by the White settlers in the area, after the Indians left in 1802. They continued to use it until about 1808 when it burned to the ground. There is no record of what denomination eventually utilized this early meetinghouse. Certainly the Presbyterian Church did not continue the mission efforts much beyond the Brainerd years. As a result, other denominations established a foothold.

Hartford Meeting and Burial Ground

As early as 1805, Upper Evesham Preparative Meeting (Medford) had purchased three acres of ground on Stokes Road near Schoolhouse Lane for a schoolhouse and burial ground. A one-room school was erected there about 1806. It may have substituted as a meetinghouse for religious services as well. It was known for many years as the Hartford School and later as the Old Indian School, even though the Indian natives had long since left the area and never attended this school.

E. W. Hawkes, the archaeologist, had excavated human remains from the burial ground in the vicinity of the Hartford School in 1916, supposing they

Hartford Friends Meeting and Schoolhouse, erected circa 1806.
(Photo courtesy of Everett F. Mickle.)

were of Indian origin. Perhaps they were, but they could also have been the remains of early Quakers or others who worshipped in this old schoolhouse.

In Dr. James Still's autobiography, the premise that this one-room schoolhouse also substituted as a church meetinghouse is quite apparent. The Stills' nearest neighbors were an Indian family headed by Job Moore. Dr. Still was very friendly with their son, also named Job. Still relates that old Indian Job was often drunk and was run over by a wagon full of wood and killed. He was buried in the graveyard behind the meetinghouse. One night when Still and young Job were attending a meeting, they heard a shrill sound from the graveyard. Job said that was the ghost of his Daddy. Still writes, "My father sent me to the same schoolhouse where the meeting had been held at another time." Later he recalled walking back to his home, which was up a hill where an old house had been in ruins. Today when walking from Schoolhouse Lane toward the site of the former Still homestead on Stokes Road, one encounters a slight elevation just before the intersection with Oak Shade Road.

STILL FAMILY BURIAL GROUND

There is a small burial ground on Stokes Road located in a cluster of trees about 100 yards across the road from the Still Homestead historical marker. There are no headstones to mark the graves. At one time there were two large fieldstones marking the graves, but they have long since disappeared. It is known that Dr. Still's parents, Levin and Charity Still, are buried here. Levin died on December 24, 1842, and Charity died April 23, 1857. James Still's first wife, Angelina Willow, died June 22, 1896, and she also lies buried here. Many other family members are here as well, but their names have not been recorded.

LOG CHURCH—TABERNACLE

A log meetinghouse once stood near the present cemetery in Tabernacle. It has been written that this log church was established by John Brainerd in 1778 and was known as "the Tabernacle in the Wilderness." Brainerd had left the Brotherton Reservation in 1777 to pastor a church in Deerfield. No documented evidence has been found to support one writer's supposition that this was Brainerd's mission. The building was later used as a school until 1885, and then dismantled.

TABERNACLE CEMETERY

A cemetery was established near the center of Tabernacle as early as 1805 on land deeded by William and Sarah Wilkins to be used by residents of Tabernacle "as long as the wheels of time shall not cease to roll."

Many early residents of the area are buried here. These residents include members of the Bowker, Brown, Pointsett, Lamb, Sorden, Crain, Piper, Bozearth and Bozarth, Moore, LeMunyon, Doughty, Wright, and Wills families. Many others lie here but their headstones are either illegible or simply fieldstones with no markings.

It is in this cemetery where Indian Ann Roberts lies buried in a plot to the rear along the fence. The grave was unmarked for many years until Nathaniel Ewan, local historian, located her grave, and a suitable monument was installed. The carpenter who built Indian Ann's home, Samuel L.

Tabernacle Cemetery. Many of the pioneer families of Shamong and Tabernacle are buried here. (Photo by the author.)

Doughty (born September 14, 1845, died April 3, 1906) lies here, as does his wife Selena (born March 27, 1842, died April 3, 1920). There are numerous Civil War veterans interred here as well.

METHODIST-EPISCOPAL CHURCH, TABERNACLE

A small frame church had been built near the cemetery as early as 1800, but it became run down and was eventually abandoned. The existing church was erected in 1880 on land deeded by Joseph Mathis. Today it has a thriving congregation and remains a vibrant part of the local religious community. The church structure is almost identical to the one in Indian Mills, erected in 1879 most likely by the same builder.

AFRICAN METHODIST-EPISCOPAL CHURCH

A frame church that once stood on the Great Road to Little Egg Harbor (now Carranza Road) was founded, in part, by Ann Roberts in the mid- to late 1800s. The church was abandoned and demolished in 1935.

Tabernacle Methodist-Episcopal Church, erected 1879. (Photo by the author.)

The adjoining burial ground is still in use today, but, sadly, many of the graves are unmarked. A Civil War veteran named George H. Eares, of Company E, 25th Regiment, New Jersey Volunteers, lies buried here. Frank Crummel, a great grandson of Indian Ann, reportedly also lies here in an unmarked grave.

BURIAL GROUND AT EAGLE

Near the site of the old Eagle Tavern, in a remote section of the Pines, lies a small graveyard enclosed with an iron railing. Only one headstone remains, that of Charles Wills, son of George and Mary Wills, born April 27, 1859, died July 18, 1859. There are other graves here that were formerly covered with pine slabs, but these have long since succumbed to the elements.

Burial ground at Eagle lies deep in the pines. There are many unmarked graves here as well. (Photo by the author.)

INDIAN MILLS UNITED METHODIST CHURCH

The United Methodist Church at Indian Mills was erected in 1879. Although the congregation celebrated a 100-year anniversary in 1975, commemorating the date of incorporation in 1874, the church was founded many, many years earlier.

As early as 1830, Methodists were worshipping in small gatherings in area homes and at the district schoolhouse. Then, on July 4, 1844, Godfrey Hancock and wife, and Nicholas S. Thompson and wife, transferred to Isaac Brown, Charles Brown, Josiah Wills, Nicholas S. Thompson, and Benjamin Reeves, Trustees of the Methodist-Episcopal Church at Hartford, two certain lots or pieces of land. The transaction instructed that they should build or cause to be erected and built thereon a house or place of worship for the use of the members of the Methodist-Episcopal Church of Hartford.

In a short time, a modest house of worship was erected, which serviced the congregation until a newer and more commodious building was built in 1879.

Indian Mills Methodist-Episcopal Church, erected in 1879, as it appeared in 1907. Note the carriage stalls to the west of the church.
(Photo courtesy of Edna M. Hagerthey Madden.)

A portion of a news article dated March 23, 1876, addressing a Baptist Church dedication, evidences that an earlier church stood here for many years before the present one. It reads, in part, "The Methodists talk of erecting a new church at no distant day. They need one badly."

And so they did. In a new deed made May 18, 1874, there is a notation stating,

> In the original deed of 1844 the amount of money to be paid in consideration for title and possession of two lots or pieces of land is not stated and is represented by a blank space, and doubts having arisen in minds of some persons concerning validity and perfection of said title, therefore for purposes of

removing such doubts a new deed was executed for $10.00. The following persons are named as grantors; Godfrey Hancock and Ellen, his wife, N. S. Thompson who is now deceased, Hester A. Prickett, nee Thompson, wife of Mahlon Prickett, Barzillai L. Thompson and Margaret, his wife, Edward T. Thompson and Sarah J., his wife, Joseph S. Thompson and Eliza, his wife, Jesse R. Thompson and Lydia, his wife, and Elizabeth Zelley, nee Thompson, wife of Isaac Zelly to Isaac Brown, Josiah Wills, Nicholas S. Thompson, Charles Brown, Benjamin Reeves and to their survivors.

The name of the church was originally the Methodist-Episcopal Church of Hartford, and was later changed to the Indian Mills United Methodist Church.

Indian Mills United Methodist Church as it appears today. (Photo by the author.)

CENTENNIAL BAPTIST CHURCH

The large edifice presently standing at the southwest corner of Stokes and Willow Grove Roads is being utilized as a children's nursery. It has had a number of uses in recent years, but was once the home of a Baptist Church appropriately named the Centennial Baptist Church, in commemoration of our nation's 100th anniversary in 1876. Reverend Elijah Brant initially organized it and held services in the one-room district schoolhouse nearby until sufficient funds became available to erect a larger and more appropriate building. E. S. Engle, who lived a short distance away, donated the land for the church.

On March 9, 1876, the following appeared in the *New Jersey Mirror*:

> The new Centennial Baptist Church of Shamong Township near Indian Mills will be dedicated to the service of Almighty God on Thursday next the 16th inst. The Rev. A. H. Lung of Camden will preach the dedication sermon at 10 A.M. There will also be services in the afternoon and evening. The public in general is Cordially invited to attend. There will be conveyances at Medford by horse and carriage from the Medford Station to meet the morning trains and carry persons to the church.

It must have been quite a procession by horse and carriage from the Medford Station.

The actual dedication service had to be postponed until March 30 due to inclement weather, although services were still held on March 16 with the *Mirror* reporting,

> The Baptist Church recently erected at the Indian Mills, Shamong Township was opened with religious services on the 16th. Although the day was stormy a congregation of 125 persons assembled to listen to the sermon by the Rev. Mr. Lung of Camden from the words, today shalt thou be with me in Paradise. Subscriptions and collections were taken up amounting to $225. This meetinghouse is one of the neatest

Centennial Baptist Church/Red Men's Hall, erected during the centennial year of 1876. Isaac Wright, a local farmer, is seated in the carriage.
(Photo courtesy of Mabel Mingin Baker.)

and prettiest small meetinghouses that is [sic] to be found in this county. Shamong is improving and someday it will be a very beautiful and important township in this county.

Henry C. Shinn, Ivins Davis, Emlen S. Engle, and Leander B. Fox were trustees of the Centennial Baptist Church of Shamong. They are mentioned in a deed dated February 26, 1876, wherein Emlen S. Engle and his wife Elizabeth A. Engle deeded the lot of 56/100th of an acre to the trustees for $112.

Apparently the church did not meet with much success, and by 1881 services were no longer being held there. Perhaps the nearby Methodist Church attracted most of the local residents. The mortgage of $1,400 was in default and eventually required a Sheriff's sale on complaint of Mechanics and Workingmens' Building & Loan Association of Camden, New Jersey, dated March 23, 1892. James M. Armstrong of Indian Mills purchased the property for $775, subject to the existing mortgage balance of

$1,400. The deed describes the property as Edgepillock Hall, formerly Centennial Baptist Church.

RED MEN'S HALL

When James M. Armstrong purchased the property, it was already known as the Edgepillock Hall, and perhaps the lodge known as Edgepillock Tribe #168 Improved Order of Red Men N.J. was already using the building for their meetings and ceremonies.

During the ownership of the Red Men's Lodge, the church steeple was removed and an upstairs floor was installed. This required the realignment of the height of the first floor windows. The building soon became the central point and gathering place for the entire township, with local elections and township committee meetings held there regularly from 1894 through 1923. In earlier years, these meetings had been held at various hotels in the area.

By the turn of the 20th century the building now known as Red Men's Hall had become a social gathering place with few recalling that it had once been a house of worship.

Mabel Mingin Baker remembered that, at the turn of the 20th century, square dances were held every two weeks during the winter months. Her uncle, John Mingin, made arrangements for the music. The musicians included Joseph and Raymond from Philadelphia who played the violin and harp. Early in the 1900s, the musicians had had to travel to Medford by train. Butler Jennings, who owned a livery stable in Medford, provided the transportation to Indian Mills by horse and wagon. Following the dance, he would drive them back to Medford and arrange for overnight lodging. Upon arising, the musicians would board the train to return to Philadelphia.

Eayre B. Joyce, father of Edna Joyce Riches, purchased the livery stable from Mrs. Riches's uncle, Butler Jennings, in 1910 or 1911. Mr. Joyce followed the same routine in transporting the musicians. They were overnight guests in the Joyce home before taking the train back to Philadelphia. Mrs. Riches recalled that her mother played the piano in the living room, with the musicians joining in on harp and violin.

Red Men's Hall prior to restoration by the Schauman family.
(Photo courtesy of George Atkins.)

During the summer months, the Red Men's Hall provided a portable platform for dancing. The platform was transported to Gardners Grove just down the road for the annual Red Men's Picnic, after which it was returned to the hall. This dance floor was placed on the lawn for the summer dances. Despite the fact that refreshments were not served (other than at the annual picnic), guests regularly traveled from Medford, Red Lion,

Vincentown, Atsion, and Tabernacle to attend these affairs. Joseph and Raymond continued to play during the summer months as well.

Lewis Shrider Jr., who owned considerable land in the vicinity and had built a home just across Stokes Road, purchased the old hall from Edgepillock Tribe #168 Improved Order of Red Men on July 20, 1964. It had been vacant for many years and was badly in need of reconstruction.

The Schauman family eventually purchased the building and extensively remodeled it. In the 1970s the building was a grocery store, and then it stood vacant again until recent years when it became a nursery school.

In 1975 the author and his son, Scott, placed a historical marker in front of the old building. As they were doing so, Mrs. Shrider came out of her house and across the road. She looked at the wording on the sign, and then exclaimed, "There was never a church there! That's always been Red Men's Hall!" When informed of the history of the building, she walked away, shaking her head, apparently unconvinced.

SAMUEL RICHARDS'S CHURCH AND BURIAL GROUND

Samuel Richards, a skillful businessman and ironmaster, and son of William Richards of Batsto, was the lord of the manor at Atsion for more than 20 years. During that time he caused a church to be built for his workers, along with an adjoining burial ground for their use.

The property was deeded to Jesse Richards, Thomas S. Richards, John Richards, Samuel B. French, Thomas Sorden, Samuel Bareford, and Henry Brown on August 6, 1828. It was to be used by "all religious denominations professing Christian religion." And so it has over the years, with nearly all Protestant faiths represented. The church is still an important part of the Atsion community and the surrounding area it serves.

Area church members are still using the adjoining burial ground. Also interred there are many of the workers' families and residents of the area from the days of the Richards regime, as well as subsequent owners of the various enterprises that flourished in Atsion proper, and those who continued on here during the Wharton era.

151

Samuel Richards's Church and Burial Ground, erected in 1828.
Photo taken in the late 1800s. (Photo courtesy of Clyde LeVan.)

The oldest visible gravemarker is that of Sarah Dunlop, which dates from 1837. There are most likely older graves that were either unmarked or marked by pine boards that have long disappeared. Curiously, there are none of the iron markers that were so common at other furnace community grave-yards in South Jersey at the time. Many of the dead were of Irish descent, possibly from Northern Ireland given that the Scots-Irish community was well established in the Pines, and its citizens frequently sought employment at the various local ironworks.

ANCIENT ATSION BURIAL GROUND

The most ancient burial ground in Atsion is frequently referred to as the "Catholic Cemetery," but this may be a misnomer that originated due to the burial of many who were of Irish descent.

What is so heartrending about this particular cemetery on the south shore of Atsion Lake is the wanton destruction of this hallowed ground over the 20th century. Sadly, little has ever been done to protect the gravesite.

Ancient Atsion burial ground. Photo taken in 1916 showing numerous old headstones. Reportedly the burial ground contained 60 graves, possibly many more. (Photo courtesy of Clyde LeVan.)

In the past, numerous stones were to be seen, but gradually they were stolen or otherwise vandalized. The burial ground was eventually allowed to deteriorate and it became so overgrown with underbrush and weeds that it was unknown to all but the local history buffs who treasure such things. The author recalls more than a dozen or so stones still visible in his lifetime.

The burial grounds at Atsion were once reported to contain at least 60 graves. Some archaeologists have suggested the grounds covered an area of approximately 100 square feet, indicating a plot 10 feet by 10 feet, but this is hardly an accurate estimate. The author personally recalls the burial ground covering at least 1,600 square feet, or an area about 40 feet by 40 feet.

Over the years, some of the names of the deceased have been recorded. The oldest known was a John Ross, son of John and Dolly Ross of the Parish of Magilligan, Ireland, who died February 22, 1804, at age 20. It should be pointed out that this particular parish is located in present day Northern Ireland in County Derry. There is a Presbyterian parish called Magilligan, as well as a Roman Catholic parish by the same name. It would be difficult to determine if the Ross family was Presbyterian or Catholic without actually researching these parish records in Northern Ireland.

Other graves identify an Eliza McNeal who died January 5, 1886, age 86, and also a Daniel McNeal, "A Native of Ireland." The Registrar's Records for Shamong Township show that a Michael McNeal, died January 28, 1900. He was a day laborer who was born and died in Burlington County. He was single, age 66, and the son of Daniel and Eliza McNeill. He was born circa 1834 and may also be buried in this graveyard.

With all the obvious evidence of an extensive burial ground here, and the need to protect it, the members of the Indian Mills Historical Society were assured that every protection would be forthcoming when construction began on the recreational complex at Atsion Lake in 1974. Unfortunately such was not the case! When underground cable was being laid, bones appeared on the surface of the ground some 60 feet from the existing gravestones. Archaeologists identified the remains of one woman and one child, who were to be reinterred after they had been evaluated. Handmade nails in the coffins appeared to be made prior to 1825.

The headstone of Eliza McNeal is one of the few that survive today.
(Photo courtesy of Clyde LeVan.)

Photo of the ancient Atsion burial ground taken in the winter of 1974.
(Photo courtesy of Indian Mills Historical Society.)

This discovery alone should have alerted state officials that the burial ground area was far larger than the 100 square feet initially estimated. The number of other graves that lie beneath the asphalt of the present parking lot we probably will never know.

There is no doubt in the author's mind that this cemetery, or what is left of it, contains the graves of many of Atsion's earliest settlers and workmen. What a shame that today only three partial headstones remain, enclosed by a small iron fence. This is a poor substitute for historic preservation.

CHAPTER 11

The Schools of Old Shamong

There were originally five school districts in Shamong Township: Tabernacle #90, Free Soil #91, Hartford #92, Union #93, and Atsion #94. The earliest school board minutes the author could uncover begin September 4, 1876. Much of the information appearing in this chapter is drawn from the Minute Book of School District #93 of the County of Burlington, which lists the original five school districts.

TABERNACLE SCHOOL #90

Tabernacle School #90, built in 1856, was once located in the center of the Village of Tabernacle, near the intersection of Carranza Road and Medford Lakes-Tabernacle Road, across from the cemetery. It functioned for many years until eventually portions of it were moved and incorporated into the schoolhouse still standing across the intersection, which was built in 1936. Among the teachers engaged at the early Tabernacle School were Esther Scull and Portence Johnson, who were paid $35 per month.

FREE SOIL SCHOOL #91

The Free Soil School #91, a one-room schoolhouse, was built on land donated by local resident J. Crain, who lived on an adjoining farm. It was in use by 1858 and may have been operating somewhat earlier. It later became known as the Baker School, as it stood a short distance across the intersection from the Baker Hotel. Free Soil School was located where there is now a WaWa convenience store parking lot on the northeast corner of Indian Mills and Oak Shade Roads.

The records list a number of teachers. Hannah Taylor taught in 1900 at $35 per month. In 1906 Nellie Stokes was paid $33 per month and in 1907

Julia Gaskill was paid only $30 per month. Not much inflation in those days. By 1914 a Norbert F. Diesch was paid $40 per month and by 1917 (through 1919), Maud A. Smyth was paid $40 per month, which was raised to $75 a month in 1920.

By 1922 the school had closed. It was sold to Vernon Drayton at a public sale on July 29, 1922, for $633. Drayton later converted it into a private home and lived there with his family for many years. It was later abandoned and stood vacant for many years until the late 1970s when the Indian Mills Fire Company burned it as part of a routine fire drill.

*Free Soil School/Baker School once stood where the present day WaWa is
located at the northeast corner of Oak Shade and Indian Mills Roads.
The photo was taken in 1969 when the schoolhouse had been a private
dwelling for many years and then abandoned.* (Photo courtesy of Frank Convery.)

Schrider once recalled that this bell rang louder than the one at the nearby Methodist Church. The circumstances of the fire are not known.

Nathaniel R. Ewan once wrote that he had heard a tale about this schoolhouse being used as a still during Prohibition, and to his knowledge it was in operation as such when it burned to the ground. Perhaps this operation could have led to the fire.

OLD ATSION SCHOOL #94

The first schoolhouse at Atsion Village was erected in 1872 on Quaker Bridge Road. It had two windows on each side, each with a single large shutter, and was a single story of frame construction on a jersey sandstone foundation. The school was built during the Maurice Raleigh ownership of the Atsion property. Amanda H. Sooy was a teacher there in 1906 at a salary of $33 per month. Ruth Etheridge Gerber recalled that her mother Mary McCann Etheridge also taught there in the year 1912.

As early as June 21, 1913, the school board entertained the thought of replacing this school with a new and larger one. The plans were eventually

New Atsion School erected in 1916 replaced an earlier schoolhouse that stood a short distance east on Quaker Bridge Road. This recent photo graphically illustrates the desperate need for restoration and preservation at Atsion. (Photo by the author.)

approved. On December 11, 1913, the sum of $1,100 was appropriated to erect a new school and purchase furniture and supplies. The old school was either taken down or burned.

NEW ATSION SCHOOL

A larger schoolhouse, built in 1916, replaced Atsion School #94 and was located approximately 30 feet west of the old school on the south side of Quaker Bridge Road. It had four windows on each side of the building, and was larger than the other schoolhouses in Shamong with the exception of Old Indian Mills School.

The first teacher hired for the new school was Margaret E. Fernwalt at a rate of $45 per month. Marion Keeler taught there in 1917 at the same salary. Ruth Gerber also recalled a Miss Brooks, a Miss Jenny, and a Miss Millie Weeks teaching there, as well as a Mr. Sullivan. She did not remember his first name.

The new schoolhouse was used a scant five years when the board agreed to transport the pupils to the Old Indian Mills School and combine the student bodies. This was in preparation for all students to be enrolled in the new Indian Mills School, then under construction at a cost of $11,900.

Following its closing, the school at Atsion was used as a private dwelling for many years. It has miraculously survived all these years without being torn down or burned to the ground. It is the only one-room schoolhouse still standing in old Shamong.

INDIAN MILLS ELEMENTARY

Indian Mills Elementary, a three-room frame schoolhouse, was completed in 1922 and opened for instruction in September of that year. The Old Indian School and Free Soil School had been sold at public auction July 29, 1922. Margaret C. Nichols was hired August 7 to teach the Primary Room at $100 per month. Miss Alice C. Fairbrother was hired April 2, 1923. Etta Garron, Verna Wright, Doris Wright, and Verna Colton were

Old Indian School that replaced the Hartford School.
(Photo courtesy of Mabel Mingin Baker.)

Mrs. Paxson continued,

> It was quite a problem for me to get home. Mr. Crain picked
> me up at school at 2:00 P.M. with the horse and wagon through
> sand and gravel roads to Medford. Sometimes we went on the
> shoulder of the road and into the woods because of the snow.
> Then from Medford to Mount Holly by train, then by trolley
> from Mount Holly to Burlington, then by train to Yardville. My
> parents met me at the station in their Ford automobile and I
> finally arrived home at 7:00 P.M.

What an experience it must have been for that young woman who had
only recently graduated from high school herself. She had gone to Ocean
City for summer school before starting to teach in Indian Mills, where she
taught for 1-1/2 years. She then taught for 45 years in Hamilton Township,
the last 39 of them in the same room teaching first grade. She continued to

163

Martha Sharp (married name Paxson) was a teacher at the Old Indian School.
She began teaching right out of high school.
(Photo courtesy of Mabel Mingin Baker.)

attend summer school in the early years until she received her permanent teaching certificate.

Other teachers at the Old Indian School were Carson Adams, Ethel K. Warlow, Helen W. Wilson, Josephine S. Gardner, and Margaret Smyth.

The Old Indian School finally closed its doors when it was sold to Lewis Schrider Sr. at a public sale on July 29, 1922, for $555. A year later Schrider sold it to Blair Chew, who used it as a cranberry packinghouse. Chew bought the land where the school was located at the public sale with the stipulation that he remove the old schoolhouse within one year. When the school was burned down, it still had the schoolbell in it. Mr.

attending the old school while the new schoolhouse was being built. He was about 8 or 9 years old at the time.

UNION SCHOOL # 93

All of the early school board meetings were held at the Union schoolhouse, which was on Old Indian Mills Road approximately a quarter mile north of Tuckerton Road. The structure was built around 1859 and was used as a school until 1920. In 1879 Lizzie S. Haines taught there at a salary of $27 per month. The board passed a resolution not to pay more than $2.50 for a cord of wood. Miss Haines had to agree to keep the schoolhouse in a "warm and comfortable position."

On December 7, 1878, records reflect that a proposal was made to close Union Schoolhouse for three months of the year and to rent and renovate the African Methodist-Episcopal Church on Tabernacle and Hampton Gate Road (now Carranza Road) to be used as a school for those three months. Only one trustee of this church could be found that was still living, and he could not legally do anything, so the idea was abandoned. The Union School was utilized until 1920 and then closed. Students were then transported to the Tabernacle School, to which an extra room was added.

In March 1883 a suggestion was made to the school board in regard to building a new schoolhouse and to prepare plans and an estimate. The matter came to a vote the following month, and the school board rejected the resolution by a vote of 14 to 9. Instead of erecting a new school, a sum of $50 was to be raised in the district to repair the old schoolhouse.

On March 20, 1888, a question was asked of the board in regard to paying various teachers for the time there was no school on account of the great snow storm (the blizzard of 1888). It was decided to write to the county superintendent for his opinion on the matter. There were no subsequent entries on this subject.

On July 28, 1899, a resolution was passed that Atsion School be kept open for 8-1/2 months, Free Soil for 7 months, and Tabernacle, Hartford, and Union for 9 months. The District Clerk ordered that a wood house be built at Atsion, 10 feet square with wood to be purchased at $3 per cord.

In July 1900 the board ordered a coalhouse to be built at Free Soil Schoolhouse. Following this entry, subsequent meetings were held at Hartford Schoolhouse in Shamong Township, beginning August 3, 1901. This was due to the formation of Tabernacle Township, created from parts of Shamong and Woodland, on March 22, 1901. Board meetings had always been held previously at the Union School, but this was now located in the newly created Tabernacle Township.

THE OLD INDIAN SCHOOL

The Old Indian School replaced the Hartford School, with building completed in 1907. It was a good deal larger and more commodious than the Hartford School and even had a steeple with a bell.

In February 1914 there is a notation that the board called for the resignation of Helen Hymes, no later than February 6, 1914. On May 13, 1914, M. Prickitt was appointed to get counsel for the Hymes case. No further details on the circumstances of her dismissal are given.

Mrs. Martha Sharp Paxson, who remembered coming to Indian Mills in 1915 to finish the term of a teacher who had been discharged, provided an interesting recollection.

> I boarded with Mr. and Mrs. John Crain. He was president of the school board at that time. I started teaching in the Old Indian School with 45 to 50 children of all ages. The school was ungraded. There was a wood stove that sat in the middle of the room. The boys carried in the wood, but I took care of the stove. The boys and girls carried a bucket of water from the creek, and we all used the same cup for drinking, and the same basin for washing.
>
> There was one small blackboard and very little chalk. Paper, pencils, and books were in very short supply. The helping teacher from Moorestown came to my rescue about once a month with materials.

HARTFORD SCHOOL #92

Around 1805, Upper Evesham Preparative Meeting purchased three acres of ground at Brotherton for the purpose of establishing a school and burial ground. In 1806 the committee of Friends reported that they had taken title to the property and it was to be called Hartford School.

According to Harold Bozearth, a lifetime resident of Shamong, the schoolhouse faced away from Wrights Lane (now Schoolhouse Lane). Bozearth, who was born in 1897, started school there at the age of seven. He died in the early 1980s.

Mabel Mingin Baker also recalled being a pupil there at an early age. She remembers that the drinking water was carried in buckets from the stream behind the school. She commented that the inside of the building looked more like a church than a school. She described the floor as being in tiers or levels, as in many churches. The seating consisted of flat benches with

*Pupils outside the Hartford School around 1897 or 1898. Left to right. Top Row:
Mary Woolman, Leeson Small, Joseph Wells, Marriott Gaskill, Lillie Pickett, Bertha
Weeks, Alma Prickett, Laura Sorden, Emma Bozearth, and Sally Taylor-Teacher.
Second row: Mary Miller, Sarah Woolman, Rachel Wright, Olive Sorden, Julia
Gaskill, Ella Small, Helen Gaskill, Ella Miller, Viola Waters, Bertha Small, and Edna
Hagerthey. Boys seated: Earl Taylor, Alva Gaskill, Wilber Hagerthey, Harrison Piper,
and James Vaughn. (Photo courtesy of Edna Hagerthey Madden.)*

no backs. There was a coal stove in the middle of the room. The boys sat on one side of the room and the girls on the other. Teachers included Allen Clymer, Sadie Small, and Bertha Weeks.

The physical description provided by Mrs. Baker seems to support the theory that at one time this school also functioned as a Friends Meetinghouse. She did not remember anything about a burial ground, but there was one there as reported by the archaeologist E. W. Hawkes in 1916.

On June 26, 1905, the school board consisted of William H. Brown, George H. Taylor, Harry F. Wright, Charles D. Sorden, and John W. Crain. The board authorized a new schoolhouse to be built where Hartford Schoolhouse now stands, as well as a purchase for schoolhouse furniture and other necessary equipment not to exceed the sum of $1,000. They authorized issuance of 10 bonds, one a year for 10 years at $100 each. Benjamin J. Mingin purchased all the bonds on December 15, 1905 at 4 percent interest per year.

The old Hartford School was sold at a public sale to Thomas Gardner on January 17, 1908, for $87.55. Harold Bozearth remembered that he was still

Hartford School circa 1903 when Sadie Small was the teacher. Students shown are Edna Hagerthey, Lizzie Crain, Mary Miller, Clement Miller, Leah Prickett, William Miller, Eva Dellett, Laura Bozearth, Merle Prickett, Ruth Waters, Bertha Small, Carrie Patterson, Raymond Crain, Mabel Mingin, Viola Waters, Carlton Bozearth, Eddie Cline, Harry Miller, Fremont Gaskill, Harold Bozearth, Wilber Hagerthey, Samel Waters, Alvin Gaskill, Norman Bozearth, and Asbury Cline. Names listed in no particular order. (Photo courtesy of Mabel Mingin Baker.)

The sale was held on November 22, 1862, after being advertised for four weeks in the *N.J. Mirror* and *Burlington County Advertisor*. Manasses Dellett was the highest bidder and purchased the property for $2,525. The property was then known as Dellett's Inn or Hotel.

DELLETT'S INN

Manasses Dellett owned a large home and farm along the present day Oak Shade Road where he also operated a grocery store. His son Thomas Dellett then operated the hotel until his death in 1879 from tuberculosis. After his son's death, Manasses tore down the old Josiah Smith Hotel and rebuilt it on the southeast corner of the same intersection, and on a much larger property. It continued to operate under the name Dellett's Inn.

Manasses Dellett died March 22, 1893, and was survived by his wife Rebecca, who died June 3, 1896, of tuberculosis at age 75. Both are buried at the Atsion Cemetery. They had been married in Camden, N.J. on March 11, 1842. Most of the Dellett family lies buried at St. Mary's Catholic burial ground in Pleasant Mills.

Before her death, Rebecca Dellett had deeded the inn to her daughter, Anna B. Patterson, on April 6, 1894. Rebecca, who had married Alfred H. Patterson on April 6, 1872, carried on the hotel that in trade directories of the time was listed as the Forrest Hotel. It then passed to their son, Fremont Patterson, on October 6, 1904.

PATTERSON'S HOTEL

Fremont Patterson died intestate December 16, 1935. The children of Fremont Patterson deeded a portion of the estate that encompassed the hotel property to his widow Delilah on May 31, 1955. By that time the old hotel had become known simply as Patterson's. Over the years, it had frequently been used for township meetings, dances, wedding, and other social affairs.

According to Hamilton Patterson, a lineal descendent, the dance floor was on the second floor and the bar was downstairs. He remembered two large barns behind the hotel where the stagecoaches changed horses. One barn was called the Stagecoach Barn.

Through the years, this landmark hotel, nearly 100 years old, became abandoned and neglected. The author remembers exploring the old property many years ago. A thick column about 10 inches square had been used to shore up the sagging barroom ceiling on the first floor to support the dance floor above. The building that could tell so many stories was now in ruins and had become too dangerous to be allowed to stand any longer. On the orders of the Shamong Township Committee, the old hotel was torn down on April 2, 1975. A bulldozer dug a huge pit behind the old hotel. It was then demolished, pushed into the pit, and covered over with dirt.

CLINE'S TAVERN

Ephraim Cline owned considerable land on the southern edge of the Brotherton Reservation that he had purchased in the late 1700s into the early 1800s. One of his purchases was of 215 acres of pinelands at a place called "Edgepillock," in 1796. Another purchase was of 108 acres at a corner of the Indian lands commonly known by the name of Edgepillock that same year.

Cline opened a tavern on the main stage road into Atsion in 1798. Mention is made in early road returns of extensive orchards west of this tavern property. The tavern stood on the west side of the road that now leads to Goshen Pond campground, fronting on Atsion Road.

The tavern became known as the Indian King. It was in an ideal location for the workmen at Atsion, a short distance down the road. They frequented the place, as did some Indian natives until Brotherton closed in 1802. In the *New Jersey Mirror*, an ad appeared December 23, 1818, advising to the public that "20,000 Cedar Rails will be sold January 18, 1819 at Ephraim Cline's Tavern near Atsion about 10 miles from Vincentown and 9 miles from Medford." A road was laid out May 1, 1839, and was called the Road from Cline's to Hammonton. On an accompanying sketch was a notation about Samuel Richard's new mill on Fleming Pike, showing a canal and stating the road was not laid over the dam.

PIPER'S TAVERN

John Piper Sr. of Evesham purchased 53 acres of land from Jonathan Oliphant and his wife, Mary, on February 1, 1791. The price was 74 pounds of gold or silver money. This land was bordered on the north by the boundary of the Brotherton Indian Reservation. The tavern, later to be called the "Buck" tavern or "Sign of the Buck" tavern, was opened for business in 1793. It was located on one of the busiest stage routes from Upper Evesham (Medford) to Atsion Iron Works. This was one of the few taverns that was in close proximity to the reservation lands, and it was here that the Brotherton lands were auctioned off at public sale in 1802. John Piper Sr. had also purchased a 100-acre tract from the Indian Commissioners in 1802, which was adjacent to the gristmill property.

John Piper, Sr. died in 1807, and the home and tavern property were willed to his wife, Martha. His estate was extensive and included numerous tracts of land in the area as well as considerable personal property, furnishings, horses, livestock, and all manner of household goods that would befit an inn or tavern. Many items listed in the estate inventory would be an antique collector's treasure. The inventory lists fan-back Windsor chairs, a pine writing desk, and a considerable amount of pewter ware.

The will was written October 2, 1807, naming his beloved wife, Martha, and his trusted friend Lewis Mingin as executors. Josiah Foster (former Indian Commissioner) and William Thompson were appointed administrators of the estate. Piper bequeathed other lands he owned to his son John, Jr., his gun to his grandson John Foster, $50 to his married daughter Sarah Foster, wife of Thomas Foster, and $30 to his grandson Solomon Williams. The 100-acre tract of reservation lands he had purchased was bequeathed in equal half portions to his daughters, Ann and Hannah. There is also a record of the release of a mortgage that Jacob Austin held against this property of Jonathan Oliphant. It was not recorded until April 11, 1803, when the matter appeared before Josiah Foster, one of the judges of the Court of Common Pleas for Burlington County.

John Piper's widow, Martha Piper, operated the tavern from 1807 to 1811, and then a William Emley was the tavern keeper from 1811 to 1822. It then passed to Josiah P. Smith.

JOSIAH P. SMITH'S TAVERN

Josiah P. Smith purchased the "Buck" or "Sign of the Buck" tavern and hotel in 1822 and remained as its proprietor for many years thereafter. In the 1850 Federal Census, Josiah Smith's age is given as 70. His children are listed as Sarah, age 35, John, age 22, Mary Ann, age 18, and William, 18; a boarder Keziah Mingin, age 85, is also listed.

The tavern and hotel, located at the busy intersection of Atsion Road and what then was known simply as "the Road from Red Lion to Josiah Smith's," prospered for many years.

Josiah P. Smith passed to his eternal reward on November 3, 1855, at age 75. He lies buried in the Baptist Cemetery in Medford. John P. Smith and his sister Mary Ann, who had married George Bozearth, a nearby neighbor, then held the property jointly. In 1859 George Bozearth is listed as innkeeper.

Manasses Dellett had purchased a portion of the tract from John P. Smith, for on September 11, 1862, he petitioned the court to divide, in two equal parts, the Josiah Smith Tavern and property between Manasses Dellett and Mary Ann Bozearth, wife of George Bozearth, the owners and proprietors. The judge rejected his petition and ordered the entire property sold at public sale.

> The Tavern Stand and Farm attached known as Josiah Smith's Tavern is situated on the main stage road between Medford and Atsion, distant about 4 miles from the Raritan Bay Railroad, now complete. The house is large and convenient and well supplied with sheds and stabling about it.
>
> The Farm consists of about 60 acres of land, the soil of which is well adapted to the growth of grain or grass; the whole well fenced with cedar fencing, and in a good state of cultivation. The premises will be shown previous to the day of the sale by the subscribers, or Manasses Dellett, living adjoining. John S. Irick, Franklin W. Earl, and William Braddock, Commissioners.

CHAPTER 12
Hotels, Inns, and Taverns

In the Pine Barrens of Old Shamong, there were once numerous taverns and accommodations for travelers along the stage routes that crisscrossed the wilderness areas of the day. Civilization has largely bypassed these tavern sites, which in most cases lie protected within state forestlands.

Most of the stagecoach routes in Burlington County led from Cooper's Ferry in present day Camden. Most were not established until after the Revolutionary War. There was Daniel Cooper at the foot of Cooper Street, William Cooper at Cooper's Point, and Joshua Cooper at the foot of Federal Street. These same roads, however, were heavily traveled before the war by teamsters hauling wood, charcoal, and products from the iron furnaces and forges that dotted the landscape in the pines. They would travel to wharves on the Rancocas in Lumberton, where barges transported the goods to and from Philadelphia. This was a much faster route than by water from Tuckerton, which would require sailing down the Atlantic Coast, around Cape May, into Delaware Bay, and then upriver to Philadelphia. The overland wagons to Lumberton were also less easily detected by enemy troops during wartime.

By 1784 there were no fewer than 57 taverns in Burlington County alone. Most of these were simply known as "jug taverns," meaning that a jug could be filled with liquor for consumption on the journey. Most of these taverns provided a bed, a meal, and a jug of spirits of one sort or another. They were usually built of logs or frame construction with one story and a loft to one-and-a-half-stories high, and usually had fireplaces for heat. They provided a modest meeting place for residents in the area and often provided a site for local elections to be held. This description fit most of the jug taverns of the day.

In 1818 an eyewitness account of the times was recorded by a botanist named John Torrey, in a letter he sent to his friend named Zachariah

Collins. He was accompanied on his journey into the Pine Barrens by a William Cooper. The letter reads in part,

> Some places we put up at were not fit for an Arab. At a place called Ten Mile Hollow or Hell Hollow we expected to sleep in the woods for it was with difficulty we persuaded them to take us in. This was the most miserable place we ever saw; they were too poor to use candles. No butter, sugar, etc. A little sour stuff, which I believe they called rye bread, but which was half saw dust, and a little warm water and molasses, were all we had for breakfast. For supper I could not see what we had for we ate in the dark.

What a harrowing experience this must have been, but it gives the reader a brief glimpse of what life was like then to the traveling public.

Each county eventually began regulating the stagecoach industry with respect to rates and accommodations for inns and taverns. Burlington County was no exception, establishing "Rates for Regulation of Tavern Keepers and Innkeepers in 1824." The stage routes across the pines were well entrenched by this time and had been for many years. In those days it was usually a two-day trip from Philadelphia to Tuckerton. A simple breakfast or supper cost 25 cents, the noontime meal was priced at 31 cents, and lodging was 12 cents. Stabling a horse for the night was 20 cents, with pasturage for the night an additional 12 cents. Oats for horses cost 3 cents, and a quart of corn was 4 cents. These rules were strictly enforced. The proprietor's license could become void in the event of a violation, with an additional cost of a $4 fine for each offense. The current rates of the establishment had to be posted as soon as received and, if they were not, then a $4 per-day fine was imposed until they were.

None of the taverns covered here were in operation during the primary years of the Brotherton Reservation with the exception of the last decade or so prior to its demise in 1802. Indians had to either travel a considerable distance to procure strong drink or merely buy it from nearby settlers. And so they did, as Brainerd frequently mentions abuse of alcohol as one of the Indians' common weaknesses.

Indian Mills Elementary when newly constructed in 1922.
(Photo courtesy of Isabel Brown.)

also teaching here between 1923 and 1925, by which time the salary was $100 per month for a teacher.

The 1922 school still survives, though there have been numerous alterations and additions. The author's three sons, Scott, Shawn, and Shane, all attended the school back in the 1970s. The school, which has provided the treasured foundation of basic skills to all who have attended, remains a vibrant part of the local educational community.

Municipal Building, where the Indian Mills Historical Society maintains several showcases of memorabilia.

FOX CHASE

Fox Chase Tavern was located on the Great Road from Red Lion to Little Egg Harbor and was established around 1800 during the heyday of stagecoach travel. One of the earliest proprietors was William Fox. Later, Hosea Moore operated the tavern for many years and became well known to the traveling public. Nothing remains now but an historical marker erected by the Tabernacle Historical Society. All opportunities to excavate this site have been lost, as the tavern site is now the entrance to Seneca High School, which opened in September 2003.

HAMPTON GATE

A tavern known as "The Gate" was formerly kept on the old Tuckerton Stage Road near where it forms the boundary between present-day Shamong and Tabernacle Townships.

The first proprietor of the tavern appears to have been David Cavileer, who purchased the tract from his father-in-law, Caleb Cramer, on April 9, 1812. Both men were originally from Little Egg Harbor Township. Cramer, a large landowner in the county, had purchased the tavern property from the heirs of Restore Shinn, on April 7, 1802. It is doubtful Cramer ever operated the tavern, and it can be assumed David Cavileer originated this business venture.

The tavern was located on the heavily traveled stage road leading from Cooper's Ferry to Tuckerton and was also close to the Hampton Iron Works and other furnace communities in the area.

The various taverns scattered throughout the Pines were popular with furnace workers as can be attested to in the various diaries of those times. Drunkenness of several days' duration was commonly reported.

The Gate Tavern was at the base of a series of hills known in early deeds as "the stone hills." These hills are unique in the otherwise flat terrain of the surrounding area. One can still see the large depressions in the hills caused by mining them for building stone. The stone from these hills supplied the foundations of many a home in the area and for the Gate Tavern, as well, as evidenced by an item that appeared in the *New Jersey Mirror*, October 19, 1838. In it Samuel Goforth advertised a 25-acre tract of land and cedar swamp "situate on the road from Alanson Whites to Hampton Gate and near the latter place on which stands a large stone house built for a tavern and which is considered a good stand for that business."

David Cavileer maintained the tavern until his passing in 1824. His will is dated March 17, 1824, and was proved June 16, 1825. His widow, Mary Cavileer, and Jesse Evans were named as executors. The will is quite interesting. He initially requests that his entire estate be left to his wife. In the event of her death, he then leaves the estate to "my friend" Mary Smith (late Mary Taylor), and after her death to her children by the present husband equally. He then adds that David Cavileer Smith, son of Mary Smith, be given separate from the other children 200 acres with dwelling house, barn, and outhouses, but only after his wife's death.

Exactly what Cavileer's relationship was with Mary Taylor Smith and her son David Cavileer Smith has not been determined, though it is curious that the boy bore the first and last name of the subjects. It is known David Cavileer had no children, although he also leaves in his will the sum of $100 to a Caroline Lawson, described as "the child I brought up."

A further glimpse of what comprised the tavern and adjoining property can also be made as the will continues to bequeath 200 acres "beginning at a large pine marked DE and SL about 15 chains from the bridge near my dwelling house to a large pine standing in the line along the pasture fence and from thence to the top of the little stone hill."

His inventory dated June 15, 1825, offers additional information as to the tavern itself when it quotes "a lott of tables, chairs, clock, and sundries in the parlor, bar room, and kitchen, Beds and bedding in the up chambers, also sundries in the cellar and garret." Also listed are "one half dozen silver tablespoons, one half dozen silver teaspoons, and two silver watches." Livestock and farm equipment consisted of,

> seven cows, four calves, one pair of oxen, two yearlings, a
> bull, two heifers, one red and white heifer, one pride bull, one

Tavern Property with two barns and 20 acres of land, lying on the northerly side of Tuckerton Road; a part of the land is very superior bottom meadow, some timber land and part is excellent cranberry land that is now producing fruit and more can be easily put into cultivation and flooded at little expense. The balance is upland suitable for grain and vegetables.

Apparently no sale was made at Small's as it was adjourned until Saturday, December 29, 1877, at the Arcade Hotel in Mount Holly. The property was then purchased by John Henry Clay Jennings. The tavern property has remained in the Jennings family ever since. The late Jerome Jennings once told the author he remembered the barn across Tuckerton Road from the tavern. His paternal grandmother had it taken down many years ago and moved to the Jennings farm down the road. The beams were all hand hewn and pegged together. It was then added to another barn and later taken down altogether. Nothing remains today of this once prosperous tavern location except the farm home and store of Mahlon Pettit nearby.

Several writers have quoted passages from the Martha Furnace Diary regarding Martha employees being drunk at the Half Moon and referring to the Flyatt Tavern. In the excellent and scholarly work *Heart of the Pines*, author John E. Pierce sets the record straight with the help of the brilliant historian and archaeologist Budd Wilson. The Half Moon of the Martha Furnace Diary was just four miles from Martha at Chips Folly on the old Martha-Wading River Road. It had been converted to a gun club and later, in 1901, was burned to the ground. In September 1975, the author, Bob Jones, and Don Catts, members of the Indian Mills Historical Society, obtained permission from Jerome Jennings to attempt an excavation of the Flyatt Tavern site. A 10-foot-square test trench was dug, which uncovered a 4-foot section of the sandstone foundation wall and also a hard-packed clay cellar floor. Excavations continued until the owner of the property became concerned that someone might get injured as the excavation was at a busy intersection and had been gaining notoriety, even though the activity was not made public. The owner requested that all further digging be stopped. This was done and the trench filled back in. Thus ended what may have been the first excavation conducted of a Pine Barrens tavern.

Foundation uncovered at the site of the Flyatt Tavern (Half Moon and Seven Stars Tavern). Note the clay cellar floor. (Photo courtesy of Bob Jones.)

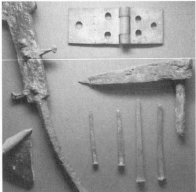

Artifacts excavated at the site of the Flyatt Tavern (Half Moon and Seven Stars Tavern). (Photos courtesy of Bob Jones.)

The preliminary digging had uncovered hand-forged strap hinges, buttons, slipware fragments, an 1803 one cent piece, 1862 and 1863 Indian Head pennies, and several domino-like items that may have been part of a game. These items are on display in the courtroom at the Shamong Township interim apparently leased the premises because Mahlon Pettit had obtained a license in 1836,

> to keep a Public House, Inn, or Tavern at Fliatum Hotel on the Public Road Leading from Medford to Tuckerton and a number of Iron Works and a place where an Inn or publick house has been kept for a number of years past.

The Orphans Court in the May term of 1838 decreed that the property was to be sold at public auction at the house of Mark Moore on May 3, 1838, later adjourned to the house of Daniel Coates in Medford, December 1, 1838. Tract #1 was described as,

> a tavern stand and plantation situate in the Township of Evesham (known as the Fly-at Tavern) and adjoining lands of John Craine, Thomas Morris and others, and at the crossroads where the Medford and Hampton Road crosses the road from Red Lion to Josiah Smith's containing about 70 acres of land. The improvements are a large frame tavern house, barn, stable, wagon house, horse sheds, a good apple orchard and other fruit trees, 12 acres of which is in good meadow and remains arable, well adapted to grain and grass, all under cedar fence. Tract #2 was a farm being part of the original tract and adjoining same containing about 30 acres with a two story frame dwelling, home and stables all new and young apple orchards, and all under cedar fence.

Elizabeth Lewallen, widow of Isaac Lewallen, deceased, relinquished any dower right she had to the Farm and Tavern House to Mahlon Pettit for $100. The entire tract was sold to Mahlon Pettit at $19 per acre. He continued to operate the tavern until about 1863 when it burned to the ground. He was then living just down the Oak Shade Road toward Small's Tavern and operating a store from his home. This home is still standing but has been considerably altered since its original construction.

Mahlon Pettit home as it appears today, much altered from its original appearance. (Photo by the author.)

The 1850 census lists Mahlon Pettit as age 55, his wife, Sarah, age 51, a daughter Eleazer, age 24, and three daughters, all age 18, Mary Ann, Sarah Jane, and Beulah. Mahlon Pettit died April 18, 1876, in his 82nd year and is buried next to his wife, Sarah, at the Baptist cemetery in Medford.

On November 22, 1877, the property was advertised in the *New Jersey Mirror*. The first purchasers failed to comply with the terms of the sale and a new sale was scheduled at the hotel of Benjamin Small just down the road. It describes the,

> Homestead Farm of the late Mahlon Pettit deceased situate on both sides of the road from Benjamin Smalls Hotel and the old Flyatt Tavern containing 112 acres of land, part of which is very superior bottom meadow, well watered, a few acres of maple timber, and the balance is upland most of which is of good quality. The improvements are a good two story Farm House, storehouse, barn, cow house, wagon house, tenant house, apple orchard and other fruit trees. The Old Flyatt

Ephraim Cline was very active in Washington Township politics. He served as Tax Collector in 1806 and on the Township Committee in 1805, 1826–28, 1833, and 1838. He was married to Rachel Salter, daughter of Joseph Salter, who was one of the family owners of Atsion Ironworks. By the middle of the 19th century, the tavern had burned to the ground and in later maps is shown merely as the "burnt house"; nothing but the faint traces of a cellar hole remains today. A nearby road heading northwest from the tavern site was known as Burnt House Road for many years.

EAGLE TAVERN

One of the most prominent taverns in the Pines was on the stage road from Mount Holly through Washington and on to Tuckerton. Because most of the furnaces in the Pines employed hundreds of workers and related craftsmen and colliers, it was only logical that taverns would be established nearby. Eagle Tavern was located a short distance from Speedwell Furnace, much to the delight of the workmen there.

Gideon Pharo was licensed as the tavern keeper in 1798. Jacob Barnhart followed him, changing the name to Barnhart's Tavern. Others followed by the names of Abner Cross and John Shield. By 1826, James McCambridge Sr. was the owner. Workers at Speedwell were still using the tavern, but that business was considerably reduced when Speedwell closed about 1840. James McCambridge purchased what remained at Speedwell on January 30, 1850, but mostly as a land investment as he continued to make his home at Eagle, which by then was no longer an active tavern.

James McCambridge was born in 1800 and died September 28, 1886. His wife, Ann, was born in 1804 and died December 27, 1855. His son, James Jr., died December 30, 1864, at age 30. Mary A. McCambridge died May 16, 1880 at age 47. All are buried in the Catholic Cemetery at Pleasant Mills. Two other children who list their parents as James and Ann McCambridge have their deaths recorded in Shamong Township. William, single, farmer, died November 28, 1917, age 76, and Sara McCambridge died January 30, 1918, single, age 81.

Site of the Eagle Tavern, once located on a heavily traveled stagecoach route that is now just a quiet and remote sand trail in the Pines. (Photo by the author.)

HALF MOON AND SEVEN STARS TAVERN AT FLYATT

A cluster of century-old red cedar trees stands as a lonely sentinel to a time long past at the intersection of Tuckerton and Oak Shade Roads. This was once the site of the Half Moon and Seven Stars Tavern that faced the old Tuckerton Stage Road.

John King opened the tavern here in 1800 and continued to operate it until his death in 1813. Reuben Lewallen then became the proprietor and operated the tavern until 1815, followed by Amos Troth until 1818. It was in February 1818 that John King's son, William, petitioned the courts stating that his father John King died intestate, also stating that he left issue naming the following: William King, Mary, wife of Samuel Wills, Ann, wife of James Allen, Samuel, Moses, Lewis, Sarah, Margaret, Lucy, and John, all minor children.

On June 13, 1818, the court commissioners sold the tavern property and 101 acres of land to Isaac Lewallen for $1,500. He continued to operate the tavern until 1836 when his health began to fail. He died in 1838 but in the

George and Hannah Baker and their grandson Fred. The Bakers were proprietors of Small's Tavern, then known as Baker's Hotel, from 1903 to 1922. (Photo courtesy of Mabel Mingin Baker.)

The guests included a locally prominent physician, Dr. Braddock of Medford, and a mortician, William Reily, also of Medford. They were frequently called upon to attend the needs of the local residents. These were still horse and buggy days and travel was much slower than today. Prohibition was enacted in 1919 and the hotel operation was discontinued. Mr. and Mrs. Baker then used the building as a private residence until they sold it to a Mr. and Mrs. Carter of Penna. in 1922. During the

Baker proprietorship many church activities were held at the old hotel and grounds. Mr. Baker showed great respect for the church and whenever a significant church activity occurred the bar was always closed. His five children were all abstainers.

The property passed to Charles and Mamie Jennings in 1930 and continued into the late 1960s. It then went by the name "Tumble Inn" and is still referred to by that name by many of the older residents of Indian Mills. The hotel and tavern property has had many owners since, and undergone several name changes, but to historians it will always be known as Small's Hotel or simply "Small's." From its erection in 1830 to the present it has remained a gathering place for local residents. Through the years it has been used for elections and town meetings as well. It is the sole edifice linking us to the by-gone tavern days in Shamong.

KEMBLE'S INN

The hostelry known as Kemble's Inn was erected in the mid 1800s on the Great Road from Eayrestown to Tuckerton, although by that time many of the stage lines were beginning to fade away in favor of the railroads and local carriage rentals. Charles S. Kemble, farmer and blacksmith, operated this inn for many years. In addition, he served in local politics as a member of the Shamong Township Committee from 1860 through 1863. He had also been a member of the New Jersey Assembly from 1855 to 1859 and was the Burlington County Sheriff at the time of his death in 1869.

Shamong Township meetings and local elections in 1861 and 1863 are recorded as being held at the "House of Charles S. Kemble at the Tabernacle." Today the building remains the only existing older inn of present-day Tabernacle and has been carefully restored to reflect the heritage of yesterday.

ORIENTAL AND NAYLOR'S CORNER

It has been written that in days of old nearly every house along the old stage routes was at one time or another a source of refreshment and lodging

Benjamin W. Small, owner of Small's Hotel, stated that Dellett Jr. had been at his hotel-bar on the night of January 19 and had about three drinks of whiskey, bought a half pint, and left the hotel about midnight. He also stated that about three months prior to the shooting, McNeal and Dellett were in his hotel, engaged in a card game, when they suddenly began fighting, with Dellett being the loser of the fight and bruised badly. However, according to Small, Dellett seems to have held no further ill feelings toward McNeal.

On Wednesday, May 1, 1889, the jury brought in a verdict of "Not Guilty" after deliberating for nearly three days, and John McNeal was acquitted and released from prison, and returned to his home and family.

The accused, John McNeal, had lived in what is known today as the Gatley Farm on Indian Mills Road just a short distance from Small's Hotel.

The background of this property is quite interesting. Arthur Thompson of Evesham, who was once proprietor of the tavern at Quaker Bridge for many years, originally purchased this 100-acre lot from the Indian Commissioners on June 10, 1802, for 250 pounds. On December 17, 1832,

The John McNeal House on Indian Mills Road was the scene of the murder of James Dellett Jr. The home is now occupied by the Gatley Family. (Photo by the author.)

187

Elizabeth Thompson, Arthur's widow, conveyed the property on Murphy Road, now known as Indian Mills Road, to Robert McNeal. This is when the farmhouse was most likely built, as Elizabeth Thompson was still operating the Quaker Bridge Tavern until 1836. Robert McNeal died April 25, 1855. His will gives his nephew "John McNeal, son of my brother Daniel, one half of the farm of 110 acres, two horses and wagon, and two cows." He was not to inherit this bequest until the death of Daniel. "Unto my brother Daniel McNeal, all the remainder of this farm and all my money and proveable property to his and his heirs." Daniel died intestate on October 23, 1876. His son John then purchased the farm on March 25, 1877, from the heirs Hugh, Michael, and James McNeal, James and John Platt, Mary Dellett, James Dellett Jr., Annie McNeal, and Daniel McNeal.

In 1833 a John, Daniel, and Robert McNeal are listed as ore raisers at Atsion Iron Works. The Daniel and Eliza McNeal buried at the oldest cemetery in Atsion are most likely of this same family, as would be their son Michael who died January 28, 1900, at age 66.

The property remained in the McNeal family until March 22, 1920, when it was purchased by Lewis Nelson Carty and Mary, his wife, of Philadelphia. They in turn sold it to John Shinski of Shamong on April 6, 1920. It was next sold to John T. Gatley Sr. of Camden on March 25, 1925, and has remained in the Gatley family ever since.

Small's Hotel was a short distance from the McNeal farm. The tavern property was purchased by William E. Haines from the estate of Thomas Crain on March 24, 1898, and was resold to Elizabeth Haines that same year. Tacy Haines of Shamong bought it from Elizabeth Haines of Cramer Hill, Camden, on August 8, 1898. William E. Haines and Tacy, his wife, then sold it to David Sharp of Mansfield, December 26, 1899.

On September 24, 1904, George W. Baker and his wife, Hannah, of Medford purchased the property, tavern house, and tract of 64 acres of land on the corner of the Murphy Road and Red Lion Road for $2,150. The tavern was then named Baker's Hotel. The family consisted of five children: Herbert, Edward, Rose, Fred, and Bertha. The Bakers accommodated overnight guests and served meals.

Mabel Mingin Baker recalled,

resulted in the fatal shooting of a local patron. Thanks to the diligent research in the old *New Jersey Mirror* by historian Frank W. H. Convery, the following articles from January and May 1889 were discovered.

Murder at Indian Mills, N.J. January 19, 1889. On Saturday night about 12:20 A.M., John McNeal shot and killed Mr. James Dellett, Jr. both of Indian Mills, N.J. Mr. Dellett, who had been drinking earlier on that night at Small's Hotel, although he was not intoxicated, went to the home of Mr. McNeal about midnight and began pounding on his back door. Mr. McNeal and his wife Margaret were asleep on the 2nd floor and also his children, Robert McNeal aged 14, and Dora McNeal about 16 years of age. Also Michael McNeal, and a brother of John McNeal, was living there at the time.

Mrs. McNeal awakened her husband and reported the pounding on the door. McNeal then opened the 2nd floor window and demanded to know who was there, but received no answer although the pounding continued. Mr. McNeal then put on some clothes and proceeded downstairs and took down his gun from the wall. He then stood inside of the back door and demanded to know who was there and what they wanted. Shortly a voice from the outside said, "I want you". Mr. McNeal then opened the door and a man he could not identify made a lunge at him. Mr. McNeal then fired both barrels into the man, killing him instantly. He fell partly lying in the door and part of his body out of doors. Closer identification proved the man to be James Dellett, Jr. a friend and neighbor of Mr. McNeal. Mr. McNeal then went immediately to the home of John Cotton "Justice of the Peace" who lived nearby, and explained the situation and gave himself up. He also went to the home of his nearest neighbor, James K. Naylor, and finally "Constable" Theodore Miller was aroused about 3 A.M. on Sunday morning and took McNeal into custody. On Sunday morning Constable Miller and Henry Wright took McNeal in a horse and carriage to the Mount Holly Jail and turned him over to Sheriff Harbert, and he was then placed in jail. On Monday, Jan. 21st, a coroner's inquest was held at Small's Hotel. Jurors selected were Henry Wright, Hugh McSwiggan, John Mingen, Charles E. French, Leander B. Fox, James M. Armstrong, Joseph Small, Hezekiah Stokes, and Clayton Buckage. The little hotel was crowded with people. John Cotton, Justice of the Peace, presided at the inquest, and Dr. Richard Braddock and Dr. Josiah Reeve of Medford, N.J. held a Post Mortem examination. Andrew Applegate, a friend of the deceased said he left Small's Hotel on the night of the murder with James Dellett, Jr. and he was not intoxicated when he last saw him. At the end of the coroners inquest the Jurors statement was as follows: We find that James Dellett, Jr. came to his death on early morning of January 20th between 12 and 1 A.M. from a gun shot wound willfully caused by John McNeal.

John McNeal remained in jail at Mount Holly from January 20, 1889, until the April Term of Court in 1889, and he was then brought to trial on April 20th for murder. He was described as a large man with sandy gray hair and beard, 54 years old, who had lived near Indian Mills a long time and was of an arguing nature.

James Dellett Jr. was described as of average height, thick set, about 48 years old, leaving a wife and three daughters, and living at the home of his father, James Dellett Sr., well known resident of the Indian Mills area for many years. Also living there was Ebenezer Cramer, an aged man described as a friend of the family.

During the trial, several witnesses appeared to give testimony. James K. Naylor, whose house was only 500 yards from McNeal's, said McNeal came to his home shortly after he shot Dellett, highly excited and crying, and explained the shooting to him.

Ira Crain, who lived about two miles from McNeal, stated that he went to McNeal's house the night of the shooting and observed that it was a bright moonlit night, but said it was impossible to identify anyone near the house due to the shadows cast by the many tall trees near the house.

Dun horse, one gray mare, one stud colt, a two-horse wagon,
one old light wagon, wagon harness, two harrows, one old
plough, one new plough, saddle and bridle, poultry, grind-stone
and crank, log chain, and two hives of bees.

This appears to reflect quite an active establishment.

Mary Cavileer apparently continued to operate the tavern for some time
after her husband's death. However, the 1849 map of Burlington County
shows J. Smith's Hotel at that place. A birth record filed in Shamong
Township March 6, 1858, for twins Richard and Anna Bozarth lists their residence as Hampton Gate and their father's occupation as innkeeper. A subsequent birth entry of October 26, 1859, for Isaac Bozarth also shows Andrew
Bozarth as an innkeeper, but this time his residence is listed as Flyatt.

The 1860 and 1876 maps of Burlington County merely list Hampton
Gate as Atsion Property. Exactly who, if anyone, operated the tavern after
1849 is problematic. Certainly the J. Smith shown on the 1849 map was not
Josiah Smith of Indian Mills but rather a son or relative of Mary Taylor
Smith. Perhaps the cartographer of the 1860 map was in error, for a
recorded deed of 1875 shows that Mahlon Prickett purchased the tavern
property from the heirs of David Cavileer and then in turn sold it to
Maurice Raleigh of Atsion in March 1878. From then on, it remained as
part of the Atsion holdings and eventually became part of the vast Wharton
State Forest.

No tangible remains of the tavern can be found today, and its precise
location remains a mystery. The approximate location would be at or near
the entrance or gate to the lane leading into Hampton Furnace. Some years
ago, the author walked this wooded trail from the furnace dam to Hampton
Gate along with his trusty Irish setter, Brandy. It is an arduous task at best,
the trail being overgrown with brambles and bull briars. The old road is
barely discernable today, being not more than a footpath in many places as
it makes its way from the old Tuckerton Stage Road.

As with so many historic sites in the Pines, only one's imagination can
suggest what once may have been, and only continued research will shed
new light on the many human stories that remain as mysteries in these won-
drous pinelands.

SMALL'S TAVERN AND HOTEL

The sole remaining tavern from the early 19th century that still stands in present-day Shamong Township was erected in 1830 by Israel Small. He had originally purchased the property from the estate of John King, deceased on June 13, 1818, for $184.93. When initially erected, the building served as a farmhouse, only later becoming a tavern and hotel.

On November 4, 1850, Israel Small sold the property to his son Benjamin for $1,000. Benjamin Small was licensed to operate a tavern there from 1855 to 1879, trading as Small's Inn. Thomas Crain purchased the property on April 19, 1879. It had been seized by the sheriff, Benjamin F. Lee, to satisfy a debt of $275.26. After all those years, the farm and tavern had passed from the Small family.

Ironically, Theodore Small was licensed there in 1881 trading as Hotel Shamong. Benjamin Small was also licensed there from 1855 to 1889. Theodore Small again was licensed in 1893. Perhaps the hotel and tavern still trading as Small's Hotel was being leased from the actual owner Thomas Crain.

While the hotel was under the ownership of Thomas Crain but under the proprietorship of Benjamin Small, a shocking set of circumstances

Carriage sheds that once stood to the rear of Small's Tavern. Now a miniature golf course has taken their place. (Photo by the author.)

Kemble's Inn was operated by Charles S. Kemble for many years. It was located on the main stage route from Eayrestown to Tuckerton. (Photo by the author.)

for the weary traveler as well as the stagecoach horses that carried them. One such place was at Oriental, also known as Naylor's Corner. This property faced the old Tuckerton Stage Road at its intersection with Taylortown Road, now known as Old Indian Mills Road. Isaac Wilkins originally purchased this property from the Indian Commissioners on January 20, 1803, and he later conveyed it to Joseph Naylor on October 12, 1825, who in turn conveyed one half part to his son John on October 22, 1825. Joseph Naylor had also bought 50 acres from Barzillai Branin and his wife, Susanna. The Branins had originally purchased this land, Lot #26 of the Indian Lands, from the Indian Commissioners on January 7, 1803.

A blacksmith shop once stood at the northwest corner of this intersection, with the Naylor home on the northeast corner. The home stood there as a landmark well into the 20th century. It has never been recorded as an inn or tavern, but it may have served in such a capacity or at least as a refreshment stop frequented by the stage drivers.

Early maps of 1849, 1858, 1860, and 1876 only record the Naylor home at or near this intersection, yet local traditions have also identified a home that

Naylor's Corner at Oriental. Building to the left was a blacksmith shop. The Naylor family occupied the two-story frame home in the center for many years. The home to the far right, in the background, is the only one standing today. (Photo courtesy of Rutgers University, Alexander Library, William Augustine Collection.)

still stands 600 feet east of Naylor's Corner as having been a stagecoach stop where passengers rested and changed to a fresh team of horses. This was also a store and post office known by the name of Oriental. The construction of this home, which includes barns and outbuildings, appears to be late 19th century, which would explain its absence from maps of an earlier day.

Another tradition persists regarding the old Oriental Road that once veered off Tuckerton Road a short distance past Naylor's corner on the south side of the road. In recent years, this unpaved road was vacated to accommodate a housing development, but it is believed to have once passed near a spring of fresh water where the stagecoach drivers may have watered their horses before proceeding out the Oriental Road back to the stage road. A portion of this old road begins again on the east side of Forked Neck Road and is called Oriental Road to this day.

CHAPTER 13
The Forges and Furnaces

ATSION

Charles Read was the pioneer ironmaster of the Pine Barrens. At one time he owned Batsto, Atsion, Aetna, and Taunton Ironworks. He had also been one of the Indian Commissioners who, in 1758, negotiated the purchase of land in Burlington County for the exclusive use of the natives as a reservation. The Indians then knew the land as Edgepillock.

Read subsequently purchased large tracts of land in the vicinity of the reservation, much of it bordering the reservation boundaries. An entrepreneur of the first order, in 1765 he erected a forge known as Atsion Forge.

Read was familiar with the names of the various native tribes in West Jersey, and the name Atsion must have appealed to him, although this particular group of Indians never actually lived in the immediate vicinity. The Atsion band, once numbering 200 warriors, was located near Crosswicks Creek in 1650. Cartographers of the 17th century corrupted the Algonquin word "achsin" meaning rock, and "onck" meaning place, into the word "atsayonk" or place of rocks. Read was a scholar and no doubt liked the sound of this word, which eventually became Atsion. The large quantities of bog ore may have resembled a "place of rocks," causing him to use this name, but this is only conjecture.

Read formed partnerships with David Ogden of Newark, and Lawrence Saltar of Nottingham, Burlington County, but always retained a controlling interest in Atsion. Saltar actually lived at Atsion and appears to have been in charge of the day-to-day operations of the forge. By 1770 there were four forge fires and numerous dwellings had been erected for the workmen.

Charles Read held various political offices, eventually rising to Chief Justice of the Supreme Court in New Jersey. But he had not planned well financially and was heavily in debt by this time. In March 1773 he sold his interest in Atsion Forge to Henry Drinker and Abel James of Philadelphia. His former partner David Ogden sold his interest to Lawrence Saltar and a new partnership was formed trading as the Atsion Company.

In the meantime, Read fled New Jersey, leaving countless creditors behind. A great man in his day, who had held numerous high offices and kept company with kings and royal governors, died a lonely, destitute individual in Martinburg, North Carolina, on December 27, 1774.

The new partners erected the first bog iron furnace at Atsion in 1774. A gristmill and three sawmills were also built around that time and the furnace community seemed to be prosperous. While Lawrence Saltar was manager of Atsion, he had his workers dig a canal from the Mechescatauxin Creek to the Atsion River. This canal, designed to improve the flow of water downstream that powered the forge and furnace apparatus, was the focus of many lawsuits. The now dry and overgrown canal bed is still visible today, which local inhabitants know as "Saltar's Ditch."

A 1930s aerial map of Atsion and surrounding area. The extensive farm fields are now covered in forest. Most of the buildings have disappeared. (Photo courtesy of Rutgers University, Alexander Library, William Augustine Collection.)

During the Revolutionary War the Atsion Company produced salt-evaporating pans and camp kettles, but there is no record of any cannonballs or shot being produced as at nearby Batsto, which had become one of the primary providers of munitions for Washington's Army. One possible reason munitions were not produced at Atsion was the pacifist influence of the Drinker family, who were strict Quakers.

Shortly after the war, in 1783, Lawrence Saltar died. Abel James declared bankruptcy in 1784 and Henry Drinker bought his share of the company. Henry Drinker and the Saltar heirs now controlled Atsion, which continued to prosper under their management for many years, though not without adversity. In 1794, after being destroyed by fire, the furnace was rebuilt at considerable cost.

In 1805 the Saltar heirs placed their share of Atsion on the auction block. The Atsion Estate then included some 20,000 acres of land. There were listed 19 houses for the workmen, a forge, furnace, gristmill, blacksmith shop, two sawmills, a dwelling house for the owner, and numerous outbuildings. Henry Drinker retained his half share in the estate, and his son-in-law Jacob Downing purchased the Saltar heirs' share. The community again seemed prosperous for many years, making a variety of household implements including kettles, stoves, firebacks, and anvils. By this time, a self-sufficient community of several hundred workers and their families depended on the Atsion Works for subsistence.

Hard times came again during 1815, and Jacob Downing eventually sold his half interest to Samuel Richards, the son of William Richards of Batsto, in 1819. By 1823 the Atsion Works were in ruins. A famous traveler of the day, John F. Watson, who was born at Batsto, gives a first-hand account of Atsion in his Annals of Philadelphia and Pennsylvania in the Olden Time. He records,

> was much interested to see the formidable ruins of Atsion Iron Works. They looked as picturesque as the ruins of abbeys, etc. in pictures. There were dams, forges, furnaces, storehouses, a dozen houses and lots for the workmen, and the whole comprising a town; a place once overwhelming the ear with the din of unceasing, ponderous hammers, or alarming the sight with fire and smoke, and smutty and sweating Vulcans. Now all is

hushed, no wheels turn, no fires blaze, the houses are unroofed, and the frames, etc. have fallen down and not a foot of the busy workmen is seen.

If J. F. Watson were to pass through Atsion today he would find even more desolation than he did in 1823.

Samuel Richards purchased the Atsion property following Jacob Downing's death in 1823. He created an entirely new forge and furnace community that traded under the name, The Atsion Company. Richards rebuilt Atsion by erecting a large mansion house in 1826, a store to service the community with all sorts of supplies in 1827, and a community church in 1828. The Richards regime prospered for many years and the social elite of Philadelphia were entertained at the Richards Mansion on many an occasion.

At one time the village store had a large cupola on the roof, and some historians have entertained the notion that this was a belfry to summon the men to work or to sound an alarm. No records have come to light to support

Photo of Atsion Mansion taken by N. R. Ewan in 1948. (Photo courtesy of Burlington County Historical Society, N. R. Ewan Collection.)

this theory. The noted folklorist Henry Beck had questioned a lifelong resident, James M. Armstrong, in the 1930s, who lived just down the Atsion Road from the store. Armstrong had never heard of a bell atop the store and neither had his father, William K. Armstrong, who had lived in the area since the store was built. Supplies were once stored in the loft, as evidenced by the large door in the eaves at the front of the building, it has been suggested that this cupola was merely built to provide ventilation and not intended as a belfry.

Atsion Store with cupola before restoration by the State of New Jersey.
Note the building had been smooth coated over Jersey sandstone construction.
(Photo courtesy of Ruth Etheridge Gerber.)

Restoration by the State of New Jersey has removed the cupola altogether. If it were not for old photographs of the store and the fading memories of some of the older residents, a passerby would never know it existed. Such is progress, but we do have the bathing beach to admire across the highway.

The Richards Mansion, the village store, the small white community church, and a worker's home (now used as a deer-hunting clubhouse) are all that remain of the Samuel Richards era on the north side of the river. There

Atsion Store as it appears today. It has been used as a Forest Ranger Station for many years. (Photo by the author.)

is also the ruin of a small worker's cottage, which remains hidden in the trees down by the river and almost directly across the river from the furnace location. A large brick open-hearth fireplace still stands in the ruins of this one-room cabin. It, too, may possibly be from the Richards era or even earlier.

On the south side of the Atsion River along the raceway of the former paper mill ruins, stands a slab-sheathed house that was erected during the 1870s. Since the passing of Mrs. Rose Lane in 2003, it lies vacant, and there are no immediate plans for its future use. Mrs. Lane had rented this small home for more than 50 years and, in effect, prevented it from being destroyed by vandalism and arson, a fate that has befallen many of the nearby buildings.

Samuel Richards died January 4, 1842, and with him also went the future of the ironworks at Atsion. The bog iron furnace communities throughout South Jersey gradually began to fail, yielding to competition from the Pennsylvania anthracite furnaces. The Atsion Estate was left to Samuel

Ruins of a worker's cabin on the north side of Atsion River. There were once at least six of these in the area. The remains of pilings for a small foot-bridge may still be seen in the river at this point. (Photo by the author.)

Slab-sheathed house, circa 1870, in foreground. An early view of the cotton mill is in the background. The small frame building in front of the mill was a blacksmith shop. (Photo courtesy of Catherine Morris Wright, a granddaughter of Joseph Wharton.)

199

Richards's two children. William Henry Richards, who had no interest in his father's business ventures, moved down Atsion Road where he lived the life of a farmer and country gentleman. Maria Lawrence Fleming, Richards's married daughter, and her husband, William Walton Fleming, moved into the mansion house, which they used primarily in the summer months, maintaining a home in Philadelphia the rest of the year. They attempted to continue the iron business at Atsion but this was doomed to failure. Fleming then built a paper mill near the site of the old iron furnace. It was a two-story construction of native Jersey sandstone and bog iron, possibly built in part from the ruins of the furnace.

The precise location of this early bog iron furnace had eluded historians for many years. A short distance behind the paper mill, just east of its foundation, are the remains of the furnace's last blast with huge slag heaps and molten debris littering a small area. While doing research in the Gloucester County Courthouse in Woodbury, New Jersey, during the late 1970s, the author came across records detailing the location of Atsion Furnace. The record, which appears in *The Boundary & Divisions Book B,* pages 302, 303, and 304 in the Gloucester County Clerks office, is dated June 1834. It reads,

> Beginning at a stake in the middle of the main water course of a branch of Little Egg Harbor River, called Atsion Branch, which is the line between the counties of Gloucester and Burlington and runs from thence on a course of South 44 degrees and 45 minutes west, the following intermedial distances to wit: 2 chains to a furnace stone, planted on the shore, from which stone the easterly course of the Chimney of Atsion Furnace, bears south 1 degree and 25 minutes east, the southwesterly corner of Samuel Richards Mansion House bears north 22 degrees and 35 minutes west, the southeasterly corner of the church or meeting house bears north 63 degrees and 45 minutes east, and the westerly corner of the grist mill bears north 49 degrees and 45 minutes west, thence from said stone, 6 chains to the Race going to the Furnace, thence 1 chain to the house where John Mingin lives, the line striking about 1 foot on the

southeast corner of said house, thence 12 chains and 50 links to
a stone on the northwest side of the road leading from Atsion
to Israel Chews.

On the first clear day, after obtaining this information, the author and
fellow members of the Indian Mills Historical Society, Don Catts and Bob
Jones, proceeded to Atsion. Catts was a professional surveyor, and with his
help, we were able to follow the coordinates as directed in the records and
pinpointed the location of the furnace stack. It was, as presumed, just a
short distance east of the paper mill ruins.

Economic conditions were in decline after Maria and William Walton
Fleming attempted to revive the community with the paper mill venture,
collapsing around 1855. William was heavily in debt and fled the country
to Belgium, where he was later joined by Maria after a lengthy search. They
never returned, instead living out their days in Belgium.

The Richards's estate was finally sold in 1861 by the numerous creditors
to a land speculator named Jarvis Mason, who sold it a year later to Colonel
William C. Patterson at a handsome profit. Patterson created a company
called the Fruitland Improvement Co., which he formed to initiate a large-
scale real estate development, almost unheard of in those days. This
planned community, which was to be known as Fruitland, never got off the
ground financially and Patterson went bankrupt. The estate, then consisting of the mansion house, store, four barns, 12 tenant houses, one gristmill,
two sawmills, and a paper mill with no fixtures or machinery was sold in
1871. It is doubtful the paper mill ever went into operation. The description
of livestock listed in the auction brochure describes in more detail how
extensive the farm property was. There were 23 Alderney cows and heifers,
eight bulls, 25 cows and heifers, one stallion, 16 horses, mares, and colts, as
well as 65 boars, hogs, sows, and pigs. Seven hundred acres of cultivated
land was also listed, and it is hard even to imagine such a widespread use of
this land at the present day.

The Atsion property was purchased by Maurice Raleigh on May 10, 1871,
for $48,200. Raleigh immediately began the rebuilding process. He greatly
enlarged the paper mill to four stories, with massive additions, and turned it
into a cotton mill. He is also credited with erecting the first public school at

Atsion, in 1872. The cotton mill eventually employed 170 persons. By this time, the railroads were in operation, bringing goods to and from Atsion; the venture was profitable. The cotton mill is said to have produced 500 pounds of yarn per week. On January 10, 1882, at the height of his success at Atsion, Maurice Raleigh died.

The earliest section of the cotton mill is to the right. Stone from the ruins of Atsion Furnace, which stood nearby, probably were used in its construction. Note the brick arch for the mill raceway. (Photo taken in early 1900s, courtesy of Indian Mills Historical Society.)

Raleigh's heirs attempted to continue the operation of the cotton mill but the business declined, and was forced to close in 1883. His heirs attempted another real estate venture, selling a small number of lots along the north shore of Atsion Lake. Most of the homes standing there today date from that period.

In 1892 Joseph Wharton bought the old Atsion Estate and added it to his already extensive holdings throughout the Pine Barrens. The cotton mill was then converted into a cranberry sorting house and remained so well into the 20th century.

The State of New Jersey purchased the Atsion Estate along with the rest of the massive Wharton Estate in the mid 1950s. Since then, the Etheridge House, long used as the manager's house, and built about 1830, was severely vandalized and then torched by an arsonist. The cotton mill was slated to be torn down by the State of New Jersey, which was spared the effort when the building fell victim to another arsonist's torch on March 27, 1977. All but one of the railroad era homes were torn down. This lone reminder of

A later view of the cotton mill, in 1974, and one of the last before arson destroyed the mill in 1977. (Photo courtesy of Indian Mills Historical Society.)

another day now stands surrounded by fencing and barbed wire. It may fall down of its own accord due to lack of preservation. What remains of this once thriving community is only a small reminder of what once had flourished there.

Miraculously the village store, now a forest ranger's station, the mansion house, the slab-sheathed house, a gun club, church, and schoolhouse are all that is left. The mansion house is one of the finest examples of Greek Revival architecture in America. The exterior was partially restored many years ago. The interior, which exemplifies the manor house of an early iron-master, continues to deteriorate, and the remaining buildings are prime targets for vandalism and arson. What a sad commentary on our commitment to preservation.

The history of Atsion has been well documented and recorded in many excellent books and pamphlets. The written word may help in some measure

Ruins of the gristmill with Atsion Mansion in the background.
(Photo courtesy of Clyde LeVan.)

to replace the wanton destruction of this treasured place. Personal recollec-tions of those who called Atsion home have also added immeasurably to Atsion's history.

John Jennings once told the author that his grandfather, John Clyde Jennings, was the last miller at Atsion before the gristmill was struck by lightning and burned to the ground. Today the ruins lie partially beneath the modern highway Route 206 and a portion of the foundation can still be found along the embankment.

Anna Hyland was born in Atsion, the daughter of George and Irene Hyland, in the building now owned by the Gloucester Stag Deer Club. She married George Cavileer, who was born in 1888 and died in 1964. He and his forebears, back numerous generations, were from Lower Bank. In 1924 Cavileer built the first gas station in New Jersey, which he and his wife oper-ated along with a breakfast bar for many years at a place called Dutchtown a short distance below Atsion. Anna recalls that her mother, in addition to

The Ice House on Atsion Lake, circa early 1900s. (Photo courtesy of Everett F. Mickle.)

working in the mill, was a dressmaker, a midwife, and an undertaker's helper. In the old days ice was cut on Atsion Lake and shipped by train. Anna remembers going with her mother to ice a corpse in the days when ice was the embalming medium. "I said to my mother, you know what? Supposing I'm afraid. She said, I never want you to be afraid of anything or anybody, and I never was."

Anna went to work after grammar school, pulling brush from the cranberry bogs, sorting cranberries, and cutting wood. "We all worked hard but we had everything we wanted and my family liked to work." George, her husband, at one time worked on the railroad in Bridgeton and was also employed by the DuPont plant near Pennsgrove. Above all, he was a sportsman trapping fox, coon, muskrat, and skunk for fur, and guiding hunters to deer. Anna cooked for the hunters, sometimes as many as 125 of them. "Big pots of cabbage, potatoes, and soup. A lot of deer too. Everybody cooked deer. Coon was very rich, otters were hard to catch. Their fur was worth a lot of money. They'd tear the dams apart and take the water off the bogs."

Anna's brother-in-law Samuel Cavileer was concerned about the declining number of snapping turtles, so he gathered up their eggs and buried

The concrete horse barn constructed during the Wharton era, photo circa 1930s.
(Photo courtesy of Lillian Bozearth.)

them in the sugar sand. "I'd see 75 or 80 snappers, each with one grain of sand on its back."

In continuing conversations with Gail Currier of Indian Mills, Anna recalled that James LeMunyon had a wagon shed at the railroad crossing on Quaker Bridge Road. There was a cow barn next to the large concrete horse barn.

There was a beautiful chestnut pegged wheel, which was used to generate power, under the raceway of the cotton mill. It was quite large in size, approximately 12 feet across. John Etheridge tore that part of the mill down and sold the equipment. Anna recalled several homes on Quaker Bridge Road past the railroad tracks toward Stone Bridge. There was the Spangler home, the William Hyland home, the home of a Mrs. Jones, and the Jacob Claypool home. The slab-sheathed log cabin home, long occupied by Mrs. Lane, was referred to as the Race House and used for Sunday school classes.

She described the railroad spur to Atco as coming very near the icehouse on Atsion Lake so the cut ice could be loaded and packed in sawdust for shipping all over New Jersey and New York. When the ice business ceased to be profitable, it closed down. The manager's home next to the icehouse was used as a dance hall with bands coming to play from as far away as Hammonton.

The elder Clement Miller once told the author of a large field on Atsion Road that is now all in trees. It was called "fills field" and consisted of a house, barns, and stables where a tenant took care of the horses and cattle for the people at Atsion.

In 1973 Gail Currier also had a conversation with Mrs. Helen Bailey, who had spent her summers in one of the Atsion worker's homes for well over 65 years. (She still had the rent receipts from Leeson Small, the rent collector for the Wharton Estate.) Mrs. Bailey recalled that there were at least four double homes, all unheated. She also remembered the site of an old iron forge two or three streams back in the woods, though couldn't recall the precise location.

Ruth Etheridge Gerber, daughter of John Etheridge and granddaughter of Andrew Etheridge, remembered many of her childhood days at Atsion in conversations with Gail Currier. She described an open-air dance hall on

Photo of a railroad era worker's home taken in 1974. Only one
of at least six homes is now left standing and lies on the verge of destruction.
(Photo courtesy of Indian Mills Historical Society.)

Quaker Bridge Road, a short distance past the church. Even as a small child she remembered that many fine dances were held there. As did Anna Cavileer, she described a silver-color water wheel lying on the ground very close to the cabin where Mrs. Lane lived near the mill raceway. She recalled the blacksmith shop was near Mrs. Lane's cabin and was quite a large building.

Ruth recalls that there was once a general store a short distance behind the present ranger's station. The ruins could still be seen and the foundation was there for many years. Ruth said,

> My grandfather, Andrew Etheridge, was caretaker of Atsion from 1890 till his death in 1925. My grandmother was Phoebe Leek Etheridge of Batsto. My uncle, Leeson Small, married Bertha Etheridge and became caretaker of Atsion in 1925. My

aunt, Mamie Etheridge, was bookkeeper for the Wharton Estate
for 50 years. She also kept the store books for many years. She
recalled the old cotton mill being a busy place during cranberry
season when all the berries were being sorted and packed.

When the Phillips family lived at Atsion their house stood
directly across from the railroad station at Atsion. It was also
known as the Lantry house. My aunt Rachey Bareford would
meet the mail train and take the mail to the post office. At the
top of the hill, coming from Quaker Bridge Road were the
remains of the old gristmill. There was no electricity at Atsion,
till 1937, till then all our lights were kerosene. The general
store at Atsion was kept supplied by some local merchants, feed
from Kirby Bros. of Medford, and Freihofer Bread. There were
barrels of beans and flour, beautiful yard goods, and especially
the Coca-Cola trucks.

*The caretaker's home at Atsion in 1928 where the Etheridge family lived for
many years. It is now just a cherished memory having succumbed to wanton
neglect and vandalism. (Photo courtesy of Clyde LeVan.)*

For several years in the early 1970s, Gail Currier received letters from Helen Phillips of Red Bank, recalling many of her memories of Atsion and Indian Mills, and also stating in part,

> My father Hugh J. Phillips, Sr. was born March 16, 1868 at Indian Mills. His parents, Mr. and Mrs. John Phillips, owned a large farmhouse with a wide front porch completely across the front of it. It stood just north of the Gardner Farm. There was a crossroads between the two farms. There was some kind of a meeting house or church on the southwest corner. My father insisted he knew more than his teachers did so he left school at 13 years of age and went to work on the railroad. He worked his way up from section foreman to supervisor, and then to maintenance superintendent of the Central Railroad from Greenwich near Delaware Bay to Jersey City. In the 1930s his diabetes became so severe he had to have both legs amputated which forced his retirement.

The family had been living in a large home in Red Bank but Hugh Phillips wanted to go to Atsion.

> No one of us argued with him. We all knew he had owned 200 acres of Pine Barrens since a boy principally to grow cranberries. My father was now wheelchair bound and had to have a young man drive us to Atsion. On arrival there he asked John Etheridge, the stationmaster, if there were any houses for sale in Atsion. John pointed to the old Atsion Hotel across the tracks from the station. My father found the owner and immediately bought it. After that every spring and fall we had to go to Atsion, in spring to have the weeds pulled, and in the autumn to have the cranberries picked, packed, and shipped to Philadelphia. This went on every year until he died March 14, 1943.

The Atsion Hotel once located across the tracks from the railroad station.
(Photo courtesy of Orville Wright.)

In subsequent letters, Helen Phillips remembered Hobart Gardner buying the old Atsion railroad station while they were living at the Atsion Hotel property.

> He later moved it to his farm in Indian Mills. When my mother died, the State of New Jersey bought our house and my father's 200 acres of cranberry bogs. The state tore down the old house or Atsion Hotel and left barren land there to add to their pine barrens.

In another letter, Dr. Helen Phillips states,

> I think my father bought the cranberry bogs when he was 14 years old. About 80 acres he bought as a young man approximately 1-1/2 to 2 miles east of the railroad crossing on Quaker Bridge Road, east of the Etheridge House and the old school.

Atsion Railroad Station as it appeared in the early 1900s. It was later moved to the Gardner Farm in Indian Mills where it was used to house migrant workers. It was eventually dismantled. (Photo courtesy of Everett F. Mickle.)

His bogs were called Stone Bridge Bogs. This was along the north side of the road and named for the bridge that goes across a branch of the Mullica River there, the Old Bogs and Banjo Jack Bog. Many years later, with Anthony Tassone Sr., the fore-man of the Atsion gang on the Central Railroad, he bought the Abe Woolman Bogs on the east side of the state highway, north of Atsion Village. My father sold some of his bogs to Anthony Tassone Sr., although Tony never owned any part of the Quaker Bridge Road bogs. He and his children worked there for my father. Tony owned a half share of the Abe Woolman Bogs on Route 206.

In further remarks about Atsion, she recalls,

Home was the Atsion Hotel. My father had extensive remod-eling done there. A bar was on the first floor for the cranberry workers. My mother died in 1958. Atsion property was left to their nephew.

Dr. Phillips stated she had the Atsion Mansion furniture in her living room in Red Bank. Her parents bought it at the Wharton Estate sale. Lewis Shrider gave it to her years ago from the old Shrider farmhouse. Kathryn Phillips Shrider was their grandmother. Their homestead was the first home heading west on Stokes Road from Red Men's Hall.

Perhaps the day will come when once again the Atsion Estate will be restored to its former splendor. At the very least, the old Richards Mansion and schoolhouse should be preserved, opened to the public, and enjoyed by future generations. Both would provide an excellent location for museums dedicated to the history of Atsion Village and the early iron industry in the Pines.

HAMPTON FURNACE AND FORGE

Few maps today chart the location of Hampton Furnace, once a thriving iron industry for many years. Those who wish to venture there should take the old Shamong Trail, once a famed Indian trail, now known as Stokes Road. Approaching Route 206, you bear right and travel south until you come to a gravel road on the left, just north of Atsion. This is the Hampton Furnace Road and easily traversed in dry weather, although the going can be a bit rough after heavy rains or snow.

Turning off Route 206, you are at once plunged into the serenity and stillness of pine and cedar that form a straight corridor for more than a mile. During this course, you will pass the old Shamong Trail as it crosses Hampton Furnace Road heading for Quaker Bridge. The Shamong Trail is rarely traveled in this section except by the most ardent of Pine Barrens enthusiasts. After proceeding farther you cross the bridge at Springers Brook and then the road bears sharply to the left. After a short distance you bear to the right, crossing the bridge at Deep Run. (The Deep Run Bogs community once flourished here for many years.) The road then remains straight for approximately one mile through the Pines. Many deserted cranberry bogs

*Deep Run cranberry bogs on the road to Hampton Furnace of Rt. 206,
circa 1920. Workers' homes can be seen in the background.*
(Photo courtesy of Ruth Etheridge Gerber.)

are frequently seen. There were once a number of homes for workers here as well, but they disappeared many years ago.

The road turns left again, and you are at once amazed at the change in terrain and foliage. You enter a large clearing scattered with century-old sycamore trees and overgrown with tall Indian grass. A sense of foreboding seems to fill the air, and you may feel you are taking a giant step into the past. This was once the Village of Hampton Furnace. Clayton Earl and Richard Stockton, who purchased the land from Restore and Mary Shinn, built the furnace in 1795. Later the property passed to George and William Ashbridge. William bought his brother's share in 1810, and then was sole proprietor of the furnace for many years until his death in 1824. A newspaper advertisement of the sale provides a more vivid description of the place.

> The property contains about 20,000 acres of land adjoining
> lands of Batsto and Atsion. There has been erected on the prem-
> ises a large Mansion House and Furnace, two Forges, a Grist and
> Sawmill, also stabling sufficient to accommodate four teams of
> horses, and a number of dwelling houses for the workmen.

Samuel Richards obtained ownership in February 1825 and added Hampton to his other extensive holdings. The furnace had burned and was not repaired. The Hampton Forge, however, was rebuilt and operated until around 1850 as part of the Atsion Works.

The Lower Forge, also known as Washington Forge, was another of the iron forges that operated in conjunction with Atsion. It was located a short distance above Quaker Bridge on the Batsto River downstream from Hampton. A visit to Washington Forge still reveals the remnants of a dam over the river and a woods road from the west near Stone Bridge that dead-ends these days at the water's edge. There remains the telltale evidence of a settlement here. Once pieces of bar iron could be readily found near the dam. They characteristically showed no signs of rust, even after more than 100 years.

Continuing the journey through Hampton Furnace, one finds that the forest has reclaimed this once sizeable community. Cellar holes and remnants of the cranberry workers' homes are evident. These are of later construction, having been built, most likely, after 1850. The mortar between the bog iron foundation stones reveals that crushed slag was used in the mixture. The road lined with crushed slag and cinder of furnace days, continues across the dam of the Batsto River where, to the left of the dam, one beholds the furnace pond that once provided waterpower for the bellows of the furnace. The pond was later a cranberry bog, and today it is overgrown with cedar, maple, and oak saplings. To the right stood the furnace stack, although no structure remains. The only evidence of the furnace are the huge slag banks extending on both sides of the Batsto River for some 200 feet.

Across the dam and to the right are the ruins of the Ryder and Wilkerson cranberry-sorting house that once kept lonely vigil of the surrounding area. Ryder and Wilkerson once owned and managed their cranberry business here for more than 50 years. Three generations of the Wells and Kell families made their home here when working and managing the bogs for the Ryder and Wilkinson families, who also owned Deep Run Bogs nearby.

To the rear of the sorting house ruins are abandoned grape arbors and vines that have been a delight to the local deer population judging by the tracks and droppings there. In front of the sorting house is an intersection of several roads. To the left, the road leads to Hampton Gate and the old Tuckerton Stage Road, where furnace products were once hauled by teams to landing places in Lumberton. The road to the right leads a short distance to the Hampton Forge with its tumbled down dam. Forge slag littering the ground is noticeable, contrasted to the slag found at the furnace site. Forge slag appears more as burnt cinders or ash. Furnace slag has the appearance of molten glass. To the left of the road is the Forge Pond created from the Roberts and Skit branches of the Batsto River. This pond once provided waterpower for the forge hammers, but is now drained, revealing acres of marsh and Indian grass and abounding with beaver and muskrat.

Brief comments about Hampton Furnace appear in Henry C. Beck's books. Beck mentions a cemetery of wooden tombstones and ruins of furnace workers' homes, but these could not be located in the 1930s, and their exact location continues to elude the author.

Wagon axles, flat and round bar iron, kettles, skillets, and hollow ware were made here until the industry closed around 1850 due to competition

A pig of iron from Hampton Furnace. (Photo by the author.)

216

from Pennsylvania iron furnaces. The industry of cranberry growers, who prospered here for many years, replaced the iron furnace community.

What was once a thriving and industrious community is now a place of desolation. There is hardly any evidence of the many facets of the iron industry that flourished here for so many years. The furnace tract is now part of the extensive Wharton State Forest and perhaps in time will be developed for some historical purpose. For the moment, the area remains as it is, with its eerie yet beautiful stillness that so exemplifies these marvelous pinelands of South Jersey.

CHAPTER 14

The Sawmills and Gristmills

The earliest known sawmill in Shamong Township appears to have been located on Mekendum (Muskingum) Brook around 1717 near the head of present-day Indian Mills Lake. Little is known about the owners of this mill. At that early date, it would have been of primitive origin and very crude, with the sawing likely done over a pit with one man down in the pit guiding the saw and the another on top of the log that straddled the pit. Such operations were eventually improved to incorporate a more modern "up and down sawmill," using water power to drive the saw vertically. These old sawmills created huge amounts of sawdust, remnants of which have been found in very remote areas of the pines. Blueberry farmers, leaving little evidence behind, carted much of the sawdust away over the years using it as mulch around the blueberry bushes.

INDIAN SAWMILL

The reservation Indians operated a sawmill for many years near the dam at the pond behind the Indian Mills firehouse, referred to as the Sawmill Pond, even to this day. Following the exodus of the Indians in 1802, the sawmill was purchased by Josiah Foster at the reservation auction. But Foster only retained it for a short while before selling the property to Samuel Reeves in October 1803, with sawmill and improvements. This was the same mill mentioned in the autobiography of James Still. Still tells of his father, Levin Still, living and working at the Indian Mill owned by Samuel Reeve. When Reeve (sometimes recorded as Reeves) died, there was considerable litigation by the heirs, as he died without a will. This seemed to be a common occurrence in those days. Commissioners were appointed to divide the Indian Mill Tract and the estate, including the sawmill and dwelling house, which were finally sold to Eber Engle on March 16, 1824.

In a subsequent sale, the deed mentions a sawmill that had recently undergone a thorough repair. Eber Engle died intestate and the property again passed to the highest bidder, Godfrey Hancock, in 1841. Hancock sold the sawmill and other buildings to William A. Woolman, on March 20, 1847.

Nicholas Sooy Thompson purchased the mill tract at a sheriff's sale on October 4, 1851. The defendants were William A. Woolman and Maria, his wife, and John M. Christopher. The sawmill tract next passed to Joseph S. Thompson when commissioners sold the estate of Nicholas Sooy Thompson, who died intestate. The sale took place on September 8, 1856. The property was described as,

> The Farm and Saw Mill property containing 198 acres of land. The Saw Mill is in good running order, and capable of cutting a large amount of lumber during the year. There are upon the property a good comfortable two story Dwelling House, Barns, three Tenant Houses, and a Blacksmith Shop. This land is of excellent quality, about 40 acres of which is cleared, the residue is handsome Young Oak Timber, excepting what is occupied by the Mill Pond.

It was sold again to Josephus Sooy Jr. on November 14, 1863, and later passed by Sheriff's sale to Charles Gaskill on July 29, 1876.

Under the proprietorship of Charles Gaskill, the sawmill flourished and was one of the busiest mills of its kind in Burlington County. However, adversity seems to have plagued this mill, as the tract including water power, sawmill, and 197 acres was again sold at a sheriff's sale on March 20, 1886, and passed to Levi B. Woolman, Albert W. Woolman, and Catherine, his wife.

The sawmill remained in the Woolman family for many years before finally passing through a Master's Sale, Chancery Court, State of New Jersey, on the complaint of Sara Wright against Anna Shinsky and others dated November 5, 1919. Benjamin Mingin was the highest bidder. The sale was actually held in Abraham Woolman's old cranberry house on January 21, 1920. This old cranberry-sorting house was later converted into a private dwelling and still stands on Burnt House Road. During the ownership by the Woolman brothers, their home burned down and a new one was erected in its place.

Benjamin Mingin may have been the last proprietor of the sawmill before it burned to the ground early in the 1920s. Mingin died on August 21, 1927, and in his will bequeathed the sawmill tract to Isaac N. B. Wright. On September 4, 1935, Isaac Wright and Amanda, his wife, deeded the tract to the Cinnaminson Bank and Trust Co.

Site of the original Indian sawmill. Photo depicts the sawmill that took its place and operated in the 20th century. (Photo courtesy of Frederick Miller.)

The sawmill property subsequently changed hands many times up to the present day. Homes were erected on the south shore of the mill pond, very near the ancient Indian burial ground that lies on the south banks of the pond.

Goshen Sawmill

Another sawmill was located near the main stage road from Philadelphia to Atsion a short distance east of where it crosses the upper reaches of the Mullica. James Inskeep owned the sawmill for a time during the mid-1700s. Inskeep later sold the property to Charles Read of Atsion in 1765, but he only deeded the rights to dig ore in the vicinity and not the sawmill itself. In John Hunt's diary of the 1770s, he mentions a small settlement of homes at Goshen. Traces of the mill raceway and scattered fragments of brick and stone can still be seen at this site, but all else has vanished.

There were numerous other sawmills throughout the Shamong area, at the Atsion Village as well as at Hampton Furnace. Bard's Mill Branch of the Batsto River got its name from a sawmill run by Bennet Bard in 1739, though nothing remains to identify the site.

Friendship Sawmill in present-day Tabernacle Township was located near the YWCA Camp known as Inawendewin. William Burr operated this mill in 1795 and a small settlement of homes was located here. Nearby, an early boundary stone for Southampton, Shamong, and Woodland Townships can be found, placed there prior to the formation of Tabernacle Township in 1901.

Boundary stone where Shamong, Woodland, and Southampton Townships meet, located at Friendship. (Photo by the author.)

LITTLE MILL

The area that today comprises the Goshen Pond campground off Atsion Road once boasted a sawmill along with a small settlement of homes. No more remains in testimony other than a few scattered bricks and fieldstones. This operation is not to be confused with the Goshen Mill, which was located further upstream. Little Mill is mentioned many times in the Shamong Registrar's records.

In 1765, Thomas and Tanton Earl were operating the Mount Skitt Sawmill, located where the Roberts branch and Skit branch of the Batsto River meet deep in the pinelands, close to the Hampton Furnace tract.

There were many charcoal kilns at Sandy Ridge off Carranza Road in the old days, and a sawmill also operated there into the 1920s. In later years, it was steam powered. The workmen lived in small tarpaper shacks and eked out a meager existence far back in the woods. It was a lonely life with little time off for leisure activity.

Many more unnamed sawmills existed in the Pines of Shamong and Tabernacle Townships. At one time, sawmills were commonplace as the only

Charcoal kilns that once dominated Sandy Ridge.
(Photo courtesy of Ruth Gerber.)

source of lumber to build homes, other than a log home. It is not uncommon when hiking through the Pines to occasionally come across piles of shavings, sawdust, the occasional brick, a few hand wrought nails, and fragments of crockery or bottle glass, indicating the site of an undocumented mill.

ATSION GRISTMILL

A three-story gristmill once stood near the dam where Route 206 crosses the Atsion River. Early in the 20th century, this mill, which was built in the 1830s, was struck by lightning and burned. Some ruins and foundation stones of bog iron are still visible at the eastern edge of the highway near the bridge and toward the Richards Mansion. At one time additional water-power was provided by Wesicamen Creek, which flows into the river nearby.

The Atsion Gristmill appears to the left of the photo
in the background. (Photo courtesy of Lillian Bozearth.)

INDIAN GRISTMILL

The Brotherton Indians had a gristmill at the head of Indian Mills Lake, which for many years was known as the Gristmill Pond. It had initially pro-vided a source of income for the natives in processing cornmeal and flour for area settlers, but after being burned down in 1762, the mill was not replaced. It may have been there prior to the founding of the reservation in 1758 but was most likely erected by the colonial government for the Indians' use, to encourage them to be self-sufficient.

The milldam had apparently survived the gristmill fire of 1762 and was probably reconstructed and improved upon after the demise of the Brotherton Reservation in 1802.

The gristmill property was auctioned off at the general sale of the reservation lands at the tavern of John Piper in 1802. Stacy Haines of Chester Township purchased the property known as Lot #21. The property deed describes the location of the old milldam as near the forks of the road corner to Lots #21 and #14 between the two mill seats. An equal half part was also sold to Aaron Engle and wife. Stacy Haines and his wife, Susanna, and Aaron Engle and his wife, Esther, jointly sold the property to Thomas Bedford on September 22, 1806. Bedford, a Philadelphia accountant, and his wife, Jane, then sold the property to Joseph A. Bedford, also of Philadelphia. The relationship between these Bedfords is not shown. The deed was recorded September 24, 1807.

An interesting agreement recorded on October 10, 1804 (and a related agreement dated January 23, 1807), between Thomas Bedford and a man named John Murphy refers to the building of a sawmill and a gristmill on this tract of land as a joint concern, and mentions the premises already standing. Joseph A. Bedford was entitled to one-fourth part of the profits of said sawmill and gristmill for a specified time between the dates of the agreements mentioned.

Thomas and Joseph Bedford, both residents of Philadelphia, apparently did not live here, but did own the property. John Murphy was most likely the proprietor and lived in the dwelling house, serving as operator of the mills. This home is still standing, and facing it from the road is the left hand portion of the two-story frame dwelling, erected circa 1805. This is the oldest existing house in Shamong Township. The right hand portion was added in 1835. Many early deeds of the period refer to the present day Indian Mills–Medford Road as the road to Bedford Mills and also as the Murphy Road. Because there were no established villages in the area of the gristmill, the names of the roads simply referred to the owners of the mill.

Looking west on Willow Grove Road. A portion of the Indian Gristmill is on the far right. Photo was taken when Benjamin Mingin operated the mill. His home is in the right center partially hidden by trees. (Photo courtesy of Edna Hagerthey Madden.)

Joseph A. Bedford died in 1814, leaving the property to his widow, Ann Bedford, and children, Thomas, Susanne, Isaac, and Sarah Bedford. The Bedford family continued to operate the sawmill and gristmill complex for many years under the name Bedford Mills.

On April 15, 1833, Ebenezer Engle bought the gristmill from the executors of Ann Bedford. In 1835 he erected a large addition to the two-story frame dwelling that had stood since 1805. The entire building stands today with the twin chimneys at the eastern end.

Nicholas Sooy Thompson of Mullica Township purchased the property from the executors of Ebenezer Engle, who died intestate. The property had been advertised in local papers for one month prior to the sale on December 7, 1841. The deed was recorded February 1842. The tract at the time included a gristmill, sawmill, and dwelling house on 100 acres of land. Nicholas S. Thompson died intestate, and his executors sold the property to his son Edward T. Thompson at public auction on September 8, 1856.

The sale was advertised in two newspapers, the *New Jersey Mirror* and *Burlington County Advertiser*, and also the *Mount Holly Herald* each week for four weeks prior to the sale. The mill property is described thus:

> Grist Mill and Water Power. The Homestead Farm contains 132 acres of land, about 40 acres of which is in a high state of cultivation. The residue is in young Cedar Timber and Mill Pond. The Grist Mill is of modern build, and lately put in good repair, with 2 run of Stones, and a never failing stream of water. The Dwelling House is a large two-story Frame Dwelling with 4 rooms on a floor, Kitchen adjoining, new Store House, Barn, and other necessary out buildings, together with a Tenant House, all of which are in good repair. Also a thrifty young Apple Orchard.

The "two run of stones" described in the 1856 newspaper ad shows this to have been a well-equipped mill. A "run of stones" refers to a pair of millstones.

The three-story gristmill that once stood at the head of Indian Mills Lake.
Note the millstones on the ground to the left of the mill.
(Photo from the Charles Philhower Collection.)

227

The lower stone was stationary while the upper one revolved on top of it, causing a grinding action. This mill with two runs would have had four mill-stones, their size anywhere from 6 inches to 2 feet in thickness. No one seems to know what happened to these stones after the mill burned down in the early 20th century.

During Edward Thompson's ownership, he had the sawmill and gristmill as well as a small store and post office located in the older portion of his home. On November 26, 1877, the property was sold to James Jacquette of Camden, who resold it to William Stiles of Camden the same day.

George Taylor purchased the property from William Stiles on March 14, 1881, and continued to run the mills and store until June 30, 1896, when the property was sold to Benjamin J. Mingin. The deed mentions the road leading from Aetna Mills (now Medford Lakes) to late Bedford Mills. The end of the mill came in the form of a fire during the early 1900s while it was under Mingin's ownership.

Home of Frank Gaskill once located across the road from the Mingin Gristmill. He once operated a steam-powered mill to the rear of his home on Muckingom Brook. (Photo courtesy of Edna Hagerthey Madden.)

After Mingin's death on August 21, 1927, the executors sold the property to P. Anthony Colasordo of Hammonton. Colasordo turned the millpond into a cranberry bog, which operated well into the 20th century. In the intervening years, the property has been sold, resold, and divided many times.

All that remains today of the once elaborate gristmill complex is the mansion house, which stands vigil near the dam at Indian Mills Lake. The modern garage next to the home sits at the approximate location of the gristmill. During severe storms in the early 1980s, the dam overflowed and exposed what had been the mill raceway between the garage and the mansion house, along with sections of the ironstone foundation of the mill. When the former millpond was converted into a cranberry bog, a simple sluice box controlled the flow of water over the dam. This would repeatedly cause flooding near the mansion house. In the 1980s the dam was completely rebuilt with a more modern and efficient spillway. During the construction of the new dam, archaeologists kept a watchful eye for any artifacts from reservation times, but none were recovered, other than some timbers and pilings, possibly from an earlier mill.

CHAPTER 15
Notable Citizens

Through the course of history, numerous residents of old Shamong have made their mark. Profiles of some of these individuals are cited here and others have already been mentioned in preceding chapters.

JOHN JAMES GARDNER

John James Gardner was born in Atlantic County, New Jersey, on October 17,1845, the son of John and Jane Gardner. Shortly before his 16th birthday, he enlisted as a private to serve in the Civil War. He was inducted August 9, 1861, for three years and was a member of Company G, 6th Regiment, New Jersey Volunteers. He was mustered out September 7, 1864. He attended the University of Michigan in 1866 and 1867 and then became involved in the real estate and insurance business.

In 1867 he was elected an alderman of Atlantic City. From 1868 through 1872, he served as mayor of Atlantic City and again in 1874 and 1875. He became a member of the common council and also coroner of Atlantic County in 1876.

His interests then turned to national politics. He became a New Jersey Senator from 1878 through 1893 and was president of the New Jersey Senate in 1883. In 1884 he was a delegate to the Republican National Convention in Chicago. From 1893 through 1913, he was repeatedly elected to serve as a United States Congressman from New Jersey, and served 10 consecutive terms. He was unsuccessful in his bid for re-election in 1912 to the 63rd Congress.

In his later years, Gardner purchased a 100-acre farm from Robert Given located on Stokes Road near the village of Indian Mills. He continued to purchase additional tracts of land in the immediate vicinity until his farm was quite extensive.

Given, the former owner of the original farm homestead, was a retired U.S. Navy Chaplain from the Civil War. Tradition tells us that the eastern

Congressman John James Gardner. (Photo courtesy of the Gardner Family.)

wing of the mansion was added on by Given so his visiting sailors would have suitable quarters. Reverend Robert Given purchased the homestead farm shortly after the Civil War, on March 23, 1867, from the executors of Daniel Milbine late of Mount Holly. Milbine had originally purchased the property from John M. Christopher, on November 2, 1851.

Christopher had purchased from James McCambridge on October 5, 1847. James McCambridge of Washington Township purchased from John and Mary McAllister of Washington Township, March 4, 1827, who had bought the original 100-acre tract from the Indian Commissioners, on November 8, 1802.

The present day Gardner Mansion, most likely erected by Robert Given in the mid-19th century, is still owned by the Gardner Family. Congressman

Congressman Gardner near the Indian Treaty Tree.
(Photo courtesy of the Gardner Family.)

Gardner continued to live in the home until his death of heart disease on February 7, 1921.

JAMES HUGH SNOW

James Hugh Snow was born in England in 1827 and came to America in 1841. During the Civil War he served as a corporal in Company G, 4th Regiment, New Jersey Volunteers. During his military service, he was held as a prisoner of war in a Confederate prison in Virginia, from June 27 to September 13, 1862. Some 21 years later, he received compensation by the Federal Government for his 79 days of captivity at the rate of 25 cents per day or a total of $19.75. He later served his country again in the war with Mexico.

After returning from his military days, Snow settled down in a small home along the Tuckerton State Road near Sooy's Tavern in Washington Township. This was just north of Batsto. In 1879 he purchased a small two-story frame home in Shamong Township across the Dingletown Road from Indian Ann Roberts, where he lived with his wife, Mary, and two sons, James and Walter.

The small frame home of James Hugh Snow, a Civil War veteran, once located on Dingletown Road. (Photo courtesy of Frank Convery.)

After his wife, Mary, died, Snow married Angeline Dixon Cotton, the widow of Ambrose Cotton. James and Angeline Snow had one son, Herbert, born in 1890, and two daughters, Mary Ann, born in 1892, and Elva, born in 1896. Mary Ann, affectionately known as "Mamie," married Charles Jennings. They had two sons, John and Jerome, and two daughters, Burnis and Vision. For many years, Charles and Mamie Jennings were the proprietors of the old Small's Hotel, operating it under the name of "The Tumble Inn."

James Snow died suddenly while splitting wood at his home in Dingletown, on June 20, 1900, at the age of 73. He is buried in the old cemetery at Tabernacle. His home on Dingletown Road, now known as Forked Neck Road, stood vacant for many years into the 1980s. The author remembers it quite well. Today nothing remains to mark the spot where so many family memories were made and are still cherished by the descendants of James Snow, many of whom still live in the area today.

JAMES STILL

James Still was born on April 9, 1812, at the Indian Mill owned by Samuel Reeves. His parents were Levin and Charity Still who had once been slaves in Maryland. After much hardship, they were able to buy their freedom and a new life in New Jersey. James Still's father worked as a sawyer for Samuel Reeve.

After a short time, the family moved into a home owned by a man named Cato. The Still family and Cato all lived in this old log house, which was one-story high with an attic. It had one door, a large fireplace, and no glass windows. There were two rooms on the first floor and one in the attic. After one or two years, Levin Still bought some land from Cato and built a simple log house on it that once stood on the south side of Stokes Road near the trap-shooting club grounds. An historical marker is in place at the site. The Still homestead had one door and no glass windows. The family lived in the poorest of conditions. James Still recalled, "Often half starved for food, half naked, barefooted, with no one to look up to but a poor dejected father, who feels the same sting."

The nearest neighbors were an Indian family headed by Job Moore. His son, also named Job, was James Still's constant companion during his boyhood years. They were no doubt a family of Indians that chose to remain in the area after the Brotherton Indians left for New York State.

At the age of 18, James was "bound out" to Amos Wilkins in Medford for a period of three years. His father received $100 for his son's services. James

235

Dr. James Still, the famous "Black Doctor of the Pines."
(Photo courtesy of Everett F. Mickle.)

was also to receive three months' schooling, one month each winter, at the nearby Brace Road School. Other than this brief schooling he received as a child in Indian Mills, he had no formal education. He learned to read and write in this brief time and then became an avid reader and lifelong self-taught learner.

After many years of hardships, Still eventually became a renowned herbalist and physician, and was referred to as the "Black Doctor of the Pines." His miraculous cures became legend in the area, and with this service came a reasonable amount of wealth. He purchased considerable land in the vicinity of Medford. His home on Church Road, at CrossRoads, was a fine two-story Victorian dwelling with an office attached. The home was

The former office of Dr. Still located on Church Road in Medford, as it appears today. (Photo by the author.)

destroyed many years ago, but the building once used as an office by Dr. Still survives today as a private dwelling.

At one point, Dr. Still was considered the third largest landowner in the Medford area, and one of the wealthiest. He had endured many hardships in his lifetime, not only from poverty and the loss of loved ones, but also from prejudice because of his race. He overcame these adversities to become a very highly respected man in his time, even by those of the medical profession who initially derided him. He was a self-educated and self-made man, and set an example that many have tried to emulate.

James Still's death occurred in his 70th year. He lies buried in the small graveyard to the rear of Jacob's Chapel, in the Colemantown section of Mount Laurel. A suitable monument marks the grave of this remarkable individual. His autobiography should be required reading for all schoolchildren today. It is an inspiring story of one man's struggle to survive and succeed against seemingly insurmountable odds.

WILLIAM STILL

Another member of the Still family, the youngest brother of James Still, also made his mark in the world. He, too, was born in the little log cabin of Levin and Charity Still on October 7, 1821. Like his older brother James he was "bound out" for a time to a local farmer, but left the area when he grew up and spent most of his adult life in Philadelphia.

William Still became very active in the Anti-Slavery Society in Philadelphia prior to the Civil War. He was a clerk and then secretary of this organization for some 14 years. He became active in the Underground Railroad movement, which assisted escaped slaves from the South in gaining their freedom. He lived for many years at 244 South 12th Street in Philadelphia. It was there he wrote his monumental literary work entitled

William Still, brother of Dr. James Still. He was a prominent leader in helping escaped slaves during the Civil War. (Photo from *The Undergound Rail Road*, Plexus Publishing, Inc., 2005.)

The Underground Rail Road, published in 1872. It was a very large volume of 780 pages with many illustrations. The volume contained Still's records and first-hand accounts of slaves who had escaped to the north prior to the Civil War. The book was of such significance that it was exhibited at the Centennial Exposition in Philadelphia in 1876. In 2005, Plexus Publishing, Inc.—working in cooperation with the Still Family Society—returned the book to print.

Besides his involvement with the Underground Railroad, William Still was also a successful businessman who operated a large coal yard and sold stoves and other heating equipment. He was a dedicated servant of his people and strove throughout his life to secure equality for them. He was a civic leader in many organizations in Philadelphia.

In his later years, Still developed Bright's disease, and the last six years of his life were spent as a partial invalid until his death on July 4, 1902. He, like his brother James, rose from a humble beginning in a log cabin in the wilderness of Shamong, to become a great leader of his people.

JOHN MINGIN

John Mingin, the son of Franklin Mingin and Sarah Cline, was a mason by trade. He was born in Batsto on April 3, 1846.

He met and married Elizabeth Miller while she was working at the Atsion Cotton Mill. After a time, they acquired property on Atsion Road west of Jackson Road where they eventually turned to farming. He became quite an active farmer, growing peaches, apples, strawberries, and cranberries. There are still many active cranberry bogs to the rear of the former Mingin farm today.

Mingin's niece, Mabel Mingin Baker, recalled,

> In the early days, cranberries were hand picked, crated, and stored in the cellar until two weeks before Thanksgiving and Christmas. They were then taken to the sorting house, put in barrels, and shipped from the Atsion station. In later years, the cranberries were scooped.

John Mingin, an early ironworker at Batsto and Atsion, later owned a farm for many years on Atsion Road. (Photo courtesy of Mabel Mingin Baker.)

Mingin was also a talented violinist and was often asked to play at house parties. He never had the advantage of formal musical training, but it's said he could play any tune once he'd heard it.

There was an ice house made from logs on the Mingin farm. The ice cutter, Fremont Patterson, lived in the old Dellett Hotel property nearby. Mr. Patterson would drive his team of horses on the ice covering the bogs, and, with the help of neighbors, cut the thick ice in squares. They would then be coated with saw dust and stored in the ice house for use in the summer.

Water came from a large open well. The pump was in the huge kitchen. Everyone had a pump box—a run off for excess

The John Mingin farmhouse on Atsion Road. (Photo courtesy of Mabel Mingin Baker, who lived here with her uncle John until her marriage in 1921.)

water pumped by hand. By the box there was another box with a lid that could be removed. Perishables could be lowered into the water and later retrieved when they were ready to be used. Cream for butter making was always lowered into the box. Later the cream would be churned by hand.

John Mingin had lived a full life at the time of his death of heart failure at the age of 78, on December 26, 1924.

ISAIAH BOWKER

Isaiah Bowker, an early settler of present-day Tabernacle Township, purchased the dwelling house and farm of 101 acres in 1800. It was located on the south side of Bread and Cheese Run, and he obtained it from James Dorea and his wife, Mary, for $800. The farm had changed hands repeatedly over a period of a few years. Dorea had purchased the farm from Isaac Carr on December 24, 1796. Isaac Carr purchased from John Risdon on June 12, 1794, and Risdon purchased from George Taylor and his wife, Sarah, on March 15, 1794. George Taylor had purchased from Bethuel Moore on October 15, 1791. Bethuel Moore had sold it by power of attorney from John Moore on May 12, 1790. He had obtained the property by the will of his father, Joseph Moore, deceased, dated December 6, 1783. This farm was part of the land Joseph Moore held by deed when the land was divided from Benjamin Moore, John Moore, Bethuel Moore, Thomas Wilkins, and Benjamin Wilkins, dated August 7, 1780. The Moores had sold 1/7th part of the Old Haines Tract that they had bought from Charles Read Esq. comprising 2,190 acres. Read had purchased the property from Enoch Haines on September 25, 1753. The farmhouse, most likely erected in 1780, was reportedly built with bricks from the ballast of ships from England. The house is on Patty Bowker Road, where it has stood for more than 200 years.

Isaiah Bowker House as it appears today. (Photo by the author.)

EDWARD T. THOMPSON

Edward T. Thompson was a grandson of Arthur Thompson, once long-time proprietor of the tavern at Quaker Bridge. Edward followed in the footsteps of his father, Nicholas Sooy Thompson, in operating the gristmill and sawmill complex at the head of Indian Mills Lake. He also ran a store and post office in the older portion of his home that today is considered the oldest existing residence in Shamong Township.

Thompson held various political positions in Shamong Township, and eventually became a New Jersey State Assemblyman, a post he held from 1871 to 1873.

The home of Edward T. Thompson. The gristmill once stood to the right of the home. The left hand side is the oldest portion of the home, erected by the Bedford Family, circa 1805. Ebenezer Engle added the right hand side, with the twin chimneys, circa 1835. (Photo by the author.)

WILLIAM R. BRADDOCK

William Rodgers Braddock was born on December 23, 1829. He was a descendant of General Edward Braddock, who served in the British Army of 1709. Another ancestor, Edward, son of General Braddock, served as a Major-General in the British Army during the French and Indian War.

William R. Braddock was a resident of Medford, where he served as a judge for some 30 years before being elected to the New Jersey State Legislature in 1848. He was a prominent surveyor in Burlington County and surrounding counties, and over the years accumulated vast tracts of land.

Braddock's connection with Shamong Township came about in 1850 with the purchase of large tracts of land north and south of Atsion Road. One tract included a large meadow, known locally as Sorden's Meadow, which at one time was within the Indian reservation boundaries. Braddock became something of an object of ridicule when he attempted to cultivate and market cranberries from Sorden's Meadow, with some neighbors referring to the meadow as "Braddock's Folly." He proved them all wrong. Eventually, a number of buildings and sorting houses were erected in the vicinity of the meadow to process the crop that in time developed into a successful local industry. In 1885, it was reported that an exceedingly large crop of cultivated cranberries was harvested and brought to market. Thanks to Braddock, Shamong Township has the distinction of producing the first cultivated cranberries in the region. Today the cranberry is a multimillion-dollar crop in the pinelands.

The remains of the cranberry bogs at Sorden's Meadow can still be seen, although the old bogs are now overgrown with forest and have not been used in years. An historical marker on Atsion Road describes the nearby site of "Braddock's Folly."

CHAPTER 16
Epilogue

The Shamong of olden days remains in the fading memories of aging locals and in the recorded history of the time. Gone are the gristmills and sawmills from which the village of Indian Mills received its name. Gone, too, are the iron furnaces and forges, marked today by only occasional pieces of slag or a stray brick. The ancient burial ground of the reservation Indians waits quietly for the archaeologist's trowel. With the exception of a half dozen or so farmhouses dating to the early 1800s, most that survive today were built from the 1840s onward.

What does remain, and hopefully will for many centuries to come, are the farmlands, cranberry bogs, blueberry fields, and pinelands of Shamong and Tabernacle Townships. Looking out over the broad expanse of open fields conjures up images of the past, of the many generations that tilled the land, and the families that were raised here. Many descendants of the hardworking people that settled this land more than 200 years ago are still living and working here today.

The Brotherton Reservation can still be experienced, but as open farmland. Many of the 100-acre tracts of land that were purchased at auction in 1802 can still be identified on local township tax maps. Both the Indian Mills and Tabernacle Historical Societies have placed historical markers at important sites. Anyone fond of history can travel through the back roads and byways, and let the imagination conjure up the old days.

The Atsion Village, which survived up until some 25 years ago, is now only a glimmer of its past glory. The cotton mill, Etheridge House, and all but one of the railroad era homes have been destroyed by arson or neglect. In the ancient cemetery across Route 206, which once contained more than 60 graves, only three tumbled down stones within a 10-foot enclosure remain. A parking lot now covers most of the cemetery.

The architectural masterpiece known as the Richards Mansion, at Atsion, was built in 1826 and still stands. The exterior was restored by the

State of New Jersey, but the interior has been sadly neglected. A cyclone fence surrounds the mansion, but even this may not be enough to deter arsonists and vandals. The old Atsion schoolhouse stands deserted and boarded up awaiting an unknown fate. The small white chapel erected during the Richards's regime, along with a deer-hunting club, stand lonely vigil as the only buildings of old Atsion Village still in use. The slab-sheathed house of early vintage, occupied for many years, now lies vacant, and a cyclone fence surrounds the only remaining worker's home; a structure that is badly deteriorating. The sad truth is that there is a lack of funding for restoration and preservation.

Many of the photographs in this history are of people, places, and buildings that no longer exist, but perpetuate their memory. It is hoped this volume will help to rekindle interest in our local history and protect what remains of the past for the benefit of future generations.

Photos of Old Shamong and Indian Mills

Several hundred photographs were studied and reviewed for inclusion in this book. Many were not included yet are considered noteworthy in their own right. The following pages provide images of yesteryear in Old Shamong and the village of Indian Mills. Life was more tranquil in those days. There were no super highways, no interstates, and no blacktop roads. To be sure, everyday life moved at a much slower pace. These photographs allow you to take a step back in time and relive those days of old.

This general store, operated since the Civil War, is still standing at the center of the village of Indian Mills and is now a pizza shop. Seated left on the bench is Walter Batterson and seated on the motorcycle is Raymond Crain. Standing next to the car are the owners of the store, John and Alfred Wills. (Photo courtesy of Pearl Odus.)

The front portion of this farmhouse was a grocery store during the latter half of the 19th century. The farmhouse still stands at the corner of Schoolhouse Lane and Indian Mills-Medford Road. (Photo by the auhor.)

Mahlon Prickett, shown in this photo, was one of the many proprietors of the general store in Indian Mills (known as Prickett's General Store when he owned it). Prickett was said to know just about all of the old timers' tales of the good old days. (Photo courtesy of Leah Prickett.)

This photo was taken looking east on Willow Grove Road from the intersection at Indian Mills Methodist Church. The building to the right was used as a store and had a pool hall upstairs. The sign on the store reads C. M. Gaskill—Cigars, Tobacco, Candy, Soft Books. (Photo courtesy of Frederick Miller.)

Bill Hess (on the right; unknown man on left) was a workman at the Atsion village owned by Joseph Wharton. (Photo courtesy of Ruth Etheridge Gerber.)

This photo was taken looking east on Forked Neck Road around the turn of the 20th century. From left to right: Bertha Wood and daughters Julia and Olive, Elizabeth Batterson and her son George. Bertha Wood's husband owned a blackshop nearby. (Photo courtesy of Pearl Odus.)

This home was one of the earliest built in Shamong, erected by Amos Wilkins in the early 1800s. (Photo courtesy of George Atkins.)

This great dogwood tree once stood in the field across from the Texaco station on Route 206. The tree was supposedly taken down to increase space for farming. (Photo courtesy of Mr. and Mrs. Louis Hand, New Lisbon, NJ.)

The William H. Brown home was once located along Old Indian Mills Road (near the Aristone properties). The home was eventually moved to a lot on Tuckerton Road by Marie and Richard Giberson, who lived there for many years. (Photo courtesy of Isabel Brown.)

This photo shows a typical farm family of Shamong around the turn of the 20th century. (Photo courtesy of Reginald Small.)

This photo shows downtown Indian Mills looking east on Forked Neck Road. Gaskill's Store (to the left) lies abandoned. The home to the right once stood on the corner of Burnt House Road, at which time it was occupied by the Cotteral family, but is now gone. (Photo courtesy of Rutgers University, Alexander Library, William Augustine Collection.)

This group of local Shamong deer hunters included (from left to right): John "Bull" Miller, John Brown, Alva "Duff" Gaskill, Harold Bozearth (who killed the deer), Alfred Bozearth (kneeling, father of Harold), Charles Bozearth (brother of Harold), and Walter Bozearth (son of Charles). Harold Bozearth was the Shamong Township Clerk for 50 years. (Photo courtesy of Harold Bozearth.)

About the Author

George D. Flemming is a lifelong resident of southern New Jersey and has been a student of history and archaeology since his early teens. He attended the Wharton School of the University of Pennsylvania and also the Charles Morris Price School of Journalism in Philadelphia. He holds membership in many historical and genealogical societies and is a 51-year member of the Archaeological Society of New Jersey. Flemming's numerous articles on local history have appeared in area newspapers and journals. The publication of *Brotherton*, his first full-length book, is the culmination of a life-long dream.

BIBLIOGRAPHY

Adovasio, James M. 2002. *The First Americans: In Pursuit of Archeology's Greatest Mystery.* New York: Random House.

Allinson, Samuel. 1875. *Fragmentary History of the New Jersey Indians.* New Brunswick, NJ: N.J. Historical Society.

Barber, John W., & Howe, Henry. 1844. *Historical Collections of the State of New Jersey.* New York: S. Tuttle.

Beck, Henry Charlton. 1936. *Forgotten Towns of Southern New Jersey.* New York: E. P. Dutton Co.

Becker, Marshall J. 1992. *Teedyuscung's Youth and Hereditary Land Rights in New Jersey: The Identification of the Unalachtigo.* Bulletin # 47. South Orange, NJ: Archaeological Society of New Jersey.

Becker, Marshall J. 1998. *Mehoxey of the Cohansey Band of South Jersey Indians.* Bulletin # 53. South Orange, NJ: Archaeological Society of New Jersey.

Besson, Adolph. 1937. *The America of 1750: Peter Kalm's Travels in North America.* English Version. New York: Wilson-Erickson.

Bisbee, Henry H. 1971. *Sign Posts: Place Names in History of Burlington County.* Willingboro, NJ: Alexis Press.

Blackman, Leah. 1880. *History of Little Egg Harbor Township.* Proceedings of the West Jersey Surveyors Association. Trenton, NJ: Trenton Printing Co.

Boyer, Charles S. 1931. *Early Forges and Furnaces in New Jersey.* Philadelphia: University of Pennsylvania Press.

Boyer, Charles S. 1962. *Old Mills of Camden Co.* Camden, NJ: Sinnickson Chew & Sons.

Boyer, Charles S. 1962. *Old Inns and Taverns in West Jersey.* Camden, NJ: Sinnickson Chew & Sons.

Boyer, Charles S. 1967. *Rambles Through Old Highways and Byways of West Jersey.* Camden, NJ: Advertising Printing Co.

Brainerd, John. 1880. *The Journal of the Rev. John Brainerd.* Reprinted. Toms River, NJ: Courier.

Brainerd, Lucy Abigail. 1908. *Genealogy of the Brainerd Family in America.* Hartford, CT: Hartford Press.

Brainerd, Rev. Thomas. 1865. *The Life of John Brainerd.* Philadelphia: Presbyterian Publication Committee.

Brinton, Daniel G. 1885. *The Lenape and Their Legends.* Philadelphia: University of Pennsylvania.

Convery, Frank W. H. 1964. The Life and Times of William Still. *Burlingting County Herald.*

Cosens-Zebooker, Betty, & Thomas, Ronald A. 1993. *Excavations of the Burr/Haines Site Burlington Co., N.J.* Bulletin # 48. South Orange, NJ: Archaeological Society of New Jersey.

DeCou, George. 1949. *The Historic Rancocas.* Moorestown, NJ: News Chronicle.

Esposito, Frank J. 1976. *Indian–White Relations in New Jersey.* Doctoral Dissertation. New Brunswick, NJ: Rutgers University Dept. of History.

Field, Rev. David D. 1857. *The Genealogy of the Brainerd Family.* New York: John F. Trow, Printer.

Flemming, George D. 1973. The Saga of Medford Township: Prehistoric Man. *The Central Record.*

Flemming, George D. 1973. Flying High at Old Flyatt. *The Central Record.*

Flemming, George D. 1974. The Story of Indian Ann: The Last of the Delawares. *The Central Record.*

Flemming, George D. 1974. A Visit to Hampton Furnace. *The Batsto Citizens Gazette.*

Flemming, George D. 1975. Medford Pioneering Township. In *The Aboriginal Inhabitants.* Medford, NJ: Medford Historical Society.

Flemming, George D. 1979. Indians' Atsion Role Disputed by Writer. *Batsto Citizens Gazette.*

Flemming, George D. 1980. The Tavern at Hampton Gate. *Batsto Citizens Gazette.*

Harper, Robert W. 1981. *Friends and Indians in South Jersey.* Mullica Hill, NJ: Harrison Township Historical Society.

Hawkes, E. W., & Linton, Ralph. 1916. *A Pre-Lenape Site in New Jersey*. Philadelphia: Publication of the University Museum.

Kaiser, Louis J. 1943. *A Story of the Public Schools of Burlington Co., N.J.*, Riverton, NJ: Press of the New Era.

Kamler, Henry. 1996. *J. F. H. Autenrieth's Description of a Short Walking Tour in the Province of New Jersey: A report from 1795 about the Brotherton Reservation*. Bulletin # 51. South Orange, NJ: Archaelogical Society of New Jersey.

Kraft, Herbert C. 1986. *The Lenape: Archeology, History, and Ethnography*. Newark, NJ: The New Jersey Historical Society.

Kraft, Herbert C. 1994. *Re-emergent Traditions Among The Lenape/Delaware Indians*. Bulletin #49. South Orange, NJ: Archaeological Society of New Jersey.

Kraft, Herbert C. 2001. *The Lenape-Delaware Indian Heritage*, Elizabeth, NJ: Lenape Books.

Larrabee, Edward M. 1976. *Recurrent Themes and Sequences in North American Indian-European Culture Contact in the State of New Jersey*. Philadelphia: American Philosophical Society.

Nelson, William. 1894. *Indians of New Jersey*. Paterson, NJ: The Press Printing and Publishing Co.

Olson, Steve. 2002. *Mapping Human History: Discovering the Past Through Our Genes*. New York: Houghton Mifflin Co.

Pearce, John E. 2000. *Heart of the Pines: Ghostly Voices of the Pine Barrens*. Hammonton, NJ: Batsto Citizens Committee, Inc.

Philhower, Charles A. 1936. *Indian Lore of New Jersey*. Trenton, NJ: Department of Conversation and Economic Development.

Pierce, Arthur D. 1957. *Iron in the Pines*. New Brunswick, NJ: Rutgers University Press.

Pierce, Arthur D. 1960. *Smugglers Woods*. New Brunswick, NJ: Rutgers University Press.

Pierce, Arthur D. 1964. *Family Empire in Iron*. New Brunswick, NJ: Rutgers University Press.

Prowell, George R. 1886. *The History of Camden County*. Philadelphia: L. J. Richards Co.

Read, Dr. Zachariah. 1859. *Annals of Old Mount Holly*. Manuscript. Burlington, NJ: Burlington County Historical Society.

Regensburg, Richard. 1980. *The Savich Farm Site: History Culture and Archeology of The Pine Barrens*. Pomona, NJ: Stockton State College.

Shinn, Henry C. 1957. *The History of Mt. Holly*. Mt. Holly, NJ: Sleeper Publications.

Shinske, Burnis Jennings. 1993. Our Grandfather James Hugh Snow. *Batsto Citizens Gazette*.

Smith, Samuel. 1877. *The History of the Colony of Nova Caesaria or New Jersey*. Trenton, NJ: Wm. S. Sharp Publishers.

Stewart, Frank H. 1932. *Indians of Southern New Jersey*. Woodbury, NJ: Gloucester County Historical Society.

Still, James. 1877. *Early Recollections and Life of D. James Still*. Philadelphia: J. B. Lippincott Co.

Tankersley, Kenneth. 2002. *In Search of Ice Age Americans*. Layton, UT: Gibbs-Smith.

Wallace, Anthony F. C. 1949. *Teedyuscung: King of the Delawares*. Philadelphia: University of Pennsylvania Press.

Weslager, C. A. 1972. *The Delaware Indians: A History*. New Brunswick, NJ: Rutgers University Press.

Woodford, Clayton W. 1882. *History of Union & Middlesex Co.*, Philadelphia: Everts & Peck.

Woodward, E. M., & Hageman, J. F. 1883. *History of Burlington and Mercer Co.* Philadelphia: Everts & Peck.

Woodward, Carl Raymond. 1941. *Ploughs and Politicks*. New Brunswick, NJ: Rutgers University Press.

Woody, Thomas. 1920. *Quaker Education in the Colony and State of New Jersey*. Philadelphia: Author.

INDEX

Atsion Company, 196
Atsion Estate, 198–199, 202–203, *209*
Atsion Forge, 193–213
Atsion Gristmill, 224, *224*
Atsion Hotel, 210, *211,* 212–213
Atsion Iron Works, 73, 74, 135, 188,
    195–196
Atsion Lake, 154, *205*
Atsion Mansion, *196, 204,* 213
Atsion River, 194
Atsion Road, 14, 82, 133, 135
Atsion Schools, 161, *165,* 165–166, 246
Atsion Store, 73, *197, 198*
Attarrumhah, 25
Austin, Jacob, 171
Autenrieth, August, 75
Autenrieth, Jacob, 75
Autenrieth, Johann Ferdinand H., 75
axes, *7,* 14
Ayres Mill Creek, 94

B

Bailey, Helen, 207
Baker, Bertha, 188
Baker, Edward, 188
Baker, Fred, 188
Baker, George W., 188, *189*
Baker, Hannah, 188, *189*
Baker, Herbert, 188
Baker, Mabel Mingin, 149, 159–160, 188,
    239
Baker, Rose, 188
Baker School, 157, *158*
Baker's Hotel, 188
Ballinger, Charles B., 121
Banjo Jack Bog, 212
bannerstones, 8, 10–11, *12*
Baptist Cemetery, 172
Bard, Benner, 222
Bard's Mill branch, 222
Bareford, Rachey, 209

Bareford, Samuel, 151
bark lodges, 19
Barnhart, Jacob, 175
Barnhart's Tavern, 175
baskets
    by Indian Ann, 115, *116*
    trade in, 74, 77–78
batons, flaking, *18*
Batsto Ironworks, 193, 195
Batsto River, 215. *see also* Swimming River
Batterson, Elizabeth, *250*
Batterson, George, *250*
Batterson, Walter, *247*
bear, Archaic period, 5
Bears Hole Corner, Shamong Township, 113,
    125–126
Beatty, John, 79–80, 83
beaver, fur trade, 22–23
Beck, Henry C., 197, 216
Becky, service with Brainerd, 67
Bedford, Ann, 226
Bedford, Isaac, 226
Bedford, Joseph A., 225, 226
Bedford, Sarah, 226
Bedford, Susanne, 226
Bedford, Thomas, 225, 226
Bedford Mills, 226
Beesleys point, 56
Belcher, Jonathan, 37, 38
Bering Sea, 1
Beringia, 1
Bernard, Francis, 45, 47–48, 53
Bethel
    crops, 36
    Crosswicks and, 29–42
    eviction of Indians, 37–38
    foundation of, 33
    land title, 37
    school at, 36
    site of, *35*
    Thompson Park site and, 42
Bird, Dick. *see* Roberts, Richard
bison, Archaic period, 5
blacksmith shops, 50

C

Indian Ann, 111–128
Indian Chief Hotel, 133
Indian Collier, *127*
Indian Commissioners, *44*
Indian Gristmill, 224–229, *226, 227*
Indian Job. *see* Moore, Job
Indian King tavern, 174
Indian Mills. *see also* Brotherton
    Reservation; Edgepillock
    Reservation
  burial ground, 12–13
  early 20th Century, *131*
  soapstone bowl, 15
Indian Mills Elementary, 166–167, *167*
Indian Mills Fire Company, 158
Indian Mills Historical Society, 84, 179, 245
Indian Mills Lake, 129
Indian Mills Methodist Church, *249*
Indian Mills Road, 135
Indian Mills United Methodist Church,
  144–146, *145, 146*
Indian Sawmill, 219–221, *221*
Indian Site Survey, 9
Indian trails, 131–134
Inner Coastal Plain of New Jersey, 2, 6
Inskeep, James, 58, 222
Irick, Henry J., 100–101
Irick, John S., 172
Irick, William J., 89, *90,* 91, 100, 106
Irish immigrants, 137
Iron, pig of, *216*
iron nails, 60
iron works, Mount Holly
  destruction of, 65
Isaiah Bowker House, *242*

J

J. Smith's Hotel, 183
Jacobs, Henricus, 25
Jacquette, James, 228
James, Abel, 194, 195

Jefferson, Thomas, 72
Jennings, Burnis, 234
Jennings, Butler, 149
Jennings, Charles, 190, 235
Jennings, Forrest, 134
Jennings, Jerome, 179, 234
Jennings, John, 205, 234
Jennings, John Clyde, 205
Jennings, John Henry Clay, 179
Jennings, Mary Ann (Mamie), 190, 234, 235
Jennings, Vision, 235
John Woolman Farm, 111
Johnson, Portence, 157
Johnston, Andrew, 39
Johnston, Jonathan C., 85
Jones, Bob, 179, 201
Jones, David, 105, 106
Jones, Joseph, 122
Jones, Pomeroy, 84–85
Josiah Smith Hotel, 173
Josiah Smith's Tavern, 172–173
Joyce, Daniel, 136
Joyce, David, 102
Joyce, Eayre B., 149
Joyce, Ely, 109
Joyce, Walter Daniel, 108
Joyce, William, 102
jug taverns, 169
Julitown, 57
Juliustown. *see* Julitown

K

Kammler, Henry, 75
Keeler, Marion, 166
Keetawawa, 89
Kekott, Robert, 39
Kekroppamant, 24
Kell family, 215
Kemble, Charles S., 190
Kemble's Inn, 190, *191*
Killbuck, John, Jr., 63

S

W

More Great Books
from Plexus Publishing

THE FORKS: A BRIEF HISTORY OF THE AREA
By Barbara Solem-Stull

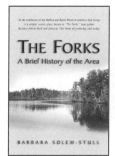

Located on a navigable waterway, yet inland and remote, "The Forks" in South Jersey was a haven for smugglers at the dawn of the Revolutionary War. This short history describes the contribution of The Forks and its inhabitants to America's fight for independence and introduces a variety of colorful characters: early settler Eric Mullica, the treacherous Benedict Arnold, visionary citizens Elijah Clark and Richard Wescoat, ship builder Captain John Van Sant, highwayman Joe Mulliner, and the fictional Kate Aylesford—immortalized as "The Heiress of Sweetwater" in a popular novel first published in 1855.

48 pp/softbound/ISBN 0-937548-51-0/$9.95

OLD AND HISTORIC CHURCHES OF NEW JERSEY, VOLUMES 1 & 2
By Ellis L. Derry

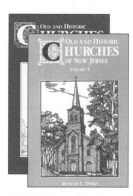

These inspirational books allow us to travel back in time to the days when this country was new—a vast and dangerous wilderness with few roads or bridges, schools or churches. It tells the stories of how our forefathers established their religious communities and houses of worship, often through great hardship and sacrifice. To be included in this two-volume history, a church had to be built by the time of the Civil War. A history of each church is given, alongside a photograph or illustration.

Vol. 1/520 pp/hardbound/ISBN 0-937548-50-2 $29.95

Vol. 1/520 pp/softbound/ISBN 0-937548-52-9/$19.95

Vol. 2/372 pp/hardbound/ISBN 0-937548-25-1/$29.95

Vol. 2/372 pp/softbound/ISBN 0-937548-26-X/$19.95

THE UNDERGROUND RAIL ROAD, 2005 EDITION
By William Still

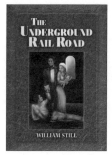

Originally published in 1872 and out of print for many years, this landmark book presents firsthand accounts of slaves escaping north via the human support network known as the Underground Railroad. The narratives were painstakingly documented by William Still (1821-1902), a son of emancipated slaves who, from his base in Philadelphia, helped guide untold numbers of fugitives to safety in the mid-19th century. The 2005 edition features the complete 1872 text, including more than 200 slave narratives, 60+ black and white illustrations, hundreds of letters and newspaper clippings, and biographical sketches of abolitionists and other contributors to the cause of freedom.

592 pp/hardbound/ISBN 0-937548-55-3/$49.50 U.S./$59.50 Canada

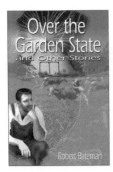

OVER THE GARDEN STATE & OTHER STORIES
Fiction by Robert Bateman

Novelist Bateman (*Pinelands, Whitman's Tomb*) offers six new stories set in his native Southern New Jersey. While providing plenty of authentic local color in his portrayal of small-town and farm life, the bustle of the Jersey shore with its boardwalks, and the solitude and otherworldliness of the famous Pine Barrens, Bateman's sensitively portrayed protagonists are the stars here. The title story tells of an Italian prisoner of war laboring on a South Jersey farm circa 1944. There, he finds danger and dreams, friendship and romance—and, ultimately, more fireworks than he could have wished for.

296 pp/hardbound/ISBN 0-937548-40-5/$22.95

PINELANDS
A novel by Robert Bateman

"A riveting story, written in a style to catch and hold the reader's attention." —Barnegat Bay Banner

"Bateman has written an elegy for one section of New Jersey and for all the places that have been devoured by progress without vision." —The News and Observer (Raleigh, NC)

In a compelling blend of history and fiction, Robert Bateman examines the seductive legacies of the past and how they are used by many to resist the abrasive realities of modern life. With its startling conclusion, Pinelands brings the reader full circle through decades of ambition, violence, love, and decadence to a present that is, perhaps, all too familiar.

256 pp/hardbound/ISBN 0-937548-27-8/$21.95
256 pp/softbound/ISBN 0-937548-28-6/$12.95

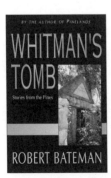

WHITMAN'S TOMB: STORIES FROM THE PINES
A novel by Robert Bateman

"Explorations of the bone-marrow loneliness of characters trying to make some sense of what's happening to them...his people and their predicaments are believable and absorbing." —The Central Record

From the author of *Pinelands* come 13 innovative short stories that chart the mysteries of everyday life. Set in and around the New Jersey Pine Barrens, the stories of Whitman's Tomb examine an often chaotic world where people struggle to preserve whatever small truths life has granted them.

With an uncanny sense for locating the extraordinary within the familiar, Robert Bateman has created an insightful collection of fiction that challenges the reader and offers a glimpse of a world that never fails to surprise.

224 pp/hardbound/ISBN 0-937548-32-4/$21.95

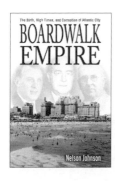

BOARDWALK EMPIRE: THE BIRTH, HIGH TIMES, AND CORRUPTION OF ATLANTIC CITY

By Nelson Johnson

Atlantic City's popularity rose in the early 20th century and peaked during Prohibition. For 70 years, it was controlled by a partnership comprised of local politicians and racketeers, including Enoch "Nucky" Johnson—the second of three bosses to head the political machine that dominated city politics and society. In *Boardwalk Empire*, Atlantic City springs to life in all its garish splendor. Author Nelson Johnson traces "AC" from its birth as a quiet seaside health resort, through the notorious backroom politics and power struggles, to the city's rebirth as an entertainment and gambling mecca where anything goes.

300 pp/softbound/ISBN 0-937548-49-9/$18.95

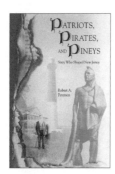

PATRIOTS, PIRATES, AND PINEYS: SIXTY WHO SHAPED NEW JERSEY

By Robert A. Peterson

"Patriots, Pirates, and Pineys is excellent ... the type of book that is hard to put down once you open it."—Daybreak Newsletter

Southern New Jersey is a region full of rich heritage, and yet it is one of the best kept historical secrets of our nation. Many famous people have lived in Southern New Jersey, and numerous world-renowned businesses were started in this area as well.

This collection of biographies provides a history of the area through the stories of such famous figures as John Wanamaker, Henry Rowan, Sara Spenser Washington, Elizabeth Haddon, Dr. James Still, and Joseph Campbell. Some were patriots, some pirates, and some Pineys, but all helped make America what it is today.

168 pp/hardbound/ISBN 0-937548-37-5/$29.95
168 pp/softbound/ISBN 0-937548-39-1/$19.95

DOWN BARNEGAT BAY: A NOR'EASTER MIDNIGHT READER

By Robert Jahn

"Down Barnegat Bay evokes the area's romance and mystery."
—The New York Times

Down Barnegat Bay is an illustrated maritime history of the Jersey shore's Age of Sail. Originally published in 1980, this fully revised Ocean County Sesquicentennial Edition features more than 177 sepia illustrations, including 75 new images and nine maps. Jahn's engaging tribute to the region brims with first-person accounts of the people, events, and places that have come together to shape Barnegat Bay's unique place in American history.

248 pp/hardbound/ISBN 0-937548-42-1/$39.95

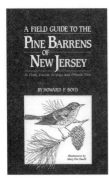

A FIELD GUIDE TO THE PINE BARRENS OF NEW JERSEY
By Howard P. Boyd

"...Howard Boyd has succeeded in the formidable task of bringing together definitive and detailed answers to questions about the Pine Barrens.... a must for anyone who is casually or seriously interested in the New Jersey Pine Barrens." —V. Eugene Vivian, Emeritus Professor of Environmental Studies, Rowan State College

With his 420-page volume, author Howard P. Boyd presents readers with the ultimate handbook to the New Jersey Pine Barrens. Boyd begins his book by explaining and defining what makes this sandy-soiled, wooded habitat so diverse and unusual.

Each entry gives a detailed, nontechnical description of a Pine Barrens plant or animal (for over 700 species), indicating when and where it is most likely to appear. Complementing most listings is an original ink drawing that will greatly aid the reader in the field as they search for and try to identify specific flora and fauna.

423 pp/hardbound/ISBN 0-937548-18-9/$32.95
423 pp/softbound/ISBN 0-937548-19-7/$22.95

A PINE BARRENS ODYSSEY: A NATURALIST'S YEAR IN THE PINE BARRENS OF NEW JERSEY
By Howard P. Boyd

A Pine Barrens Odyssey is a detailed perspective of the seasons in the Pine Barrens of New Jersey. Primarily focused on the chronology of the natural features of the Pine Barrens, this book is meant as a companion to Howard P. Boyd's A Field Guide to the Pine Barrens of New Jersey.

The two books form an appealing collection for anyone interested in the Pine Barrens of New Jersey. The Field Guide can be used as a reference tool for the types of flora and fauna and the Odyssey as a calendar of what to expect and look for season by season in this beautiful natural area of New Jersey.

275 pp/softbound/ISBN 0-937548-34-0/$19.95

WILDFLOWERS OF THE PINE BARRENS OF NEW JERSEY
By Howard P. Boyd

Howard P. Boyd offers readers 150 detailed descriptions and 130 color photographs of the most commonly seen Pine Barrens wildflower species. Other useful features include a chapter on the flora of New Jersey, notes on threatened and endangered species, a primer on flower anatomy, a glossary of terms, references to literature cited and recommended reading, and indexes to both the common and scientific names of wildflower species. The author has avoided highly technical language, and employed a useful chronological organization (by blossoming times).

176 pp/softbound/ISBN 0-937548-45-6/$19.95

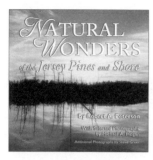

NATURAL WONDERS OF THE JERSEY PINES AND SHORE

By Robert A. Peterson with selected photographs by Michael A. Hogan and Steve Greer

In this exquisite book, fifty-seven short yet informative chapters by the late Robert Peterson celebrate a range of "natural wonders" associated with the Pine Barrens and coastal ecosystems of southern New Jersey. The diverse topics covered include flora, fauna, forces of nature, and geological formations—from birds, mammals, and mollusks, to bays, tides, trees, wildflowers, and much more. More than 200 stunning full-color photos by award-winning photographers Michael Hogan and Steve Greer bring Peterson's delightful vignettes to life. For South Jersey aficionados—young and old alike—this is a book to treasure.

312 pp/hardbound/ISBN 0-937548-48-0/$49.95

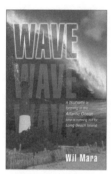

WAVE
A novel by Wil Mara

When a terrorist's plot goes awry, a smuggled nuclear device detonates off the mid-Atlantic U.S. coast, creating a massive undersea landslide. Within minutes a tsunami is born, and a series of formidable waves begins moving toward the Jersey shore. The people of Long Beach Island are sitting ducks, with only one bridge to the mainland and less than three hours to evacuate.

In this taut thriller, Wil Mara achieves a remarkable balance of science, storytelling, and characterization. From the disgraced mayor with a unique chance for redemption, to the young lovers from opposite sides of the track, to the working mom desperate to find her young sons, the lives and emotions of Mara's protagonists play out vividly against the looming disaster.

312 pp/hardbound/ISBN 0-937548-56-1/$22.95 U.S.

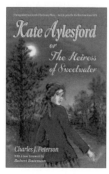

KATE AYLESFORD
OR, THE HEIRESS OF SWEETWATER
A novel by Charles J. Peterson
With a new Foreword by Robert Bateman

The legendary historical romance, *Kate Aylesford: A Story of Refugees*, by Charles J. Peterson, first appeared in 1855, was reissued in 1873 as *The Heiress of Sweetwater*, and spent the entire 20th century out of print. As readable today as when Peterson first penned it, *Kate Aylesford* features a memorable cast of characters, an imaginative plot, and a compelling mix of romance, adventure, and history. Plexus Publishing is pleased to return this remarkable novel to print.

306 pp/hardbound/ISBN 0-937548-46-4/$22.95

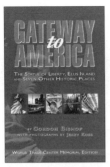

GATEWAY TO AMERICA, WORLD TRADE CENTER MEMORIAL EDITION

By Gordon Bishop • Photographs by Jerzy Koss

Gateway to America is both a comprehensive guidebook and history. It covers the historic New York/New Jersey triangle that was the window for America's immigration wave in the 19th and 20th centuries. In addition to commemorating the World Trade Center, the book explores Ellis Island, The Statue of Liberty, and six other Gateway landmarks including Liberty State Park, Governors Island, Battery City Park, South Street Seaport, Newport, and the Gateway National Recreational Area. A must for history buffs and visitors to the area alike.

188 pp/softbound/ISBN 0-937548-44-8/$19.95

WONDERWALKS: THE TRAILS OF NEW JERSEY AUDUBON

By Patricia Robinson

Wonderwalks is the first book to present all of the accessible trails, sanctuaries, and nature centers owned by the New Jersey Audubon society. This delightful guide explores the 34 New Jersey Audubon nature preserves and sanctuaries throughout the state. Both casual hikers and seasoned naturalists will enjoy this one-of-a-kind, top-to-bottom environmental tour of the Garden State. The book includes dozens of photographs, seasonal lists of birds and butterflies, trail descriptions, driving directions, and much more.

200 pp/softbound/ISBN 0-937548-53-7/$19.95

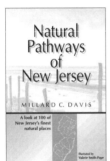

NATURAL PATHWAYS OF NEW JERSEY

By Millard C. Davis

Natural Pathways of New Jersey is a guide to 100 natural places in New Jersey. Davis's descriptions of beaches, forests, and fields include not only the essence of the landscapes, but also portray the animals and vegetation native to the area. The book is divided into sections by county, making it easy for anyone to find the cited areas. It features over 100 original watercolor illustrations by artist Valerie Smith-Pope and two simple trips that anyone can take, showcasing the best that New Jersey has to offer.

271 pp/softbound/ISBN 0-937548-35-9/$19.95

To order or for a catalog: 609-654-6500, Fax Order Service: 609-654-4309

Plexus Publishing, Inc.

143 Old Marlton Pike • Medford • NJ 08055
E-mail: info@plexuspublishing.com
www.plexuspublishing.com